Orange-Coll

Orange-Collar Labor

Work and Inequality in Prison

Michael Gibson-Light

OXFORD
UNIVERSITY PRESS

OXFORD
UNIVERSITY PRESS

Oxford University Press is a department of the University of Oxford. It furthers
the University's objective of excellence in research, scholarship, and education
by publishing worldwide. Oxford is a registered trade mark of Oxford University
Press in the UK and certain other countries.

Published in the United States of America by Oxford University Press
198 Madison Avenue, New York, NY 10016, United States of America.

© Oxford University Press 2023

CIP data is on file at the Library of Congress

ISBN 978–0–19–005540–0 (pbk.)
ISBN 978–0–19–005539–4 (hbk.)

DOI: 10.1093/oso/9780190055394.001.0001

1 3 5 7 9 8 6 4 2

Paperback printed by Sheridan Books, Inc., United States of America
Hardback printed by Bridgeport National Bindery, Inc., United States of America

This book is dedicated to the more than 2,300,000 people presently "doing time" in the United States

Table of Contents

1

Introduction

Prison Labor and Stratification

> If one convict is to be permitted to sweep the rooms of the prison, another to clean the furniture and utensils, another to keep the yard in proper order, as a substitute for hard labour, undue and improper partiality is shown, and an authority and discretion are exercised that the laws never intended.
>
> —Society of the Prevention of Pauperism in the City of New York (1822)

On an otherwise barren expanse of land sits a sprawling prison complex. Near its center, inside a concrete and steel warehouse—a grey monolith beneath an open sky—forty men stand shoulder-to-shoulder along narrow steel tables. The humidity is stifling, and the hum of industrial freezers all but drowns out the sounds of crinkling plastic as the men hurriedly assemble thousands of sandwiches. It's all part of the punishment here at Sunbelt State Penitentiary (SSP), a medium-security men's state prison complex, as it is in such facilities throughout the United States.[1] A correctional officer (CO)[2] in gleaming aviator sunglasses watches from a central office as the men assigned to the "food factory" work six-hour shifts, five days a week, preparing meals for those sentenced to live within the razor-wire confines of SSP. Civilian staff members—called "white shirts" by prisoners and badged COs alike—stroll through the site.

Sometimes they help wrap sandwiches. More often, they keep a watchful distance.

The tallest worker on the line is Soto, a broad-shouldered Mexican citizen in his thirties. At six feet, six inches tall, he towers over the tables, hunching over as he wraps sandwich after sandwich, day after day. "I have to move around," he tells me. "As tall as I am, I got to move around [or] my knees will start hurting." Still, his back and legs ache after most shifts.

Soto has worked in the food factory for the past sixteen months. With good behavior and exemplary work evaluations, he makes nearly double the wages most of his coworkers command: up to almost $0.20 per hour. But the work is monotonous. "I've lost the will to come in and work here. You know what I mean? . . . And now it's just like—it's just like [the film] *Groundhog Day*. It's just the same thing." Miming the way they slap together sandwich materials, he laughs, "Boom, boom. Cheese, no cheese. That's all that it is. That's *all* that changes—is cheese or no cheese." Soto is sociable, outgoing, and has a high school diploma, yet he has struggled to transfer to a more desirable job within the institution. His options, he explains, are limited. "I can't work certain jobs. I can't work the *good* jobs because I'm a Mexican national. They tell me I have to work here." When Soto sought to work in the prison's call center, he was deemed ineligible, because "I don't got the [citizenship] papers. Need to get them *papers!*" He also lacks the specific social ties that might facilitate a sort of labor mobility within the prison's closed society. "If I try to get into any other job—one of the jobs that people *want*—you got to know somebody to get you in. You know what I mean? I know a lot of people in that yard, but I just can't seem to get the job. I don't know what's going on."

A very different prison workplace is abuzz across the way. Here, in a building adjacent to the prison's housing bays, there is a maze of cubicles. Salesmen in orange, the incarcerated workers in the call center sit in swivel chairs facing personal computers. Their individual cubicles are adorned with sales scripts, motivational slogans, and family portraits. They speak politely through telephone headsets to customers in the outside world, pitching advertising packages to business owners who have no idea they are speaking to incarcerated men. Air-conditioning keeps the room at a comfortable temperature, and music drifts through wall-mounted speakers. The sales team works autonomously, as a single civilian staff member skims paperwork, humming along to the music in a central, window-lined cubicle. The workers occasionally crack jokes or complain about frustrating calls. When a sale is made, some cheer.

Jake, a muscular white man in his late thirties, occupies a central cubicle. Formally, he is the "inmate trainer,"[3] and although prisoners are officially barred from holding authority over one another, the other men in the call center recognize his responsibilities go beyond acclimating new hires. "I'm the trainer," he tells me. "What I do is train guys when they're brand new. And I also try to keep everybody on the same track. I guess on the outside that'd be called a manager." Indeed, his coworkers will refer to Jake as their "informal" or "inmate manager."

Call center jobs, with the comfortable work environment, mentally engaging work, and wildly higher starting pay (around $2 an hour, which is more than 20 times higher than what is offered in the food factory and many other worksites), are considered among the prison's best. Jake, with his tattooed arms and booming voice, has worked here since the early weeks of this, his most recent in a string of prison terms, and he has already accumulated a bit of savings that will help him get on his feet when he is released.[4] What's more, he has fostered a good relationship with the civilian call center manager, who promises to help Jake find employment on the outside. When I ask how he got this highly sought work assignment, Jake attributes his success to experience and connections. "When I got over here," he remembered of arriving at SSP, "I heard that they have a phone job. And I've done phones like this down in [another prison] . . . . One of the guys that was up here living in my [housing] pod, I kind of told him, 'Hey, this is what I used to do,' and this and that." After his neighbor vouched for him, Jake was hired. "I've learned a lot in the time that I've been here," he beamed.

* * *

It is, by now, fairly common knowledge that the United States has more prisons and incarcerates more people than any other nation, whether counting by raw numbers or in per capita terms. A country with just five percent of the world's population, the U.S. accounts for twenty to twenty-five percent of its legal captives, including more than 1.5 million people held in state and federal prison facilities in 2020.[5] Far fewer people realize this is a *labor force*; the vast majority of imprisoned men and women in the U.S. are put to work. This fact may conjure pop culture tropes, like stamping license plates or doing roadside cleanup along sunbaked highways, but most prisoners produce goods and provide services for penal institutions, for state and federal agencies, and, by way of complex contracted arrangements, for juggernaut corporations like Walmart, Whole Foods, AT&T, and Microsoft.[6] Incarcerated individuals like Soto and Jake note that participating in penal labor programs is vital to getting through a U.S. prison sentence. Work is how they pass their time, make money to purchase necessities, pick up or hone potentially marketable skills, and maintain positive—even future-oriented—outlooks and self-conceptions behind bars. For them, and for most American prisoners, to do prison time is to go to work. As the above accounts illustrate, however, not all prison jobs are equal, nor are all prisoners accorded the same opportunities.

SSP's administrators and front-line staffers maintain that any prisoner demonstrating good behavior and positive work performance will "automatically" move up the hierarchy of prison jobs. As one correctional officer, a man that I call CO Byrne, put it, "everybody" tends to start in the food factory—"If you're the new guy, you make sandwiches," he comments—but "if they do well, they get those good jobs. Nobody gets the sign shop who just showed up on the yard." To him, the prison labor system offers a straightforward path to promotion: "If they get three E's [reviews of "excellent" or "exceeds expectations"] in a row on evaluations, they can basically ask for a new job. It has to do with attendance, attitude, and performance." CO Byrne's perspective aligns with penal labor proponents, who contend that "prison labor provides . . . a pathway to correct deviant behavior and possibly find personal redemption."[7] Yet, although

Soto consistently received "excellent" scores on his biweekly work reviews, his pathway seemed to dead-end at the food factory; Jake, on the other hand, secured a "good job" in the air-conditioned call center, only weeks after arriving on the yard.

Both men were convicted of violent offenses. Both had clean behavioral records at SSP. And both got consistently excellent reviews from their job site supervisors. Why did Soto and Jake's job search outcomes look so different? As I show in this book, differences in race,[8] ethnicity, and nationality interact with individuals' possession of valued skills and resources to influence prisoners' positions in this closed employment system. And that variation has direct implications for prisoners' social and economic standings, their understandings of punishment and senses of dignity, and their preparations for release (more than six hundred thousand people are released from prison each year to return to communities throughout the U.S.). In this way, carceral structures—and penal labor structures in particular—reproduce and exacerbate social inequalities between groups along the lines of race, ethnicity, and class, attenuating prisoners' experiences within and beyond prison. In these pages, I explore how people inside experience, endure, and at times resist this stratified system.

The Prison and Inequality

A central question in the sociology of punishment asks: *How do social inequalities shape, and how are they shaped by, justice system contact?* The impact of the criminal justice system on disparities across communities grew readily apparent as the U.S. embraced mass incarceration in the 1970s. To unpack the processes underlying this, scholars largely focused on two related phenomena: pre-prison punishment discrepancies (in which harsh sentencing disadvantages already-marginalized segments of the population) and post-prison disparities (in which different groups fare better or worse as they reenter communities after incarceration). Work emerged as an important indicator. Labor market participation and job quality are negatively correlated with a person's likelihood of imprisonment (if you have a job, and if it is a good job, it's less likely you'll serve time),[9] and employment outcomes are commonly used to assess "success" in reentry (if you have a job—good, bad, or otherwise—you're succeeding).[10]

Today, social scientists Sara Wakefield and Christopher Uggen conclude, American prisons overwhelmingly "house the jobless, the poor, the racial minority, and the uneducated, not the merely criminal."[11] A rich body of scholarship from researchers, including Wakefield and Uggen, documents how prisoners are disproportionately drawn from communities at the bottom of social and economic hierarchies.[12] Although different socioeconomic class groups[13] participate in criminalized activities at similar rates, it is the impoverished who comprise much of the prison population.[14] Researchers show how the prison system has expanded to contain a surplus population of those who, lacking employment and social supports, have been pushed out of or kept to the margins of the formal labor market.[15] The unemployed and under-employed are overrepresented in carceral settings, they theorize, because employment gaps, contacts with social welfare services, and informal efforts to make ends meet leave them more susceptible to carceral intervention.[16] These patterns are exacerbated in minoritized communities and for black men in particular,[17] as they already receive disproportionate and inequitable attention from policing and surveillance apparatuses[18] (again, often in spite of comparable patterns in criminalized behaviors[19]). Amid the cordoning off of black and brown citizens, increasingly confined to prisons, cut off from formal labor markets, and denied the vote and other civic engagement, social scientists forcefully argue that criminal punishment both enforces and legitimates a violent racial caste system.[20]

Those who have investigated post-release work patterns consistently document disparities in which groups who were disadvantaged before incarceration face steeper odds of success, having gained the stigma of incarceration. Whole swaths of rigorous academic research examine the impacts of punishment on health, family stability and development, civic engagement, housing, and neighborhood and community dynamics,[21] often concluding that labor market access and wage outcomes are central to post-release inequalities.[22] In addition to being removed from market participation while behind bars, justice-involved people encounter continued exclusion once their sentences are completed.[23] Many hurdles prohibit these individuals from (re)entering formal employment relations for long periods (if at all),[24] and those who do successfully find work report their wages are reduced by as much as ten to thirty percent of their pre-carceral pay.[25] To be sure, all ex-captives face difficult prospects, but these are notably bleaker for minoritized individuals facing discrimination related to race, criminal history, and the combination of the two.

Bridging the Gap: Studying Prison (Work) Experiences

The study of inequality surrounding prisons has uncovered and worked to understand these and other pre- and post-prison disparities, yet there is very little in-depth observational data focused on the factors contributing to inequalities *in* prison.[26] According to a 2014 National Research Council report, "Most research on social and economic effects treats prison as a *black box*, with little detailed study of what takes place inside and its potential effects."[27] By going inside, as I do in this book, and putting observations and interviews in conversation with a wide range of scholarship, I venture to bridge this empirical and theoretical gap. Only then can we begin to understand how labor structures contour carceral experiences—in other words, how work shapes punishment in practice.

Again, Wakefield and Uggen eloquently sum up the big picture:

> Prisons tend to house those with the least human capital, financial capital, and social capital . . . . If prisons are not successful in addressing deficits—and there is ample evidence to suggest they are not— widespread incarceration reinforces existing disadvantages, to the detriment of inmates and the communities to which they return.[28]

The contemporary prison is structured such that different prisoner groups have vastly different experiences and carry different burdens. A central thesis of this book is that labor, which occupies the time of most imprisoned individuals, is key in producing this variegation. Official rhetorics aside, the institution-within-an-institution that is penal labor does not commonly confer marketable skills and positive outlooks to the imprisoned. Instead, lines are drawn—and jobs are assigned—on the basis of *existing* skills, knowledge, social ties, and demographic characteristics.

Further, opportunities to engage in stimulating, rewarding work have grown rare in the nation's prisons.[29] The opportunities that exist, recent survey research reveals, are doled out inequitably in ways that suggest discrimination tied to race, class, gender, and nationality.[30] As a result, prisoners like Soto and Jake have vastly different experiences of work—and therefore life—behind bars. Soto, hunching his enormous frame over the assembly line in the food factory, struggles to purchase enough additional food and adequate supplies to make it through each week. He labors in deskilled monotony, striving fruitlessly to acquire a "good job." Jake, however, is able to financially plan for his release, saving the surplus from his far-higher call center wages. His prison job allows the gregarious man to hone his sales skills, interact with the public, gain informal social authority as an "inmate manager," and cultivate a positive personal narrative.

These observations raise a series of questions. If there are "good" and "bad" prison jobs, and if these affect prison life, why don't we understand how the jobs are allocated? How is this labor system structured at the institutional level? How is it experienced at the personal level? And how might carceral work-sorting processes connect to patterns of inequality?

SSP, the site of my ethnographic study of life and work behind bars, is not a private prison (it is managed by the public employees of the state's Department of Corrections, or DOC). Nevertheless, the sprawling facility houses a huge number of prisoners, most of those prisoners are required to work, and SSP—like most public prisons in the U.S.—has entered many public–private contracts that intertwine private enterprise with its day-to-day operations and operating budgets. These contracts allow private firms to oversee different aspects of daily provision, such as food services and medical care, for the imprisoned, and to implement certain work programs in the name of rehabilitation and revenue-generation.[31] Still, as a public facility, the responsibility of adequately supervising and providing for the incarcerated masses ultimately falls on the government employees tasked with overseeing corrections.

I investigated this institution using ethnography: the social scientific method of systematically observing and participating in a corner of the social world as a means of study. Although I was able to freely enter and exit the facility, I spent eighteen months observing and sometimes working alongside those incarcerated at SSP. In a variety of prison contexts, I was able to observe the men's daily practices, work routines, interactions, and strategies for navigating and enduring the challenges of prison. To learn more about the practice of penal surveillance and supervision, control, and work allocation, I shadowed a number of COs as they carried out their operational duties and I conducted eighty-two individual interviews with Sunbelt's working prisoners and staff members. Any trepidation surrounding my status as an outside researcher, which was made known, seemed to fade with time; indeed, several participants expressed appreciation that someone unconnected to the institution was interested in their experiences. (The curious reader will find more information on my methodological approach and the prison fieldsite in the Appendix.)

For the most part, my research focused on the contained labor system within one medium-security unit, or "yard," within SSP. Among the biggest yards on the complex, it housed over one thousand men whose convictions ranged from minor drug possession to assault, and from money laundering to murder. Some of its residents had been moved, after years of good behavior, to this unit from higher-level custody units. To structure my visits and better focus observations on consistent processes and themes over time, I eventually narrowed my research to four specific worksites: a sign shop, an auto garage, a food factory, and a call center. Representing jobs designated "good" and "bad" by workers, these locations are described in deeper detail in Chapter 2.

Unlike survey-based studies, the ethnographic and interview-based approach I employed enabled me to capture the organization of the prison workplace and the daily, micro-level processes of carceral labor. This method also allowed me to map the meso-level composition of the prison employment system—that is, the organized system of labor complete with diverse jobs and job sites, workers, wages, perks, and established rules and norms for classifying and regulating each.[32] As I engaged in sustained qualitative data collection, my day-to-day presence helped me establish an increasing level of trust with the people within SSP (including the incarcerated and DOC staffers); in turn, this trust helped generate richer and more exhaustive data. Ethnography, as it is meant to do, revealed structures, processes, and understandings not readily accessible through (but supplementary to) other approaches.

As a result, this book outlines how the contemporary carceral institution—via its structure and the practices of agents within it—classifies its wards through penal labor, privileges those endowed with valuable capabilities and resources, and erects hurdles for those considered lacking. Social barriers are here reproduced not between the poor and rich or the incarcerated and free, but within the narrower range of social class occupied by the prisoner population. Processes of classification and exclusion on the inside generate barriers to skill development, resource acquisition, and dignity maintenance for groups already struggling against discriminatory criminal justice practices and labor market experiences. Labor is thus threaded through a chain of inequality, acting to engender and exacerbate unequal encounters before, during, and after prison.

U.S. punishment has always revolved around labor, in one way or another, which is why prison scholars Dario Melossi and Massimo Pavarini contend, "the history of the rise of the American prison is (also) the history of models of prison employment."[33] Simply by occupying a large chunk of prisoners' time, work has the potential to shape millions of carceral experiences and to do so in ways that might be considered both positive and negative (as part of the process of punishment, it self-evidently has the capacity to do great harm to men and women already at odds with mainstream society).[34] Relatedly, penal labor directly influences the wellbeing of the incarcerated in significant ways. Work assignments, for instance, impact and are impacted by a prisoner's social and economic standing behind bars. Nationally, prison wages (in the forty-five states that pay them) range from less than five cents to more than $5 per hour,[35] a dramatic pay gap that determines whether incarcerated people are able to access basic goods and services behind bars, especially as more and more of these are subject to private, for-profit administration.[36] And as is true for all workers, prisoners' perceptions of self-worth are tied to their work; within a system designed to strip them of dignity and value, employment may be particularly implicated in incarcerated individuals' self-esteem. Any way we look at it, the interaction of punishment and work is a potentially monumental force in the lives and life chances of millions.

A Brief Labor History of American Punishment

Before unpacking the linkages between prison work and the reproduction of social inequality, it is useful to review the interconnectedness of work and American punishment over time. Regardless of the "era" of punishment, legal scholar Jonathan Simon writes, "Wherever you look in the development of modernist penality you will find labor. Exhort the offenders with religious tracts, but make them work . . . . Educate them as citizens, but make them work. Treat their pathological features, but make them work."[37]

Punishment and labor in early American history

From the start of white European settlement in North America, labor has been central to social control and conceptions of justice. In the colonial era, England engaged in penal transportation, relocating convicted criminals to the colonies as indentured laborers.[38] Following the American Revolution, the cultural context in the fledgling United States brought the development of a unique outcrop of the revolutionary Enlightenment ideals animating much of Europe, as well as a full restructuring of the nation's economy and labor market. As society changed, so did its approach to punishment, and new criminal punishments frequently took the form of public hard labor or "penal servitude," a socially salient shaming ritual designed to deter crime.[39]

In 1790, the U.S. established its first prison in Pennsylvania. Like other early carceral institutions, it emphasized solitary confinement, and prisoners were, at times, left to perform their individual labors in isolation. Reformers developed the penitentiary as a means to rekindle "decency" through rationalized, uniform deprivation and control; with Protestant ideals top of mind, work was baked into this penitent punishment.[40] Rather quickly, in 1796, New York passed the first known law enabling those convicted of crime to receive compensation for their labor,[41] and penal labor was set on an upward trajectory.

Slavery would remain the legally sanctioned backbone of the U.S. economy for decades to come, although political and legislative shifts at the start of the 1800s introduced a number of hurdles to the importation of slave labor. Coupled with rapid industrial development, the country's economy began to demand new sources of free or dirt-cheap labor.[42] The factory model of corrections that emerged in the 1820s was exemplified by New York's Auburn Prison, where penality promised not only effective reform, but covetable revenue.[43] No longer following the Pennsylvania model's emphasis on isolation, prisoners in the Auburn model labored daily in congregate workshops to fulfil private industry contracts.[44] They manufactured textiles, boots, tools, furniture, and other goods in silence, then spent each night detained in solitary cells. Around the same time, convict leasing arrangements, in which private industry more fully and directly utilized captive labor, arose, although they would truly flourish after the Civil War. As the penal system evolved, the state would continue to commodify minoritized bodies in new ways.

The American Civil War amplified the need for cheap clothing and footwear, particularly for soldiers; this demand was met with an expansion of penal labor in the 1860s.[45] Following the war, in 1865, the nation ratified the 13th Amendment to the Constitution, abolishing slavery except as punishment for a crime. This "punishment clause" facilitated the near-instantaneous transformation of the newly-free labor of black citizens into "convict labor" via the intentional incarceration of masses of black men and boys.[46] That is, the prison was used to replicate core features of the chattel slavery system, providing cheap labor and racial control and containment.[47] It would continue, fueling the inordinate policing, surveillance, and incarceration of black Americans, well into the "Gilded Age." Strict laws known as the Black Codes allowed whites to exploit black bodies through the coercive force of the rapidly expanding criminal justice system.[48]

In the Jim Crow era, prisoners were subjected to working conditions nearly as harsh as those created by the institution of slavery.[49] They were compelled into tireless manual labor, laying railroad track and working in mines, factories, and farms under threat of physical punishment and further isolation.[50] The prisoner population, dominated by former slaves and their descendants, was a profit machine, with bodies leased out to private firms or set to labor within prison workshops fulfilling private contracts.[51] In the South, law enforcement officials enthusiastically and systematically fabricated criminal charges against black men simply to meet the persistent demand for cheap prison labor.[52] In this way, the state subsidized the continued production of former plantations well after the formal abolition of chattel slavery.

In the late nineteenth century, it was the rise of the labor movement that would reduce the nation's reliance on penal labor. Organized, chiefly white workers argued that prison production was driving down wages and employment on the "outside," and in areas where organized labor had the greatest influence, penal labor was abolished or constrained.[53] Still, the public and private sectors continued to rely on working prisoners where possible until the late 1920s, when states began to discontinue private convict leasing (the last of these programs, in Alabama, was shuttered in 1927). New Deal era legislation in the 1930s formally limited prison production to state goods like license plates, road signs, and uniforms. So, as private contracting was sidelined, public uses of penal labor flourished.[54]

Punishment and labor in the era of mass incarceration

The 1970s, we now understand, ushered in the era of mass incarceration. Ideological shifts, rampant inflation, and other factors, including the neoliberal rhetoric of responsibilization (explored more fully in the next few pages) forwarded by Richard Nixon and elevated (if not embodied) by Ronald Reagan, resulted in symbolic "wars" against crimes like drug use and vagrancy. Across the nation, policing focused on targeting poor and minoritized communities experiencing reduced rates of formal labor market participation. At the same time, expansions in prosecutorial powers magnified unequal sentencing patterns.[55] Overstuffed prisons were left to incapacitate and punish rising ranks of underserved people targeted by a retributive regime and sentenced to ever-longer terms of confinement.

The incarcerated labor force grew in direct proportion to the rise of imprisonment as the state's *de facto* response to more and more transgressions. Decades after New Deal legislation limited the uses of penal labor, the Justice System Improvement Act of 1979 and the accompanying Prison Industry Enhancement Certification Program (PIECP) would once more lift many restrictions on the production, sale, and distribution of prisoner-made goods.[56] The power of organized labor also declined. These changes paved the way for the renewal of private work programming in publicly managed prisons.

The Reagan–Bush years of the 1980s and 1990s were punishing in many ways and for many people, not only those directly targeted by harsh developments in penality.[57] While leaders stumped for the neoliberal cultural ideals of hard work and personal responsibility, earnings and productivity were becoming almost wholly disconnected.[58] GDP rose, as did workers' performance demands, and real earnings dropped. Inequality between elites and workers rose drastically, as did the average worker's time spent working, poverty rates, and financial insecurity.[59] Incarceration skyrocketed, propelled by a host of structural and social forces.

By the 2000s, commentators searching for a phrase to convey something bigger than *mass* incarceration began speaking of "hyper-incarceration" and pointed to the ways criminal justice targeted poor, minoritized men.[60] Although crime and arrest rates decreased into this decade, prosecutorial behavior shifted toward bringing felony charges and urging judges toward lengthy prison sentences.[61] Cost-cutting companies, hoping to employ cheap carceral labor, joined private prison corporations and other interest groups to lobby for harsher sentencing and mandatory minimums.[62] Meanwhile, states' strained budgets led legislatures to privatize programs and services in public penal facilities, and prisoners were put to work in record numbers (see Figure 1.1).

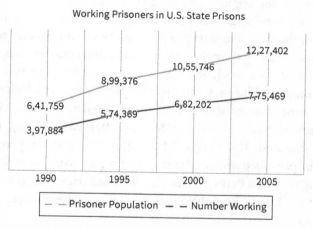

Figure 1.1 Rise of total and working prisoner populations in U.S. state prisons, 1990–2005.

These data are drawn from Bureau of Justice Statistics (BJS) reports: James Stephan, "Census of State and Federal Correctional Facilities, 1990," Census of State and Federal Correctional Facilities (Washington, DC: Bureau of Justice Statistics, 1992), https://www.bjs.gov/index.cfm?ty=pbdetail&iid=4067; James Stephan, "Census of State and Federal Correctional Facilities, 1995," Census of State and Federal Correctional Facilities (Washington, DC: Bureau of Justice Statistics, 1997), https://www.bjs.gov/index.cfm?ty=pbdetail&iid=535; James Stephan and Jennifer Karberg, "Census of State and Federal Correctional Facilities, 2000," Census of State and Federal Correctional Facilities (Washington, DC: Bureau of Justice Statistics, 2003), https://www.bjs.gov/index.cfm?ty=pbdetail&iid=533; Stephan, "Census of State and Federal Correctional Facilities, 2005." At the time of this writing, the most recent full BJS report from this series was for 2005. Statistical tables released in advance of the 2019 report confirm that 99.7 percent of state prisoners were held in facilities housing work programs, although details on how many imprisoned individuals held such jobs have not been released.

Credit: Author.

The Great Recession of 2007 to 2009, unlike the Great Depression nearly a century earlier, raised anxieties over the costs of incarceration and the criminal justice system renewed its emphasis on personal and fiscal responsibility, privatization, and the commodification of services, goods, and labor power behind bars.[63] As penal budgets thinned, facilities slashed prison programming, including work training and educational programs, and their per capita (more precisely, per captive) spending dropped precipitously.[64] Penal labor has both ensured prisons' fiscal stability and maintained the veneer of providing rehabilitative programming from that point to the present.

Today, states compel the imprisoned to work to benefit their captor institutions as well as municipalities in need.[65] Some two-thirds of those held in state prisons work. Most fill "facility support" roles, maintaining the prison or generating revenue for its operating budget, and a few work beyond the walls on state projects including maintaining public parks and roadways.[66] Most penitentiaries also house some manner of state-run "correctional industries," which are more unreservedly profit-oriented and often governed by differing sets of state and DOC policy.[67] Throughout the country, people confined in prisons perform cleaning and repair work, as well as jobs ranging from data entry to textile manufacturing, call center operation to wildland firefighting, and seemingly every occupation in between.[68]

Importantly, working prisoners—whose labor is necessarily coerced—are not formally classified as *employees*.[69] They do not have the protections and guarantees of work in the free world, and they can be sanctioned for refusing to work: "punishments for refusing to [work] include solitary confinement, loss of earned good time, and revocation of family visitation."[70] Typical Occupational Safety and Health Administration (OSHA) regulations, which aim to guarantee safety in the workplace, are absent from many facilities,[71] and workers toil without social security benefits or protective interventions like the federal minimum wage.[72] As prison wages stagnate (or, in some cases, drop[73]), prisoners are being made responsible for expenses including rising fees to access medical care, use telephones and electricity, and supplement the diminishing provision of institutional food and hygiene products. In a scheme called "pay-to-stay," many are assessed fees for the "privilege" of the prison's "room and board."[74]

Neoliberal penology after the Great Recession

Labor has been consequential throughout the history of American punishment (see Figure 1.2). The contemporary state's dependence on prisoners' labor to meet economic and operational imperatives reflects a distinctly neoliberal approach to punishment. The political philosophy of neoliberalism (which, as I have noted, rose to new prominence in the U.S. with the Reagan administration) prizes fiscal responsibility and individual self-reliance. Under this framework, the state's social welfare function is superseded by the mission of protecting capitalist markets from regulatory interventions (and occasional collapse).[75] Yet, under neoliberal "small government," the state carries a big stick. State interventions involving severe forms of policing, supervision, and incarceration are celebrated and naturalized. In fact, these practices effectively keep people judged superfluous or antagonistic to labor markets from "undeserved" access to dwindling social supports. State actors surveil the formal employment participation of the poor and formerly incarcerated, and with shocking efficiency they extract the labor of the *currently* imprisoned.

The influence of neoliberalism on penal policy and practice notably intensified following the Great Recession when politicians in the U.S. and elsewhere in the world took up the banner of fiscal austerity. Earlier cuts became gouges to government agencies' budgets, and though the U.S. prisoner population had reached new heights, per capita corrections spending continued to drop.[76] Neoliberal approaches to justice, narrated through the rhetoric of scarcity and bootstraps, expanded as institutional budgets contracted,[77] placing more of the economic

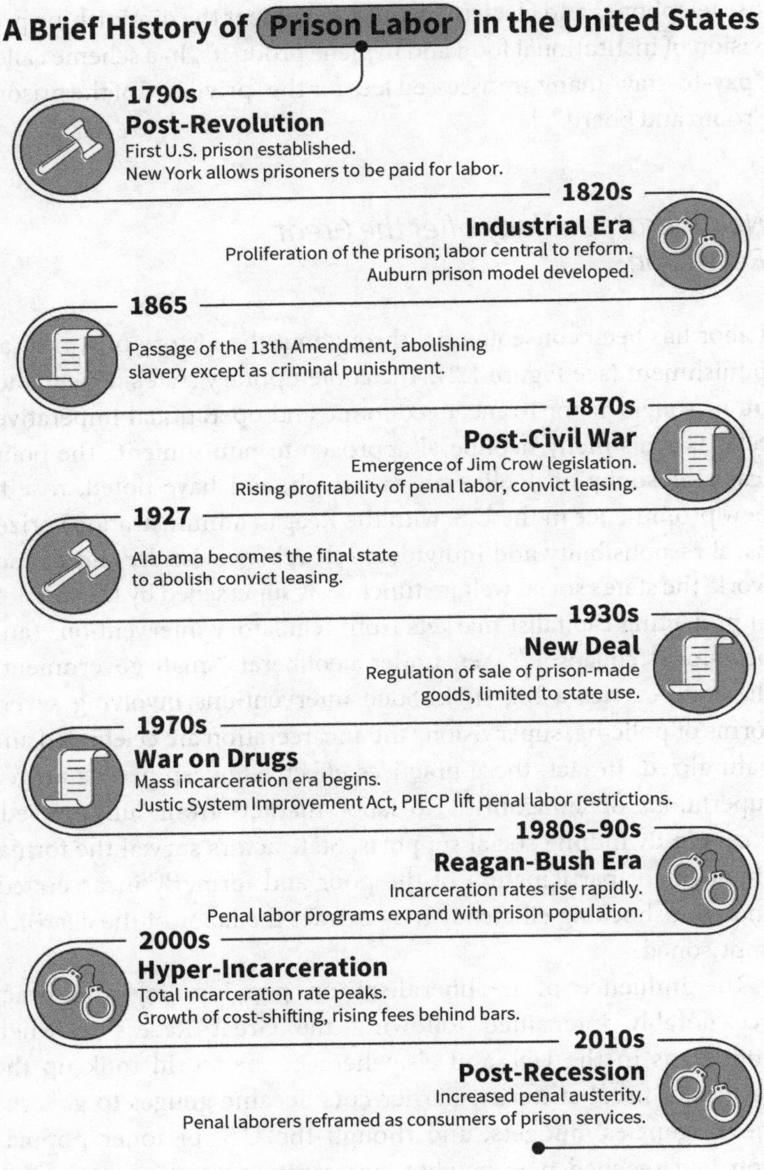

A Brief History of (Prison Labor) in the United States

1790s
Post-Revolution
First U.S. prison established.
New York allows prisoners to be paid for labor.

1820s
Industrial Era
Proliferation of the prison; labor central to reform.
Auburn prison model developed.

1865
Passage of the 13th Amendment, abolishing
slavery except as criminal punishment.

1870s
Post-Civil War
Emergence of Jim Crow legislation.
Rising profitability of penal labor, convict leasing.

1927
Alabama becomes the final state
to abolish convict leasing.

1930s
New Deal
Regulation of sale of prison-made
goods, limited to state use.

1970s
War on Drugs
Mass incarceration era begins.
Justic System Improvement Act, PIECP lift penal labor restrictions.

1980s–90s
Reagan-Bush Era
Incarceration rates rise rapidly.
Penal labor programs expand with prison population.

2000s
Hyper-Incarceration
Total incarceration rate peaks.
Growth of cost-shifting, rising fees behind bars.

2010s
Post-Recession
Increased penal austerity.
Penal laborers reframed as consumers of prison services.

Figure 1.2 Key moments in the labor history of American punishment.
Credit: Author, redrawn by Chelsea Nicolas.

burdens of incarceration on the shoulders of prisoners, reframed as "consumers" of prison services.[78]

Scholars refer to the United States' flourishing neoliberal penology, under which systems of punishment have evolved to prioritize fiscal efficiency over other outcomes, like rehabilitation.[79] The coupling of heavy reliance on carceral institutions with increasingly harsh welfare policy exposes an overarching punitive political project, through which, in the words of sociologist Loïc Wacquant, "the penal state tends, for the categories confined to the lower reaches of the social and spatial structure, to replace the social state."[80] Already, considerable scholarship has detailed the broad reaches of neoliberal punishment platforms. Zooming in, this book draws out the micro- and meso-level implications of the techniques of neoliberal penology implemented and imposed within prison walls, unlocking the doors to a contemporary site of deep and lasting stratification. In its pages, you will see how neoliberalism infuses daily prison life and how the quality of individual encounters with penal institutions has become closely tied to the individual prisoner's ability to succeed in prisons' insular work worlds. Unlike classical critical scholarship, which calls attention to macro connections between political economy and punishment,[81] we will look at the ways labor is foregrounded in the contemporary penal facility, altering prison life in accordance with each prisoner's competitiveness in the internal labor pool.

Theoretical Toolkit and Chapter Summaries

Two theoretical traditions are particularly key to my inquiry throughout this book. First, I use what may be called the social reproduction framework, derived from the sociology of culture, to make sense of the ways incarcerated individuals are sorted into distinct social positions. Second, I employ the labor process perspective, developed by scholars focused on the sociology of work, which allows me to analyze ground-level workplace dynamics and assess their impacts on personal and material outcomes. (Not every reader, I understand, wishes to absorb a precis of sociological approaches;

if that's you, a short outline of the book and its sections is only a few paragraphs away, under the heading "Chapter summaries.")

Theoretical tools

The sociology of culture teaches us that social institutions, such as workplaces, schools, and prisons, classify individuals in ways that favor those from advantaged backgrounds.[82] Sociologist Pierre Bourdieu offers a valuable template of the social world for uncovering the particular skills, outlooks, and resources prized in certain settings and how these replicate privilege and power over time. According to Bourdieu, the modern world is made up of competitive "fields" in which actors use various social resources—which he refers to as "capitals"—to secure influence or reward.[83] In this sense, capital is not only financial capital, but a range of "resources that provide different forms of power."[84] Thus, individuals may be said to have economic capital (wealth and property), but also cultural capital (embodied forms of useful knowledge or dispositions) and social capital (durable ties to influential others).[85] The social structure of actors within any given field may be "defined by the unequal distribution of capital" across those actors, according to Bourdieu.[86] Viewing the social world through this lens highlights how individuals or groups that reflect or embody valued skills, characteristics, and outlooks may be rewarded greater access to desired outcomes. Those lacking in prized areas, on the other hand, may face significant hurdles to success.

Social institutions classify social actors in accordance with which valued capitals they do or do not possess. For example, institutions may "sort and sieve" individuals along the lines of socioeconomic background and resources.[87] When rigid institutional structures demand adherence to particular dispositions or norms, groups that do not or cannot conform are likely to suffer.[88] Put differently, rather than transferring valuable resources to those who lack them, key institutions classify individuals according to the capitals they already possess and treat the groups unequally. By privileging some and punishing others, institutions operate as agents of "ritual exclusion," strengthening rather than eroding the boundaries between social classes.[89] By employing this perspective, I consider how various skills, resources, and characteristics are deployed and evaluated in the carceral job search, as well as how these unequal sorting processes stratify the prisoner population along the lines of class, race, and ethnicity, hardening disadvantage.

The sociology of work, on the other hand, has informed my view of the prison system as a labor market institution with powerful implications for unemployment rates and stratification in the free world. Scholars have even contended that penal policy directly responds to market needs by actively controlling and limiting the labor power of the poor.[90] These outcomes are of vital social consequence, but so, too, are the on-the-ground realities of combining work and punishment. Here, as well, the prison remains a "black box." People go in, people come out. We know that what happens in prisons is consequential for individual outcomes and for society writ large, but our actual knowledge of internal labor conditions and experiences remains sorely limited.

The labor process perspective turns toward ground-level workplace practices to understand patterns of managerial control, worker agency, internal and external labor market dynamics, and related phenomena across diverse labor contexts.[91] This framework recognizes that workers are not mere cogs, but agentic social actors who engage in diverse practices and strategies at the site of production. Here, sociologist Michael Burawoy's insights are particularly fruitful.[92] To learn why workers behave the way that they do—why, for instance, they work as *hard* as they do or continue to participate in exploitative labor relationships that seem to go against their own interests—Burawoy and subsequent labor process scholars have keyed into the dynamics of the shop floor. In workplaces, external and internal labor conditions interact to facilitate workers' uptake of different forms of collective action through which they endure work while seeking desired outcomes, including material rewards as well as improved senses of self-worth.[93] Managers, in turn, may mobilize such processes to evoke productivity or acquiescence to work conditions. By applying this paradigm to penal labor, I uncover a variety of strategies that carceral workforces use to cope with, resist, or try to rise above the conditions of work in confinement, taking action to secure a measure of personal and collective dignity.

Chapter summaries

I employ theoretical tools from cultural and labor analysis to investigate the manner in which imprisoned laborers secure work, the factors that shape this process, and various outcomes of unequal job sorting behind bars. Setting the stage for this effort, Chapter 2 details the expansive labor structure inside SSP. Prisoners' own accounts guide my descriptions of the work offerings, so that their assessments of what they value in a prison job, what they seek to avoid, and how they assess the management, organization, and daily realities of different worksites form a typology ranging from top-tier "good prison jobs" to bottom-tier "bad prison jobs." This chapter also introduces four carceral workplaces upon which the remainder of the book focuses (a food preparation warehouse, an auto garage, a call center, and a sign shop), outlining the organization and day-to-day experiences of jobs at different tiers of desirability and their impacts on carceral experiences.

In Chapter 3, I turn to the carceral employment system as an institution mediating social mobility—and immobility—for a distinct rung of society. If everyone is required to work, and if there are "good jobs" and "bad jobs," who decides which people get which job—and how do they make that decision? The social reproduction framework teaches us that prisoners held in the same facility and on similar charges are likely sorted into jobs in ways that correspond to their existing forms and levels of capital. After all, we know that punishment technologies are differentially deployed against prisoner groups, such that, for instance, there are differences in the treatment and experiences of people held in men's vs. women's facilities and across custody and detention levels, resulting in some groups experiencing distinctive challenges.[94] I argue that the contemporary prison, like other classifying institutions, is not truly engaged in teaching new skills or conferring novel outlooks, despite those invested in the purportedly rehabilitative capacity of incarceration. Rather, by rewarding top positions to the already endowed, it is, as Bourdieu says of elite schools, "merely teaching fish to swim."[95] Those found "lacking" are not only barred from the top, but actively relegated to the bottom of the institution's labor, economic, and social hierarchies.

Chapter 4 is devoted to unpacking the explicit role of race in job sorting and how penal labor functions as a racializing institution. Specifically, I find that the forms of capital valued in the carceral employment system are often deeply intertwined with race. As a result, minoritized workers—U.S. citizens as well as foreign nationals—accrue additional barriers to success, personal agency, and dignity under the guise of "job fit." Despite official agendas, DOC policies often contribute to penal labor segregation, as do informal codes of "racial politics," or prison-specific norms governing interactions between and behaviors within ethnoracial groups.[96] Individual acts of discrimination magnify such phenomena in what can be called a hyper-racialized space.[97] These individual- and organizational-level factors interact with arrays of capital to reproduce and reinforce processes of racialization in the contemporary American prison.

Complementing the preceding chapters' focus on job-sorting, Chapter 5 considers the internal outcomes of penal labor stratification through the comparative material wellbeing of working prisoners. At SSP, the lowest-paid laborers receive approximately $0.09 per hour and the highest-paid receive approximately $2.34.[98] How does the prisoner wage gap shape precarity behind bars and individuals' preparations for release? Disadvantaged prisoners, as mentioned above, often struggle to purchase food or hygiene products from the commissary store, and they may be unable to afford the fees charged for visiting a doctor, calling a loved one, or using an outlet to power personal electronics. The prison's black-market, in which prisoners can access healthier foods, warmer clothing, and other vital goods, may also be out of their reach. So, while everyone behind bars faces harsh treatment and limited protections, higher-paid prisoners are better able to meet their needs and perhaps a "want" or two. Like Jake, several of those assigned to "good jobs" reported amassing savings for release or sending funds home to support their families.

Chapter 6 moves from the economic to the personal, using the labor process perspective to consider how job types affect prisoners' agency and dignity. In micro-level interactions between workers and overseers, worksite variation fosters the emergence of different worker strategies (what some labor scholars term "work games"[99]). Strategic action in this context may be understood as a form of "secondary adjustments" (a term coined by foundational sociologist Erving Goffman) or arrangements "by which a member of an organisation employs unauthorised means, or obtains unauthorised ends, or both, thus getting around the organisation's assumptions as to what he should do and get and hence what he should be."[100] I document how different strategies map onto discrete approaches to dignity, enabling some to acquire or safeguard positive identities while others may be too busy resisting mortification to do the same. In this way, the structure of the prison employment system bounds different experiences of work, punishment, and self-worth. As a result, even the simplest coping strategy may indirectly contribute to the reproduction of underlying institutional structures that are detrimental to the larger incarcerated population.

In the final chapter, I return to the practice of prison labor amid the evolution of neoliberal penology. My analysis of the ground-level forces of punishment and labor inform my understanding of macro-trends in terms of the broader objectives, discourses, and techniques of neoliberalized punishment. I consider how alterations to the carceral status quo, championed by institutional actors, policymakers, and anyone invested in reconciling patterns of class and racial inequity and exploitation within the nation's penal facilities, might contribute to a more just criminal justice apparatus by building on the insights of incarcerated individuals as well as radical reformers and stalwart scholars.

* * *

In what follows, I document how carceral labor shapes prisoner experiences in ways that reproduce and exacerbate inequalities between social groups. It is important to once again underscore that this does not occur solely in "private prisons." Most U.S. prisons, including SSP, are staffed and managed by state employees, yet stratification and exploitation persist in these public institutions. I will also caution that issues of inequality behind bars cannot be addressed by simply increasing the proportion of so-called "good" jobs in this setting. All imprisoned workers, regardless of their standing in the prison labor hierarchy, faced hardships that came with serving a prison stint. By illustrating moments of struggle and suffering, as well as perseverance, cooperation, and sometimes playfulness in their accounts, this book seeks to pay tribute to the enduring humanity of these orange-collar laborers so often obscured from public and scholarly view.

2
It's Like Its Own City

The Prison Employment System

> Visiting these various establishments, we have been sur-
> prised by the order, and sometimes the talent, with which
> the convicts work; and what makes their zeal quite sur-
> prising is that they work without any interest in its produce.
> —**Gustave de Beaumont and Alexis de Tocqueville (1833)**

The View from Outside: Prisoner Labor as Monolithic

As the morning sun slowly rises over a wide stretch of interstate highway, eight men occupy a small patch of land on the side of the busy roadway. The temperature, already climbing, will exceed heat advisory levels in a matter of hours. Seven of these men sport the same uniform: vivid orange short-sleeve shirts, orange pants, and worn black boots. The letters "DOC" (Department of Corrections) are emblazoned down their shirt backs and pant legs. One of them wears an orange bucket hat, two others wear wide-brimmed straw hats fraying at the edges, and the rest wear sweat-stained orange trucker caps. All wear sunglasses and yellow reflective vests for roadside safety. A decal on the side of a nearby van announces to passersby that these are imprisoned workers from a state prison, Sunbelt State Penitentiary (SSP). As morning commuters speed past, these men haul large, clear plastic trash bags over their shoulders, most already filled with refuse collected from the side of the road. They wield pointed rods that they call "litter sticks" to pierce strewn cups, food containers, bits of plastic and paper, and other garbage that they will shake into the bags. Some hold two bags with the same hand, a sign that they are "beasting it"—a competitive game of one-upmanship that working prisoners sometimes play to pass the time by seeing who can collect and carry the most.

An eighth man stands in the shade of the van in silence. He is a correctional officer tasked with surveilling this captive crew. His collared shirt and slacks—not to mention his fully stocked and armed utility belt—distinguish him from the orange-clad workers. With thumbs hooked into his belt, he scans the surrounding area calmly, his face largely obscured by wraparound mirrored sunglasses and a dark cap pulled down low. He turns his head quickly to the left when one incarcerated worker momentarily sets down his equipment to stretch. The man in orange tilts his hat up to wipe the sweat from his brow and briefly squints into the sight of oncoming traffic and a neon truck stop sign at the next exit. Noting the officer's gaze, he picks up his bag and returns to his task.

This roadside crew represents the quintessential public image of carceral labor. For most of the morning commuters on this stretch of highway—like many Americans in general—this passing scene will likely be their only firsthand view of forced labor. Aside from the occasional news story exposing, for example, a clothing company's reliance on prison-produced textiles, or depictions of incarcerated kitchen workers on dramatic television programs, the institution of penal labor appears somewhat monolithic.

Yet the reality of prisoner work on-the-ground is quite distinct from this popular image. In the early days of my fieldwork at SSP, I would quickly learn what those on the inside already knew: that the world of work behind bars is quite expansive, diverse, and competitive. The nation's sprawling penal complexes are home to many distinct jobs, each entailing different combinations of difficulty, pay, and perks. The prison relies on codified rules to organize daily labors and govern the assignment, management, and expectations of different jobs. It is also home to numerous informal norms surrounding work, which sometimes supersede official departmental orders in day-to-day practice. A large internal workforce made up of the captive population navigates this labor system, compelled to compete for the most desirable positions. They may be evaluated based on their skills, social connections, and other resources in hiring decisions. And, as in the free world, a shrouded informal market, in which entrepreneurial individuals sell illicit goods and services, flourishes in the shadows of the formal system.

Taken together, these features characterize what labor scholars call an employment system: an organized system of labor complete with numerous jobs of different skill and pay levels, diverse workers seeking these jobs to secure wages and various perks, and basic rules and norms that classify and regulate workers, managers, and worksites.[1] The *prison* employment system is comprised of workers in the form of prisoners (although they cannot legally be categorized as "employees"[2]). They produce goods and provide services that are utilized by local, state, and federal institutions, as well as by private firms and (often unknowingly) consumers in the free world. In addition, correctional officers and other staffers may fulfil roles reminiscent of frontline managers in this setting, while DOC administrators, the state, and the private firms that contract prisoner labor oversee production and service from atop the institutional hierarchy.

In essence, the entirety of the prison is organized in one way or another around labor. A majority of prisoners spend their weekday hours working.[3] Institutional security staff coordinate and surveil these workers and their activities. On the one hand, the prison participates in the national economy through the provisioning of goods and services generated by the incarcerated workforce—acting as both a purveyor and labor market institution.[4] On the other hand, it also resembles a microcosm of the broader economy. As one staff member would put it: "The prison is like its own city, where the prisoners do all of the work."[5]

Approaching the prison as an employment system, I highlight the perspective of the unheard workers in this arrangement. How vast is the variety of labor duties that occupy their time in the penitentiary? How do they evaluate or rank the many work offerings behind bars? Put another way: For the majority today, to be sent to prison is to be sent to work; so, what does this work look like and how do prisoners feel about it? To address these questions, I illustrate the diverse world of work at SSP, chronicling the sights and sounds of the bustling institution in which so much activity revolves around labor. Drawing on the insights of the incarcerated, this chapter explores the perks and drawbacks of different worksites through their eyes. Not all prison jobs are equal, and workers' valuations inform their practices and strategies as they navigate prison life and labor. Prisons are characteristically physically removed from society, often rendering these and related phenomena invisible to the public.[6] Entering the prison to conduct ethnographic fieldwork, I was granted a rare look at this hidden and complex world.

The Diversity of Penal Labor: A Tour of Sunbelt State Penitentiary

The road to SSP is long and narrow with little to see in either direction. At 6:00 am, two snaking lines of light crowd the lanes—one long row of red taillights belonging to staffers entering the prison to begin their shifts, and one white row of headlights belonging to the departing officers whom they are relieving. It is shift change at SSP. The night crew exits, the morning shift enters, and white vans sit idling by the prison gates. These prisoner transports wait patiently for the outside work crews to be "turned out" to be taken to worksites throughout the state. Each van is already outfitted with trailers hauling portable chemical toilets, water coolers, and the appropriate tools for the day's work. An incarcerated shoeshine looks on from his makeshift station—an old desk chair atop a wooden box—as staff and prisoners enter and exit for work. He awaits instructions from any correctional officer (CO) who might require his services. Having no "customers" at the moment, he sits calmly in the chair, hands folded over his stomach.

By 7:00 am, the workday for most incarcerated laborers has begun. Just outside the gates, three grounds crewmen are spread out near the road. They wear reflective yellow vests over their orange attire. There appears to be no one immediately supervising them. Two of the men dig up weeds with ancient hoes, a third reclines *in* his wheelbarrow beneath a withered tree, one leg propped upwards. He leans forward slightly to get a good look at me over his sunglasses. Recognizing me as the visiting researcher and not a CO come to punish him for lounging on the job, he greets me with one of my prison nicknames—"Hey, *Flaco!*"—and reclines back once more. Closer to the main point of entry, another small crew drags red plastic rakes over an area of gravel. They slowly pull their tools along precise, parallel rows, like sullen Zen monks tending a garden. A CO stands by, leaning on a knee propped up on a bench. Apparently lost in thought, his thousand-yard stare peers through the men.

Beyond layers of barbed wire fencing can be spied a massive green tractor, driven by a smiling heavy-equipment operator in orange. He is dragging the interior perimeter of the complex grounds, loosening dirt and spreading it in even lines. This stretch of earth is tilled regularly as a security measure so that boot imprints will cleanly register in the fresh soil. As the tractor rumbles closer, the sight of the drab buildings of the institution temporarily melts into the thick clouds of dust it kicks up.

I walk past birds chirping from coiling razor wire perches. The shoeshine looks on as I approach the metal detector at the main entrance. A rigid CO rattles off a standard inquiry: "Any weapons, explosives, ammunition, cell phones, pagers, laptops, drugs, alcohol, currency, or any other contraband?" I answer, "No," and empty my pockets into a plastic tub before proceeding through. A perimeter patrol truck creeps by. The bulky pickup has bright spotlights bolted to the sides of its bed and a shotgun visibly mounted beside the driver. As the thick, metal double-gate croaks open, I move forward through the security line and gather my belongings (car keys, wallet, pen, and notebook for recording fieldnotes). On the other side of the armored entrance, a prisoner throws open the door of a rickety shuttle bus. He is the driver. Another batch of night-shift COs and nurses emerge from the tram while incoming employees standby to board. Inside, it smells of coffee and sweat. As they step up, each rider announces their destination: "Building 7." "Education." "Psych wing." The driver nods solemnly. Each hard plastic seat fills and one man stands in the aisle.

The shuttle weaves smoothly between massive, pale buildings encased in steel and razor wire. They seem truly impenetrable. We cruise along double layers of fencing, twenty feet high. Blinking red lights along the top remind us that security systems are armed and online.

The ride through the complex offers a detailed snapshot of the division of penal labor. As the shuttle progresses to its first stop, we pass the complex laundry where more men in orange lug bulging burlap bags out of industrial-era green machines under dim sulfur lights. We pass a row of men hunched over in a row at the side of the road, hacking at weed patches with old rakes. One gazes longingly at an airplane coasting overhead. In the distance, a yellow backhoe bounces across an open expanse on its way to some worksite within the facility, its incarcerated operator bobbing behind the wheel. We approach another shuttle and the drivers exchange nods as they cross paths.

Through several layers of razor wire fence sits the largest yard of the prison, where well over one thousand men eat, sleep, and pass the time however they can. At this moment, one hundred or so stand together outside two massive gates. They are still waiting to be "turned out" for the day to head off to their work assignments. A bus with chipped, white paint and barred windows waits on the outside for them to be directed through. Half will ride this bus to another area of the prison for work in the food factory—a food preparation warehouse in which prisoners prepare lunches for the entire complex—where they will wrap sandwiches or lunchmeat for the next six hours. The remainder will board other buses or vans to take them to different sites within the facility, such as the sign shop or auto garage, or beyond institutional grounds to collect trash from roadsides or parks.

On a later date I would view these "turn outs" from a closer vantage point. Waiting prisoners shuffle around between the sally port gates. After twenty minutes, a CO emerges through a door from the small building connected to the secure entryway and waves them on. They quickly form a rough line and, one-by-one, stand before a small camcorder, remove their hat, and state their name and identification number into the camera (a security measure implemented years ago following the escape of a prisoner who no longer resembled his file photo, enabling him to elude local police for a time). Some stare at the ground while waiting. Others joke with fellow prisoners or the COs. When the line progresses slowly, one man shouts out, "This is fucking ridiculous! I quit! Haha!" The CO behind the camera smiles and looks up, "Yeah, you *better* be playing." When the next man reaches his mark, another dares him, "Hey, sing like Aerosmith into the camera." After reciting their information, each man shuffles through the external gate and ascends the steps of a bus waiting to transport them to work, wherever that may be.

Within the nearby dust-worn buildings, others have already begun their workdays. These are the men whose jobs take place on the yard—that is, within the confines of the secured area surrounding the housing bays. Not having to exit the gates means no long waits for the bus and less exposure to additional security protocols, including the "strip shack," where carceral laborers are commanded to "strip down, squat, cough" for inspection. Incarcerated tutors help civilian educators set up their classrooms. Porters mop. "Knob polishers" buff doorknobs and brass fixtures. "Butt collectors" empty dustpans full of spent cigarette filters picked from cracks in the pavement. HVAC teams and electrical crews troubleshoot utility malfunctions. Coffee-fueled advertising salesmen are already two hours into a twelve-hour shift of cold-calling customers from the prison call center. Kitchen workers shovel out "late breakfast" to the non-working prisoners still on the yard. And, off of official prison books, those operating in the informal economy gamble, amass others' laundry to wash, clean up other men's bunks, or carefully construct artistic "hobbycraft" items—portraits, cards, or sculptures crafted with clever combinations of goods from the commissary store—to be sold in the underground economy.

These varied activities represent only a portion of the tasks that occupy the time of the men at SSP, yet they highlight the diversity of work behind bars. Each offers its own combination of perks and drawbacks. Some informally function as punishments dished out to those deemed noncompliant or uncooperative. Others are awarded to those with valued experiences and resources, as later chapters will detail. All jobs are evaluated against one another by workers navigating the carceral employment system.

Evaluating Work: Prisoners' Rankings of Prison Jobs

Incarcerated laborers draw on various criteria to assess and compare work offerings. Many parallel those valued by workers in the free world. According to the sociologist Arne Kalleberg's study of "good jobs" and "bad jobs" in the American economy, job quality may be assessed by rate of pay, skill level, degree of worker control or autonomy, security and stability, opportunities for advancement, and available perks or fringe benefits.[7] While research in the sociology of work offers a thorough understanding of how individuals assess the sites and conditions of their labor in the formal sector, such processes remain underexplored behind bars, despite work's central place in penal operations.

Though similar in key ways, worker evaluations take unique shape when filtered through the prison context. In gauging the appeal of different jobs, the incarcerated weigh the nature of the work itself alongside the carceral conditions surrounding it. Hence, some positions that might be considered undesirable in the free world are instead highly regarded behind bars, highlighting the relativity of such evaluations. Numerous characteristics informed worker opinions regarding which prison jobs they might compete to secure, and which they might scheme to avoid. I draw these together to construct a tiered typology of prisoners' informal rankings of prison jobs.

Key features of prison jobs

Wages are crucial for surviving a prison sentence today. Some American states offer no pay for prisoners' mandated labors—a fact that has only contributed to the image of penal labor as a new form of slavery.[8] Most institutions, including SSP, do provide some, if meager, payment. Yet, like in the free world, this pay is far from uniform between sites or workers. A wide pay gap divided classes of prisoners at SSP. Those at the bottom rungs of the wage ladder received around $0.09 per hour.[9] Many hovered around $0.20 or less. Working one's way up to the standard hourly pay cap of approximately $0.50 was possible, but difficult. Doing so required receiving positive evaluations from staff supervisors, avoiding disciplinary tickets, and holding a high school degree or equivalent. Meeting these prerequisites was often not enough, however, as final decisions depended on approval from the officer in charge of pay budgeting for the entire unit.

It was no coincidence that the work assignments deemed the "best jobs" were also the best paying. Two special sites were permitted to exceed the standard wage cap. First, the sign shop offered a starting pay of $0.50 and could pay up to approximately $1 an hour after periodic raises. Second, pay at the call center started at $1, well exceeding the pay of most workers. If they met sales quotas and received satisfactory reviews, salesmen became eligible for quarterly raises that could increase wages to a maximum of approximately $2.34 an hour.

The costs of imprisonment are increasingly shifted to the imprisoned, who must pay fees for things like medical care, electricity, telephone services, and more. Higher-paid working prisoners can even have room and board charges deducted from wages.[10] What's more, as the quality and quantity of institutional meal offerings decline, men and women behind bars have come to rely heavily on supplemental items purchased from the prison commissary, which sometimes cost more than in stores in the outside world (more on this in Chapter 5). According to one SSP worker, higher paying jobs "are the only ones where you can *survive* in here—you can afford food and hygiene."

Beyond pay, the skill level of jobs carried considerable weight. The institution classified worksites as "skilled" or "unskilled";[11] however, skilled or vocational programming has grown rare alongside other service degradations throughout the nation's prisons.[12] To prisoners at SSP, such jobs promised the potential to acquire or hone marketable abilities to improve their prospects for labor market reentry. One worker, Ben, related that he applied for a position in the prison sign shop solely to build up his résumé and "get real experience" to better his odds in the outside market. "I didn't think I'd live past 30," he said, "so I need a new plan for the *next* 30 years." Skilled jobs were also often mentally demanding, helping the hours in the day pass faster. This was important as prisoners frequently battled slow time over long sentences. "The perks of this job," said one laborer holding a position classified as skilled, "is that . . . time goes by pretty fast. Days, weeks, months pass by like no other job." Moreover, skilled work brought status on the yard in contrast to others who were deemed unskilled or unmotivated. As one man from a skilled site asserted, "You gotta have some *drive*. Lot'a guys don't really have that—that's why they're stuck [in deskilled jobs]."

Accordingly, any job promising greater autonomy or freedom of movement around the workspace was highly valued in the restrictive carceral space. For some, this feature took some getting used to. In the engraving shop—where prisoners crafted fine plaques for the DOC and other state agencies—workers were typically allowed to recline in their desk chairs and chat during slow hours. Shortly after getting hired there, a man called Low-Light shared with me, "It's weird when it's slow—I get nervous when the boss comes around, seeing me sit. Like, 'Oh, shit, should I jump up [and work]??' But I think it's cool. Not like in the bakery. That was slave work over there. Always working, busting your ass. They'll jump down your throat if you slack off over there."

"Sounds bad," I replied. Shaking his head, he affirmed, "*Terrible.* You don't really get breaks—only every once in a while, if they decide you do. Sometimes you have to work through lunch. You eat and work at some of the positions."

It is common in prison to be moved without notice. One may be relocated to a new bunk unexpectedly, or "rolled up" in the middle of the night and transported to a new unit in the same facility or to entirely new prisons without warning. This unpredictability is a facet of modern punishment. As a result, any semblance of consistency or stability is appreciated. Workers prized sites in which transfers, demotions, and terminations were less frequent. Those in skilled positions were often officially placed on institutional "hold," protecting them from relocation, save for security or disciplinary interventions. CO Bush, tasked with overseeing work and educational program placements, said, "You don't want these guys moving from skilled jobs—the sign shop, the call center . . . . So, I'll place a work hold on the skilled workers. They [DOC] can still move them, but it won't be part of *daily* movement. There better be a *reason* [for it]."

Still, for most outside of protected workplaces, the risk of transfer remained an everyday prospect. Certain sites were notorious for high turnover and frequent demotions or restructuring. As one staff member put it, shuffling through the captive labor force was simple because "[we] don't have to have a paper trail to fire somebody." This was apparent in the food factory, where staff estimated a monthly turnover rate of "about twenty percent." In reality, the rate was likely much higher. CO Byrne, who oversaw the eighty- to ninety-man crew in this site, said, "[I get] about two new guys each day, I'd say . . . . There's always somebody else for them to shoot in."

Another feature that penal laborers desired was the opportunity for advancement within worksites. Many housed various workstations through which prisoners might progress. One benefit of this was the possibility to learn or implement a wider variety of skills. Eli, an "old number" veteran of the prison system, looked forward to his release in twenty-one months. He shared his plan: "To learn every skill the [sign] shop has to offer—every station . . . . And this is the most enlightening [job] because the skills can be used on the outside." Another perk of mobility was the opportunity to break up the monotony of day-to-day prison life. By hopping between stations over the years, one could ensure a more diverse experience. This was particularly valued by those facing long sentences.

Some jobs boasted unique features that workers valued. For instance, food prep jobs were generally derided for their poor pay, instability, and restrictions on worker movements; however, they facilitated access to snacks and supplementary rations. According to Willie, "There's perks to working in the kitchen—you get to eat before everybody else, and then [again] after. So, you get extra meals!" Chow line workers were known to stash away edibles, which could then be sold in the prison black market. Despite the best attempts of staffers trying to curb illicit trade, the informal economy of SSP was replete with cookies, chips, meats, bell peppers, zucchinis, and other fresh produce smuggled out of the kitchens and the food factory by enterprising risk-takers. For many men ineligible for or otherwise unable to secure higher-paying jobs, gaining access to a site from which they might pilfer was a potential perk.

Finally, being assigned to some positions could cause undue conflicts for a worker. Positions such as shoeshine or staff barber, for example, were perceived by many to entail an unacceptable degree of submission as workers directly attended to the personal needs of overseers. These jobs also often required interacting one-on-one with correctional officers for sustained periods of time. As such, men who actively pursued jobs like this might be suspected of being "snitches" or "rats." Some groups collectively refused to work in such positions for these reasons. These worksite boycotts were often enforced by different ethnoracial cliques on the prison yard. (Chapter 4 will unpack the racialized social structure of SSP and its influence on labor practices and hiring.)

Three Tiers of Work at SSP

While individual prisoners might prioritize workplace features in different ways, most relied on some combination of the considerations outlined above. Many worksites were appraised in broad strokes. For instance, certain jobs were commonly referred to as "good" or "the best" jobs (e.g., "That is the best job going" or, more colorfully, "This job is gold"). Others evoked classification as "bad" or "the worst" (e.g., "That's the worst job I ever had" or, with greater specificity, "It's bullshit over there—they don't pay good and they'll work the hell out of you"). Piecing these accounts together, I adopt the language of "tiers" to capture patterns in how different positions were described. Rather than representing concrete classifications, this informal ranking system instead considers standings in more general terms. In doing so, it sets the stage for future chapters to explore how jobs along this hierarchy are allocated, as well as the outcomes of such processes.

The bottom tier of the labor hierarchy at SSP primarily represents low paying jobs classified as unskilled, or those that have otherwise been deemed problematic by prisoners. These typically exhibited few, if any, of the features that workers valued most. In many cases, laborers near-unanimously derided them as "bad jobs." Examples include scrubbing tiles on the floor crew, collecting garbage, tarring roofs, cleaning toilets as a porter, washing laundry, or raking or collecting cigarette butts on the grounds crew. Workers in such jobs often reported feeling "trapped," with little hope of advancing to better opportunities. Some of these positions were assigned as punishment. According to one worker, Hoke, jobs like "cigarette butt collector" or "rake pusher" were typically reserved for "guys that screw up." On formal disciplinary paperwork, this sanction was listed as "extra duty."

The food factory was a quintessential bottom-tier job. Here, a crew of approximately eighty to ninety workers prepared bagged lunches—colloquially referred to as "bag nasties"—and other meal items for the entire institutional population. During busy weeks, they might ship out up to sixty thousand units. A few men operated the bakery crew and the special diet prep team, which were classified as "semi-skilled" stations, but the overwhelming majority held so-called unskilled positions like wrapping lunchmeat or bread in plastic during each long workday. This was "zombie work," according to a participant called Stavo. Another man, LD, started his penal labor tenure rolling bologna in the food factory before eventually making his way to the prison sign shop. Now securely stationed in a "good job," he asserted that "the [programming] officer just throws people in the food factory. Matter of fact, if you get fired from *here*, you get sent *there* as a punishment, nine times out of ten." A private firm contracted to fulfill food services oversaw this punitive environment. In addition to a rotating cast of civilian employees of this company, a single officer, CO Byrne, panoptically surveilled the crew from his window-lined central office, regularly emerging to perform counts, oversee incoming deliveries and outgoing shipments, and check the far corners of the large warehouse building for perceived shirking or wrongdoing.

The drudgery of the food factory was derided by most. It was frequently regarded as a "prison-within-the-prison." I repeatedly heard it called "terrible," "forced labor," "the worst job," a "trap" or "trick" job, "probably the lowest job there is," and other invectives from prisoners and staff alike. Many factors were cited in these critiques, including the low pay ("most . . . make fifteen [cents] if they're lucky—this is the bottom of the bottom"); poor treatment of workers ("they treat everyone like shit!"); limited or poor training of captive laborers ("it's *supposed* to be 'corrections'!"); and despotic managerial techniques like heightened surveillance, frequent revocations of scheduled breaks, and heavy restrictions on movement. One civilian employee tasked with supervising the food factory stated, "I think the *only* jobs that benefit them are ones with skills." He gestured to a group of prisoners rolling lunch meat and continued, "This work? It doesn't help them. But they have to do it."

The middle tier of the prison employment system hierarchy captures jobs that may boast some desirable features (e.g., skill training) but are lacking in other valued areas (e.g., higher pay). Many of these positions elicited mixed sentiments from the prisoner population. Outside work crews, for instance, were well regarded by some because they guaranteed a flat hourly pay of $0.50 as well as the opportunity to venture outside of prison walls. This was not a universal consensus, however. Many regarded the outside crews as highly *undesirable* for their low degrees of autonomy. Not surprisingly, prisoners were heavily scrutinized off prison grounds by supervising COs as well as "checkers" who visited each crew multiple times daily to count workers. Certain other skilled positions were regarded in a similar light. The carpentry and welding shops, HVAC crew, heavy equipment operators, and the electrical team were referenced as "fine" jobs for those entering prison with the proper skills, but they came up short in the areas of autonomy and stability. In what were sometimes considered "white-collar" worksites, tutors, staff aides, and clerks directly assisted staff members with educational or office work. Although they were categorized as skilled, such positions allowed for little autonomy or mobility. These jobs also often involved sustained individual interaction with staffers, leading many to eye them with suspicion.

The fleet services auto garage offers a prime example of the ambivalence with which middle tier positions were often met. Generally, fleet services was considered an "okay job." It was a skilled site in which workers experienced relatively high levels of autonomy and could even occasionally operate motor vehicles to perform test drives after services. Yet, as a mechanic named Danny shared while wiping his greasy hands with a worn rag, "Not a lot of people seem to want this job." Despite the complexity of the work, pay here was limited to the standard cap. Many also disliked the fact that an officer, CO Peña, was permanently stationed on-site, closely monitoring prisoner movements and tool usage from his caged corner office. Additionally, many of the procedures and hardware that the crew used were outdated, diminishing the notion that they were truly honing marketable skills. According to one staff overseer of the garage, Boyle, "auto repair is all tech now—it's working with computers. We're not 'mechanics' or 'grease monkeys' anymore." When asked if his workers were being trained as technicians, he solemnly replied, "No, not a lot of tech work coming through here." Still, the small crew serviced every vehicle in the prison— from pickup trucks to tractors, electric golf carts to hulking transport buses. Anywhere between two and twenty vehicles could be dropped off for maintenance daily. As one Sergeant would put it, "These men work on every vehicle. *Every* vehicle comes through here. We depend on them."

Incarcerated auto mechanics commonly possessed prior mechanical experience. The "car wash" out back, however, was considered an unskilled job. Here, workers cleaned officers' vehicles. Whereas mechanics worked indoors, exposed only to their overseers, Graham and Boyle and CO Peña, car washers operated in the open air from a small, paved area outside the building. This left them subjected to the authority of any officer passing within eyesight. Passersby often ordered them to perform additional duties like clearing trash and debris from the surrounding grounds. Car washers often expressed frustrations at their lack of recourse against random officers who issued commands that exceeded their job descriptions. Divisions were magnified by the fact that these low skill jobs were more often than not filled by men pulled from the ranks of foreign nationals.

Finally, rare "top-tier" worksites possessed virtually every feature that workers valued. These were consistently regarded as the "best" jobs and were highly competitive. There were only two worksites at SSP that fit into this category of near-universal praise: the call center and the sign shop. In addition to being the highest-paid offerings at the institution, both provided engaging tasks. Each, too, was said to accord greater autonomy than could be found elsewhere, along with relatively high levels of stability and opportunities for mobility between workstations. These sites were also overseen by civilian staff members rather than badged COs, contributing to what laborers reported felt a bit less like prison and more like the free world. The subjective "general environment" of these spaces was frequently discussed. Many said they felt more "normal," received "better treatment," and could temporarily "escape" from the prison while at work. "It's not the job," maintained Gerald, "it's the environment" that matters. According to Marshall, the main characteristics of a "good job" were higher pay and the ability to "feel normal," as if "you just *sleep* at the prison." Time spent at such jobs was therefore considered "doing good time."

Working at the sign shop felt "like a vacation from prison," according to one worker named Lester. Here, around thirty prisoners could earn up to double the standard pay cap, receiving between approximately $0.50 and $1 hourly to produce street signs. The process began in metal fabrication, where a small crew operated a hulking "sign cutter" machine to stamp out metal sheets to precise dimensions. Newcomers to the shop typically started in the nearby screen-printing station. Here, they learned to pull high quality ink over mesh screens to apply text and imagery to these cut sheets of metal, creating signs of all sorts. Across the shop, men in the vinyl station designed signage digitally, which was then printed onto vinyl sheets with an industrial printer. Unlike in the food factory or other restrictive sites, prisoners could walk about the sign shop freely. Scattered laughter from mobile groups of workers resonated beneath the whirs and thuds of the sign cutter. Out back was a fenced-in smoking area complete with a sunshade, paint-chipped bench, and wall-mounted cigarette lighter. This is where workers took breathers between orders. According to one man, Ben, "It's a *real job*. I'm not saying those guys out there [in other sites] aren't working—they're just under the gun. 'Do this! Go there! Don't go there!' Here, it's like a real job. We come in, work our eight hours. If there's down time, we take it."

Across the facility, the prison call center was considered "the best job to make money at." A private firm that maintained offices in multiple states oversaw this operation. Dennis, the owner of the company, contracted with SSP for prisoner labor as well as on-site office space. Call center salesmen were the highest paid penal laborers by a wide margin, receiving between approximately $1 and $2.34 per hour. Many on the yard referred to them as "prison CEOs." This crew of thirty to thirty-five made outgoing, unsolicited "cold calls" to small businesses throughout the U.S., attempting to sell advertising packages while withholding the fact that they were calling from behind bars. Internet radio played softly over wall-mounted speakers, air conditioning kept the room at a comfortable temperature, and complimentary coffee (a luxury behind bars) flowed freely. To maintain these coveted positions, workers had to meet monthly sales quotas of $5,000, known as "five-to-survive." This resulted in high early turnover and created a stress-filled atmosphere, especially in the final days before deadlines. These pressures resemble those of call center labor in the free world in many ways.[13] Nonetheless, salesmen expressed satisfaction with how the office was run "like a business" in the "real world," and many praised the opportunity to "exercise your social abilities" by conversing with people on the outside. According to Jake, the informally dubbed "inmate manager" of the sales team, "I'm learning life skills *and* I'm making money." He added that, "you need work like this to keep your sanity."

A New Approach to Prison Labor

The typical image of penal labor held by many—as a monolithic institution distinct from the realities of work in the free world—is not entirely borne out in the contemporary prison. To be sure, imprisoned workers are confined to environments of heavy surveillance, limited rights, and coercion. Yet, whereas jobs like highway cleanup or the chow line may closely resemble popular conceptions of prison work, others, like the call center and "cigarette butt collector," reveal vast divides in the penal labor hierarchy.

It would be insufficient, however, to conclude this story here, with the revelation that there are "good prison jobs" and "bad prison jobs." While this does add greater depth to our view of work behind bars, it also raises its own questions about how jobs are assigned and what impacts this may have on prison life. The remainder of the book will draw on ethnographic insights to reveal not only how those behind bars perceive different labor offerings, but also the subtle ways that prisons operate as engines of inequality for those in bad jobs *and* good jobs alike. Exploring labor's role in generating unequal carceral experiences in this way advances our understanding of how neoliberal approaches to punishment shape life on the inside.

To unpack these phenomena, I focus on practices and discourses surrounding four prison workspaces: the food factory, the fleet auto garage, the sign shop, and the call center. These were chosen based in part on their differing statuses in the eyes of the imprisoned. The food factory, oft characterized as the worst job, represents the lowest tier of the carceral employment hierarchy. The fleet auto garage, which elicited mixed reviews from participants, represents the middle tier. Beyond occupying different levels in the labor hierarchy, these two sites also housed jobs of supposedly varying skill, according to official classifications. The food factory contained unskilled lunch preppers alongside semi-skilled bakers, while the garage retained unskilled car washers as well as skilled mechanics. This reveals the influence of status distinctions not only between workplaces but also within them. Finally, the sign shop and call center were considered the best available work offerings. From them, I observed the top tier of this status pyramid to which so many aspired. These higher-paying skilled jobs differed in that the former involved the "blue-collar" labor of fabrication and printing, while the latter entailed "white-collar" knowledge work. These reveal that such distinctions alone do not determine perceptions or experiences of value.

By documenting daily labors in these carceral workplaces, I illustrate an institution distinct from common media portrayals. This allows me to move beyond well-worn questions. For example, when penal labor is discussed in public fora, it is often in the context of debates over the fiscal and philosophical implications of privatization.[14] Private interests were instrumental in the history of American punishment, as discussed in Chapter 1, and maintain influence today. Yet, for my research participants on the inside, questions of privatized penal labor were of seemingly little consequence. Across the nation, the majority of prison jobs—including many of the most punitive offerings—are overseen by the state. From the standpoint of men at SSP, profit-seeking firms operated desirable jobs like the call center as well as objectionable jobs like the food factory. Meanwhile, the state oversaw laborers ranging from high-status sign shop crewmen to those collecting cigarette butts or tarring roofs under the summer sun. Privatization was not a sole predictor of day-to-day job quality or inequality and was therefore not a salient concern for most. The moral and political questions surrounding prisons-for-profit remain urgent. However, such debates often overshadow investigations into the structure and management of publicly run facilities and programs. "Every private prison could close tomorrow," writes Rachel Kushner in

The New York Times, "and not a single person would go home. But the ideas that private prisons are the culprit, and that profit is the motive behind all prisons, have a firm grip on the popular imagination."[15]

Another question dominating public and political discourse is whether, or to what extent, penal labor reduces recidivism—that is, the likelihood that individuals will return to criminalized behaviors after release. This is a reasonable query, given that penal labor has frequently been justified on grounds that such work transfers skills and outlooks that facilitate reintegration into society. Prison researchers, however, have repeatedly called into question such claims.[16] Moreover, while rates of prison work participation have risen in recent years, recidivism rates remain high. The early 2000s saw the ranks of state prison workers swell to new levels, exceeding three-quarters of a million captive laborers.[17] Still, approximately sixty-six percent of those freed from state prison in this period were rearrested within three years, with around eighty-two percent rearrested within ten.[18] The factors contributing to the struggles of the formerly incarcerated—including hiring discrimination, exclusion from certain jobs, diminished social supports, and more—are well established.[19] Despite prevalent evidence that carceral labor does not significantly improve reentry prospects for most navigating these barriers (because it is structural constraints and not merely personal failings that hamper prospects for most), historian Heather Ann Thompson notes, "Americans remain susceptible to the idea that a large penal system might offer society . . . economic benefits. Isn't it the case that putting prisoners to work increases their employment opportunities once they are released?" The answer, she asserts, "is a categorical 'No.'"[20]

To better understand the realities of carceral life and labor, we must move beyond these and related questions that, while important, often eclipse immediate challenges faced by people behind bars. This chapter has set the stage for uncovering how the prison sorts its orange-collar laborers into this system in ways that lead to unequal experiences of punishment.

3
Capitals and Punishment

The Sorting of Working Prisoners

> Other desirable positions, clerkships and the like, are
> awarded to influential prisoners . . . These are known in the
> institution as holding "political jobs."
>
> —Alexander Berkman (1912)

The contemporary U.S. prison is, in the words of sociologist Bruce
Western, an "engine of social inequality" and a "significant feature
on the new landscape of American poverty and race relations."[1] The
racially and ethnically minoritized and the poor are disproportionately policed, surveilled, and incarcerated. After prison, these same
populations face heightened discrimination and worsened labor
market prospects. Yet, despite mounting disparities leading to prison
and plaguing them upon release, less is known about how structures,
practices, and experiences *within* penal institutions shape inequality.
How does the quality of contact with the prison alter experiences
on the inside? Through what processes are patterns of stratification
reproduced and maintained within prison? Furthermore, given the
differences between top- and bottom-tier penal labor assignments at
Sunbelt State Penitentiary (SSP) described in the previous chapter,
how are "good" and "bad" prison jobs assigned and who or what is
privileged in this process?

This chapter illustrates on-the-ground processes that privilege
prisoners possessing marketable skills and capitals while restricting

others in the allocation of higher paying, skilled prison work. Because imprisonment occurs disproportionately in the lives of those with fewer opportunities for vocational or educational certification and training,[2] such imbalance in opportunities for skill and capital development behind bars mirror and aggravate broader systems of stratification.

Observations and interviews reveal that prior work skills, labor market knowledge, education, social ties, and demographic features such as nationality, race, and ethnicity are each influential in the prison job search. It is along these lines that the institution classifies and sorts its captive labor force. As a result, particular prisoner groups have better chances of securing desirable jobs and may experience greater mobility between stations within the workplace. In the end, it is often those who are also more likely to experience advantage in formal labor markets in the free world who are privileged in the prison employment system, while those more likely to encounter setbacks in outside markets face similar hurdles to success on the inside. As such, the socially reproductive nature of this institution affects the nation's most disadvantaged communities not just before and after, but also *during* incarceration.

Taking Bourdieu to Prison

The sociologist Pierre Bourdieu has contributed greatly to our understanding of how institutions help reproduce class and other social categories. Even institutions that are supposedly designed to help generate class mobility—through teaching, certifying, or perhaps even correcting—instead often strengthen existing barriers. Although he never directly studied the prison himself, the social reproduction framework that Bourdieu advanced is helpful for understanding how key institutions sort and classify those who pass through them.[3] He reveals, for instance, that elite schools rely on recruitment procedures that filter applicants, admitting only those "already endowed, through their background, with the dispositions they require," ensuring that they maintain control of the social benefits of education.[4] Individuals' resources and capabilities are integral to how they navigate and compete in social "fields" such as this.[5]

Operating at the opposite end of the social ladder, the prison similarly filters its wards. Extending from Bourdieu's work on social classification and boundaries, I identify five key sorting mechanisms that institutional actors rely on to allocate desirable and undesirable jobs. At different stages in the hiring process, prisoners may be sorted in terms of the capitals that they possess—that is, the knowledge, skills, and resources that they might exploit to help them gain legitimacy or social mobility.[6] Two species of capital are implicated here: cultural capital and social capital. First, cultural capital refers to demonstrable "competence in some socially valued area of practice," in the words of sociologists Jeffrey Sallaz and Jane Zavisca.[7] Imprisoned job applicants may possess cultural capital in the form of embodied skills represented by marketable work experiences and knowledge of labor market norms. They may also mobilize other forms of cultural capital in the form of official certifications that facilitate social mobility and certain styles of self-presentation that are rewarded in this system. Second, social capital refers to valuable ties to others that can be used to get ahead. Connections to influential prisoners or staffers could greatly improve a worker's prospects. In the absence of these capitals, already-disadvantaged individuals are often constrained by compounded barriers to social mobility. Nationality, race, and ethnicity are fundamental to the accumulation and assessment of these resources, which will receive greater focus in Chapter 4.

Labor organization as an arena of social reproduction

The work of prisoners has grown increasingly important in penal policy in recent decades.[8] In response to slimming budgets and shifting political agendas, prisoner work has been leveraged to financially support—or at least mitigate many expenses of—overcrowded, economically strained facilities while simultaneously contributing to custodial order.[9] Despite this reliance, proponents contend that carceral labor provides net benefits for those compelled to carry it out. Workers are said to gain marketable technical skills, positive outlooks towards labor, and "soft skills" (e.g., improved approaches to scheduling and teamwork) that will purportedly help secure gainful employment upon release.[10] Yet, even if such arguments are accepted (and studies suggest they should not be[11]), it nevertheless remains true that jobs classified as vocational or skilled are quite rare in the nation's carceral facilities. Instead, most prisoners today engage in unskilled or fully deskilled facility support positions like grounds maintenance or food service, or in public works projects like roadway trash collection.

As the incarcerated compete to attain the few jobs promising relatively higher (yet still paltry) pay or rewarding environments, administrators and ground-level correctional staff wield immense power to shape their experiences. Workers the world over are evaluated and ranked in terms of their capabilities and resources. Yet, in the prison setting, such classificatory processes serve to underscore capital disparities that already abound within this vulnerable population.

Getting a Prison Job

The fact that "good prison jobs" were difficult to acquire—and not always equitably assigned—was common knowledge within SSP. Some accepted this reality as an unfortunate but inevitable facet of criminal justice involvement: "I'm used to getting jacked around by the system," one respondent fatalistically stated. For others, this perceived injustice only added to frustrations with the institution. In a conversation during work one day with Lemmy, a gray-mustachioed, white prisoner employed in the sign shop, he muttered, "The state doesn't rehabilitate, it [just] incarcerates."

"What about jobs like this?" I asked. "Sure, but they're hard to get. I've been down [incarcerated] eleven years and I finally *just* got one."

Like many others, Lemmy had desired a top-tier job for its higher pay, greater autonomy, and other attractive features. Yet, he had failed to acquire one until he was able to develop and mobilize the necessary resources. Having worked as a craftsman for decades, he already possessed some skills necessary for the productive labors of the shop. Beyond that, he added, "To be honest, it's—a lot of it's who you know . . . . Getting hired on, I knew somebody. And moving within the company [worksite], I knew somebody. And they pulled me along." Once employed, these connections facilitated a quick transition from an entry level station to a more desirable job designing signs digitally. For every man like Lemmy who secured a sought-after job, however, there remained many others who lacked advantages that might help them navigate the prison employment system, regardless of how hiring was "supposed" to work.

The official job assignment process

On paper, the hiring process at SSP was straightforward. A prisoner had simply to fill out an application indicating their preferences and qualifications and wait for an opening in their worksite of choice. In the meantime, they might be assigned to another open position. In practice, however, this process rarely, if ever, played out as described. First, acquiring the one-page paper application for work was often easier said than done. As one young prisoner told me with a shrug, "You really gotta ask around to get an app. *Some* [housing] bays have CO clerks who might [have them]." To be sure, it took me nearly two months to track one down. Those who did not—or could not—submit an application indicating specific preferences were often automatically sent to the food factory or other unpopular facility support jobs. (As CO Byrne had claimed, "There's *always* somebody else to shoot in.") According to one working prisoner, Jake, "Once you're in their little system, they'll keep assigning you— to the food factory or wherever." Limiting access to applications helped ensure a steadier supply of labor for such vital but vilified worksites.

Once an application was eventually located and submitted, job applicants could expect to be called in to meet with a CO overseeing assignments to different prison programs. "We have about three-fourths [of our population] doing *something*, either working or in classes," she told me. "That's the best, I think. Just keeping them all busy." Many of the remaining, unassigned prisoners were those who had been deemed physically or psychologically unfit for work, or who had been marked "ineligible" for many programs after being labelled a "flight risk" (i.e., potentially likely to attempt an escape) or raising other security concerns.

Even if an individual did manage to get assigned to the job of their choosing, the most desirable worksites still relied on additional steps to vet applicants before the hiring process could be completed. Being accepted into the prison sign shop, for instance, required passing a short educational assessment. The on-site manager of the sign shop, Mr. Edwards, described this as a way to narrow down the applicant pool by assessing knowledge of "basic middle school things—shapes, colors, et cetera. Things that you and I could do with ease." Those who achieved an adequate score on the test advanced to a sit-down interview with Edwards, who would inquire into work history, skills, and general outlooks regarding work and workplace dynamics. Similarly, those applying to the call center had to pass a brief computer test—demonstrating their ability to log in to a computer and dial a call using the automated system. This was because, I was told, "most of what is done here takes place on a computer." Upon successfully completing this, applicants then had to perform a "mock sales call" with the manager of the firm, Dennis, using a provided sales script. When I asked one recent hire about the experience, he exclaimed: "It was scary. *Real* scary. Like, I started sweating within 20 seconds. I was dripping sweat!"

After being assigned to work, whether to the job that one had desired or to another one entirely, transferring to a different worksite was often difficult. According to Mr. Dempsey, a civilian staffer overseeing the sign shop: "Guys put in requests to move [to the shop] all the time, but they almost *never* go through." For this reason, prisoners in many sites—especially those employed in the bottom tier of the employment hierarchy—often expressed feeling "trapped" in their jobs.

The Role of Work-Related Experience and Knowledge in Getting a Prison Job

Prison labor is sometimes said to teach skills and outlooks that the incarcerated may lack. Yet, at SSP, skilled work assignments were often secured by those *already* possessing marketable capabilities or valuable resources. In the early days of fieldwork, a senior sign shop worker called Eli told me: "Prisons aren't too particular where they assign you, you see. Unless you have a skill in a certain area." When I inquired into this further, the programming officer confirmed Eli's proclamation, stating, "Past work history is big. [Especially] for a lot of the skilled positions: automotive, any kind of maintenance, that sort of thing." Indeed, Eli had possessed some experience in manufacturing and printing, which helped him secure his position in the shop. Another man, called Bass, had operated his own small sign shop for thirty-five years in the free world and considered his time working in the prison shop to be "valuable training" to hone his skills and prepare to improve his business upon release. Another, Clegg, worked for decades alongside his father producing signs prior to incarceration. "I [am] second generation. I mean, yeah, my father was in the sign business," he told me. "That's how I got into it, working for my dad." With a slight smile, he added, "My son's in the same business, too." Past experiences such as these were often directly mobilized in the job search. According to Clegg, "I've got twenty-five years in in the sign business, so [Mr. Edwards] hired me from that. So, yeah, that's how I got on."

Many other sign shop workers had not directly "worked signs" before prison, yet nevertheless possessed other relevant skills acquired from different production experiences. For example, Samuél had worked in metal fabrication during his pre-prison work history, which helped him secure a position in the shop's metal fabrication station. Lemmy, on the other hand, was a skilled contractor and possessed experiences and abilities seemingly analogous to parts of the printing process, which helped him join the printing crew.

Like in the sign shop, it was also well known that the fleet auto garage privileged applicants with previous experience in the trade. Noting that most of the crew had worked in automotive repair in the past, I asked one of the incarcerated workers there, "Do you think people who already have mechanic experience have a better chance of getting a job here?" Without pause, he snorted and replied, "*Oh yeah*, definitely." I would learn that the managers of the garage, Graham and Boyle, almost exclusively pulled applications from men who had repair and maintenance experience *and* who were referred by current workers. The CO overseeing the garage, CO Peña, acknowledged that although it might benefit prisoners to be trained from scratch, it was more important that the prison's vehicles were repaired quickly and properly—"And you don't have that many inmates out there who can do a tear-down of a tire or change a transmission."

Upon hiring experienced workers, fleet staff monitored them closely during a two-week "trial period" to ensure that they possessed the skills they had claimed. Boyle would recount that it was sometimes "a roll of the dice," adding, "Sometimes it works out, sometimes it doesn't."

* * *

Although transferring from a "bad job" to a "good job" was difficult at SSP, it was not entirely impossible. A man named Jared, for example, managed to move from the food factory to the sign shop during my fieldwork. He did so, I would learn, by leveraging his prior experience. When I commented that he already looked like a "pro" after only a few days on the job, he shared that he actually had years of sign-making experience and had secured his position by directly mobilizing these skills along with his ties to workers both within prison and in shops in the free world. "Clegg handed in my application for me, which helped," he said. "I also used to work signs on the outside and I mentioned that. Mr. Gale [one of the civilian staffers overseeing the shop] asked who I worked for and I told him, my best friend, who owns his own shop. He said 'Oh! I've known [him] for years!' It was mostly those credentials, though. I worked signs on the outside."

In general, workers already possessing marketable capabilities were better able to navigate the prison employment system than others. On some occasions, they managed to entirely circumvent the formal interview process. For example, in the call center one afternoon, I was surprised to see Lester, a thin, white man with a gravelly voice, whom I had seen that morning in his job as an inventory clerk at the sign shop. He walked in and sat down at a computer shortly after the sales crew had returned from lunch. He informed me that he left work at the sign shop early so that a friend could teach him the ins and outs of the call center's computer system. Although he had not yet "transferred" to the call center, he was confident that, given his computer skills, he would certainly be brought on. Sure enough, he was added to the roster the following week, foregoing the entrance tests. As one of relatively few SSP prisoners with a college degree and verifiable computer literacy, Lester was a valued commodity in the carceral employment system. "You have to try to hold on to guys who can do computers," Mr. Edwards would tell me, "because they're hard to come by."

In some cases, staffers overseeing skilled worksites actively competed with one another to secure or retain workers. CO Peña of the fleet garage got into a minor spat with another correctional officer one week over the hiring of a talented welder. The prisoner applied to and was hired by the auto garage, only to be put on "hold" at his current job, the grounds crew, before he could transfer. "We tried to hire a welder from over there," Peña recounted to me. "As soon as they found out, they said 'Nope!' They cut it off, trapped him there. [The CO] over there said '*Hell* no!' when he tried to move. 'I need him here—he's my best welder!' That's how it goes." While Lester had managed to mobilize his capabilities to traverse the labor system more easily, the welder instead found himself ensnared by his current boss *because* of his skills. This situation reveals that possessing valued capitals does not necessarily or automatically grant one autonomy in navigating the penal labor hierarchy, even if it does improve one's chances. In certain cases, it may even limit a worker's mobility.

Labor market knowledge

In addition to demonstrating relevant work skills, certain forms of labor market knowledge were valuable in pursuing top-tier jobs at SSP. Successful applicants in this pursuit were often those experienced in the job search process, including preparing materials, like a résumé or cover letter, and successfully navigating face-to-face interviews in a manner consonant with job search norms in the free world. These sorts of ingrained skills are often obtained through experience or are imparted by parents, mentors, or educators.

The value of this form of labor market knowledge was particularly apparent in the hiring process of the sign shop. Even before taking the educational assessment test that Mr. Edwards administered to hopeful applicants, individuals were first expected to satisfy his *informal* hiring expectations. Edwards revealed his process for narrowing down the applicant pool: "When guys send me applications that say, 'I'm a good worker and a fast learner,' those go *right* in the trash. Anybody can write that. Anybody can *say* that. What I want is a *résumé*. When a guy sends in a résumé or a cover letter with 'I've worked *this* job for X amount of years, *this* job for X amount of years'—*those* are the men I will interview. *Those* are the men I will hire." During the time of my fieldwork, SSP offered no programs or classes aimed at training prisoners in drafting these additional application materials. This meant that those who had not learned such skills prior to incarceration were greatly disadvantaged in the hiring process.

Those who did submit application materials to Edwards' liking usually advanced to the one-on-one job interview with the man. Here, they were asked to detail the prior work experience outlined in their application materials. "When I interview them, I ask them, what jobs have they had on the outside," he told me. Applicants were also expected to convince the overseer that they would approach the opportunity to work in the shop "with a dedication to do a job and to do it *well* and not just [with an attitude of], 'I'm here. Pay me.'" Conducting oneself "professionally" in the eyes of the interviewer remained an unspoken requirement.

The Role of Educational and Linguistic Markers in Getting a Prison Job

Beyond labor market experiences, other forms of embodied knowledge and resources were prized in the prison employment system. These forms of valued cultural capital included prisoners' educational attainment and certifications, as well as their expressive or self-presentation styles—in particular, the ability to exhibit what Bourdieu and other scholars of the cultural factors behind social mobility refer to as "linguistic cultural capital" (or simply "linguistic capital"). This is the ability to communicate using dialects, accents, and vocabulary often assumed to designate social standing.[12] Status markers such as these often serve discriminatory functions. Assumptions about education and interpretations of speech falling outside of so-called "Standard American English" may be colored by presuppositions tied to class and race, generating added biases against underserved communities.

Educational attainment

A major barrier to desirable employment for many is their level of formal education. Approximately seventy percent of incarcerated people in the U.S. lack a high school degree or equivalent.[13] For most prisoners, the absence of educational certifications severely limits their access to desirable work—and the higher wages and training that those jobs promise.

Official departmental regulations at SSP mandated that job applicants must possess a high school diploma or GED to be eligible for any position in which reading and writing skills were considered *bona fide* occupational qualifications. This included working as an educational tutor assisting teachers in the prison classroom; a clerk or aide helping staffers file paperwork and take notes; and a salesman in the call center, where workers were expected to comprehend written sales pitch scripts, calculate costs, and compose written messages to potential customers. Less clear-cut, however, were regulations which mandated the same educational requirements for positions like the sign shop or outside highway cleanup crews, where advanced proficiency in reading and writing were not necessarily required for most day-to-day activities. Nevertheless, these jobs also required high school equivalency, leaving a large segment of the population unable to pursue such opportunities.

To be sure, this educational barrier to mobility acted as a motivator for some. For example, while preparing bagged lunches in the food factory one afternoon, I worked alongside two men who had spent the last several months wrapping sandwiches. While we assembled our materials—meat, bread, cheese, repeat—the man to my left cast a sideways glance at his coworker, who seemed to be working quicker than usual. With a furrowed brow, he blurted, "Hey, why you rolling sandwiches so *fast?* You ain't gonna get no special *privileges* rolling fast like that." With a slight shrug, the speedy worker timidly replied: "I'm taking my state requirement [GED] test next week. I want to get a good job. If I'm fast *and* I pass that? I dunno—might be good." The first man shook his head as if to signal disappointment in his workmate before emitting an exaggerated "*Psh, whatever.*"

Linguistic markers

Speaking skills were highly valued in prison hiring processes and were assessed in job interviews and other official contexts. To exhibit linguistic capital means to demonstrate mastery of communication styles that are valued by institutions or by powerful persons within them. Certain dialects, vocabularies, and accents may be deemed "incorrect" or "improper" by those holding power in many formal settings. Mastering dominant dialects is tied to class upbringing and entangled with processes of racialization. According to linguistic anthropologist H. Samy Alim and colleagues, "On the job market, language-based discrimination intersects with issues of race, ethnicity, class, gender, sexuality, and national origin to make it more difficult for qualified applicants with an 'accent' to receive equal opportunities."[14] In the penal labor context, linguistic capital was reflected in individuals' ability to recognize and abide by speech patterns that administrators and correctional staffers rewarded.

Successfully recognizing and adhering to valued language norms was especially important for getting a job in the call center. In line with knowledge industry work in the free world, the hiring process here required jobseekers to speak a particular way. As urban studies scholar Karen Chapple notes, this type of work commonly expects workers to "speak like white corporate America," which includes, according to the author, the "avoidance of slang (such as Black English)."[15] To assess workers along these lines, the call center hiring process involved calling the site manager, Dennis, over the phone to attempt to sell him advertising time in a "mock sales pitch." On these calls, applicants read from pre-printed sales scripts and responded to questions from Dennis, who performed the role of an interested customer. When I asked which qualities he prioritized during the sales call test, Dennis replied that the most competitive applicants "speak clearly and slowly, come up with logical responses to questions, [do] not stutter, don't sound like they're from the *ghetto*, and have relatively good English." Along these lines, he would add, "one-third fail as soon as they open their mouth."

Dennis directly drew on perceptions of race and space in describing the qualities of (un)desirable applicants. The fact that not speaking like one is "from the ghetto" was considered a necessary qualification highlights the racialized nature of linguistic requirements. As a result of privileging narrowly-defined styles of self-presentation, the call center—the highest-paying worksite by a wide margin—was predominantly staffed by white workers. The exclusion of many applicants of color was justified on account of these dialect or accent expectations. By foregrounding hiring criteria that tended to exclude minoritized candidates, the overseers of this site appeared resigned to maintaining an ethnoracial labor hierarchy behind bars. Chapter 4 will further unravel the ways in which sorting processes were infused with perceptions of race, underscoring how penal labor is both racialized and racializing.

The Role of Social Ties in Getting a Prison Job

Knowing the right person in prison can prove invaluable. At SSP, those who could be "vouched for" by people already connected to desirable worksites possessed valued social capital, or durable ties or networks of relationships that they could draw on to "get ahead" or attain resources.[16] Unlike in the free world, in which casual, indirect, or "weak" social ties may prove fruitful in the job search,[17] in prison, close or personal ties to well-positioned prisoners or staffers appeared necessary for success.

Ties to facility staffers

Being on good terms with the officer supervising work program assignments was helpful in avoiding lower-tier jobs. One man, called Diamond, proudly told me, "I wouldn't work in the food factory. They'd have to *fire* me! . . . Actually, I know somebody in the [programming office], so I'd never end *up* over there." Noting my interest in his ability to mobilize this tie, he continued, "Prison is *all* about who you know. You know the right person, you'll *never* get stuck in a shitty job." Building rapport or trust with other staff members could prove influential as well. According to one man, "COs who see you work will give you more leeway" and may even "help you get out" of disagreeable jobs.

When overseers were reassigned to different sites across the institution, they sometimes brought prized workers along with them. Before managing the prison sign shop, Mr. Edwards oversaw an agricultural worksite. When the private contract funding that program was discontinued, Edwards was reassigned to the sign shop. Ocho, a

Chicano worker who was stationed in the sign shop's metal fabrication station during my fieldwork, was one of several prisoners who had previously worked in the agricultural program. When Edwards was relocated, he promptly hired Ocho at the new site. "This is like gold!" he exclaimed when describing the position that he was able to acquire through this tie to the boss. Like others, he attested to benefiting from his social ties. Being able to secure a good job in prison, he said, "drives you even more to stay focused and to stay healthy."

Ties to working prisoners

Despite departmental regulations formally limiting the input of prisoners into everyday institutional operations, incarcerated men who were already employed in desirable worksites were often able to informally influence hiring practices and assist others in securing skilled, higher-paying positions. According to Mr. Gale, who helped oversee the sign shop, being vouched for by someone already employed and in good standing was a virtual necessity if one hoped to secure a position there. "We only take guys who *know* each other," he stated. For example, after he had established himself in the shop, Ocho was able to begin recruiting individuals that he knew and trusted from the prison yard. When a metal fabricator position opened, he recommended Samuél, who was working as a dishwasher in the food factory at the time. This referral helped Samuél secure an interview. His relevant work history further ensured his success in the application process.

This manner of hiring was common to the sign shop. (Recall, for example, Jared's earlier recognition that "Clegg handed in my application for me," or Lemmy's acknowledgement that friends had helped pull him along.) Workers actively recruited whenever an opening on the crew emerged. Many recounted keeping a "mental list" of possible referrals for just this occurrence. Hiring only those who had been recruited by current shop workers was justified on the basis that it made the work process smoother. According to one long-standing prison laborer in the shop, Felix, "When I'm in the yard *recruiting*, I only look for guys who we can *work* with." Similarly, during a conversation about a recent vacancy, LD, a wide-eyed prisoner working as an inventory clerk, and Dempsey, a civilian manager supervising the worksite alongside Gale and Edwards, agreed on this point. "It comes through us," LD said. "With very few exceptions, the guys we hire are all referred by us." Dempsey quickly nodded and added, "Yeah. And—we don't want to empower these guys *too* much—but it works."

"If we recommend someone, they're gonna be *on time*," LD insisted. "We're gonna make sure of it. Because if they're *not*, if they aren't *reliable*, then we look bad too." According to him, not everyone on the yard was deserving of a referral, regardless of their social ties. "We sort of vet people out, make sure they're reliable for a while first." Referred applicants could prove "unreliable," for instance, by being dishonest about disciplinary records. Those who had received excessive disciplinary write-ups—or "tickets"—could expect their transfer to the sign shop to be halted by the officer tasked with approving work assignments. According to LD, "Sometimes a guy might not be forthright with us. He might have more tickets than he said. So, the [programming officer] will shut it down. I've referred *one* person since I've worked here—I made certain first that he was shooting straight with me. I trusted him, plus he was working as a tram driver, so I knew he didn't have any tickets, [in order] to work that job."

The value of social capital was not unique to the sign shop. The mid-tier fleet auto garage also relied on a combination of referrals and work history in hiring decisions. Here, too, staff members often circumvented formal application and hiring processes. "They're [the programming office] usually good about letting me pick my own people," said the civilian garage manager, Graham. I would see this in action on multiple occasions. For instance, when I first met Seth, he expressed that he felt "stuck" in his job wrapping sandwiches at the food factory. A few months later, however, he had secured a position in fleet following a referral from another mechanic, Gael. According to Seth, it was his work ethic that enabled him to finally move up in the prison employment hierarchy. "If you work hard," he said, "then CO Byrne will let you go."

In practice, however, it appeared that his social capital (making use of his tie to Gael) was the underlying factor in getting hired at the garage. When the position became available, Gael told his boss, Graham, that Seth would be a good fit. The boss then called the programming officer and requested that Seth be transferred over. The programming officer in turn called CO Byrne to initiate the transfer. A short while later, Seth was moved into a mechanic position. In a rare occurrence, Seth in fact possessed only limited mechanical experience. However, with Gael closely training and supervising him, he quickly honed his skills enough to succeed. Once he had proven himself in his fleet job over time, he too became trusted enough to recommend others just as Gael had referred him. According to Seth, whenever a position became available, "we'll go back on the yard and find people, and then give [the site managers] their application, and they'll decide if they want to hire them or not. But we'll question them on the yard about what they know, and this and that."

In the call center, workers were instrumental in hiring in a different way. Possessing ties to active salesmen could provide a decided advantage in preparing to demonstrate the requisite communication skills in the "mock sales call" test. When a position on the sales team opened, current workers often sought out friends from the yard and gave them a copy of the sales script. Unlike unconnected applicants, who received the script mere minutes before they were expected to follow it on the phone, well-connected individuals could benefit from days or even weeks of advance notice and time to perfect the pitch. Jake, the incarcerated salesman who oversaw the training of new hires, kept a stack of scripts on hand to provide to his contacts whenever a new round of hiring was set to commence. One person who benefited from this was Marino, a tattooed man with a "back East" accent. Having received the script weeks before his interview date, he spent his time doing practice runs with friends from the sales team whom he said had "helped me keep at it." With this training under his belt, he had little trouble succeeding in the interview. Months later, I would watch him extend the same assistance to others. Outside during a smoke break one day, a man approached and expressed anxiety about memorizing the script. With a reassuring tone, Marino told the man, "Hey, just keep at it. Whenever a commercial comes on [TV], take a break and study it. We'll go over it when I get off. Alright?" After the man left, Marino flicked his cigarette and told me, "He's studying the script. I'm trying to get him a job here."

For those employed in the most desirable worksites, the ability to grant or deny a referral operated as a form of power. In this way, some maintained notable influence over work programming at SSP. In such an environment, where racial politics often dictated the rules of interactions—and limited with whom one could develop strong social ties—social capital was intertwined with racial, ethnic, and national divides. Ethnoracial hierarchies were created and maintained in the prison partly via processes rewarding strong connections. Those in prized positions were typically more likely to refer or assist those from the same racial or ethnic group. This was often because, as the next chapter will outline, the racial politics of the yard curtailed their ability to build trusting relationships across these demographic boundaries.

Institutionalizing Social Reproduction

Labor stratification pervaded SSP. Ethnographic data reveal how the contemporary penal facility rewards incarcerated jobseekers already possessing the requisite abilities or resources, bolstering claims that penal labor functions largely to mitigate the costs of mass incarceration.[18] Heavy reliance on formal and informal sorting mechanisms reveals that the prison did not primarily approach work as a means to transfer skills and outlooks that prisoners lacked, despite claims to this effect from proponents of penal labor.[19]

Disproportionately few behind bars possess marketable job skills, knowledge regarding formal market procedures, valued certifications, privileged self-presentation styles, or advantageous social ties to assist in the job search.[20] Nevertheless, these and other forms of capital were regularly necessary for success in the internal prison employment system. As in the free world, it was the *combination* of prisoners' capitals which often facilitated success in this field. Those possessing an array of valued capitals—such as being able to demonstrate relevant work skills *and* being well-connected enough to earn a prized referral—tended to move up.

As Bourdieu suggests, by privileging those already endowed with the skills and dispositions that they are purportedly designed to instill, key institutions function to consecrate "sacred" groups through a "rite of institution."[21] In other words, the school and other institutions merely provide certifications to people already well-positioned to succeed. They do so, he reveals, by employing "recruitment procedures [that] are so obviously designed to guarantee them students already endowed, through their background, with the dispositions they require that we have to wonder whether, as the Romans used to say, they aren't merely 'teaching fish to swim.'"[22] I argue that the internal workings of carceral institutions play a part in the larger tapestry of social reproduction. Like prestigious educational facilities atop the social hierarchy, the prison—which instead operates at the so-called "lowest rungs" of society[23]—filters and categorizes its occupants. Inverting the school's function of consecrating an elite, the prison employment system confines the disadvantaged to the bottommost reaches of social and economic hierarchies not only following contact with penal institutions, but during contact as well.

Scholars have argued that society prepares some for continued education while priming others for prison.[24] This chapter demonstrates, however, that these institutions are more than just the endpoints of social sorting. Instead, their social functions are more directly linked in that both rely on internal classificatory processes oriented toward maintaining barriers between social classes at a more micro level. The mechanisms underlying the reification of divisions between the poor and rich—as between the incarcerated and free—therefore also act to exacerbate disparities within the narrow range of social class representing the prisoner population.

Integral to these classification processes are divisions along the lines of race and ethnicity. Race and social capital, for instance, are tightly linked.[25] Moving forward, I take a closer look at how prison racial politics shape experiences of penal labor in direct and indirect ways. More overt patterns of discrimination in penal labor sorting mechanisms emerge at every level of the hierarchy of prison jobs. The next chapter examines the prison as a racializing institution, maintaining an ethnoracial order through its labor practices.

4

There's Rules in Prison

Penal Labor as Racialized and Racializing

> I wasn't racist at heart, but I was in a world where I *had* to be
> to survive. If a little thing like this sounds complicated that is
> because it *was*.
>
> **—Gustavo "Goose" Alvarez (2020)**

At the heart of Sunbelt State Penitentiary (SSP) stands the fleet auto garage. It is, according to staffers, vital for the prison's operation. Day-to-day, a steady stream of cars, trucks, buses, and tractors operated by Department of Corrections (DOC) agents zoom about like tiny cells navigating the circulatory network of roads connecting every building in the complex. Each one must at some point pass through the garage for regular service, repair, refueling, or a wash. The main crew of incarcerated mechanics that keep these vehicles on the road is small. Gael, a middle-aged Chicano man, has the longest tenure in the shop and is typically the first to be notified about incoming jobs. Training under him is Seth, a white worker in his early thirties who moved to the garage from the food factory after Gael recommended him to his civilian bosses. While those two primarily attend to the cars and trucks in need of service, Danny, also white and the youngest of the mechanics, specializes in repairing the heavy transport buses or tractors that often need repair. Back in the facility housing units and out on the recreational yard, where racial tensions come to a peak, Gael must often refrain from interacting too familiarly with Seth and Danny. During work hours in the garage, however, they work closely together, directly collaborating on various tasks, sharing jokes and stories, eating lunch alongside one another, and generally operating in tandem to keep up with the seemingly unstoppable flow of fleet vehicle repairs.

In many ways, this portrayal of the fleet services garage—as a space where individuals can for a time escape the racial divisions of the yard—seems to align with a common refrain regarding labor at SSP. Many staffers insisted that work represented a sort of safe haven from the tensions and violence of "racial politics," or, to quote prison scholar Philip Goodman, "the patterns, norms, and rules around racialized behaviors and interactions" that dictate things like whom one may speak to, eat with, drink after, exercise alongside, or make physical contact with across ethnoracial lines.[1] For example, Mr. Edwards, who oversaw the sign shop, attested that, "On the yard, it's all politics. You get guys not wanting to associate with different races . . . . But not in here. I've got Mexican [American] guys working with black guys, side-by-side, no problem. No B.S. in here." One correctional officer would claim that, even though tensions may be high in the housing bays, "As soon as they leave the gate for crew work, they mix. They'll talk to each other, work side-by-side. But when they get back, it's back to normal—they segregate. They won't even talk to each other a lot of the time." Some prisoners made similar statements. When describing his job in the sign shop, for example, Luisito claimed, "It's like a real job. We all work together—all the races."

To be sure, certain aspects of day-to-day work practices seemed to confirm this view, as the example of the mechanics described above may attest. Nevertheless, over the course of my eighteen months studying carceral workplaces like the fleet garage, various micro-level practices that did *not* align with this narrative also emerged. For instance, around the corner from the mechanic bays where Gael, Seth, and Danny worked cooperatively, the fleet garage's car wash station revealed a different sort of division. Unlike the men laboring within the garage, the car washers were designated as "unskilled." This less desirable station was typically occupied by foreign nationals. Each long day, the introspective Raul, a Mexican citizen with gray hair that he kept pulled back in a loose ponytail, stood at the ready to wash the inside and outside of every vehicle leaving the garage. It was his third year in this job. The second spot on the two-man car wash crew was something of a rotating position—the others who took on the job seemed to get fired at a high rate. During my time there, I saw the position occupied by two Mexican nationals and one white American, all of whom were fired after stints that lasted between one week to a couple months.

In light of the frequent vacancy in the car wash station, I filled in many times to assist Raul in his tasks. As we scrubbed down a steady flow of prison vehicles, he shared his views on prison life and labor. He was openly critical of the institution and about the importance of race and ethnicity in how things were organized. With his characteristic bluntness one day, he stated that, "If you're born here—Chicanos, blacks, whites—you get a good job. Then you make [one dollar] per hour. If you're *not* born in this country, you go . . . to the food factory. Or you clean bathrooms—clean *shit* as a porter on the yard." Racial and ethnic demographics were central to his view of how the institution slotted its captive workforce into the few "good jobs" that it had to offer. What's more, he was quick to note how nationality cut across these features in key ways. For example, divisions existed *within* the population of Hispanic prisoners at SSP. While Chicano workers might actively pursue desirable positions, Raul and other Latin American nationals faced dimmer prospects. Institutional regulations barred them from even applying to the most prized prison jobs. Many also faced language barriers. "Most of the Mexicans on the yard, they clean the bathrooms," Raul said, "or they are working over there in the food factory. Why are they not working [better jobs]? Because they don't have *English.*"

As scholars like Goodman tell us, prisons are "*racialized* places, meaning they are saturated with talk and action in which race takes front stage—and inmates, officers, and administrators engage in *racializing* moves to categorize . . . inmates" along these lines.[2] Practices surrounding labor are central to this categorization.

This chapter examines how race is implicated in and constructed through work assignment processes in direct and indirect ways. Hiring decisions at SSP were ostensibly made on the basis of race-neutral skill or resource requirements, which obscured biases tied to presuppositions about different demographic groups. Moreover, the official rules of the institution and the codified (yet officially unsanctioned) rules of "racial politics" intersected to directly influence job allocations, resulting in an even more overt preservation of racial and ethnic hierarchies and white supremacy. In the carceral employment system, whiteness acted as a veritable credential while minoritized actors frequently came up against additional hurdles. Such disparities persisted despite formal policies designed to limit discrimination.

Beyond operating as a containment site for populations that society views as dangerous or disagreeable, the prison is home to practices and processes that openly manufacture and maintain a racialized labor and economic order from within. Highlighting the experiences of individuals struggling to overcome these features, I demonstrate how penal labor is racialized and racializing through formal policy, racial political rules, informal hiring practices that privilege white workers, and mobility procedures within worksites that are similarly skewed. It is important to note that the pains of imprisonment affected all who were confined to the institution, regardless of race. Nevertheless, in examining the ways that racial categorization hindered the advancement of people of color through penal labor hierarchies, I maintain that processes of racialization tied to work amplified many of these pains for minoritized prisoners.

Prison, Labor, and Ethnoracial Order

The contemporary prison is central to the creation and preservation of ethnoracial hierarchy in the United States. By serving to "warehouse the precarious and deproletarianized factions of the black working class," in the words of sociologist Loïc Wacquant, it contains a population deemed deviant and dangerous, and actively reinforces caste divisions.[3] As such, today's prisoners are disproportionately drawn from the impoverished and disenfranchised, resulting in a population that had overwhelmingly been jobless, poor, and undereducated before incarceration (and which will likely face continued social and economic marginality upon release).[4]

A key aspect of this is the prison's function "as a modern system of racialized and gendered labor governance," according to sociologist Erin Hatton.[5] By detaining full swathes of working age members of communities of color, it shapes broader patterns of employment through their removal. Yet, questions of how exclusion and classification along ethnoracial lines occurs on the inside remain underexplored. As another sociologist, Michael Walker, notes, "More contemporary studies do not directly examine the significance of race for inmate living."[6] Research in work and organizations provides useful insights for this endeavor. For instance, scholars of work in the free world have outlined how racial prejudices at times supersede merit in hiring decisions.[7] These biases may be deeply embedded in organizations, such as when overseers presume that people of color or women are best suited for less desirable positions or tasks. Such biases often remain hidden beneath discourses that regard work and workers in abstract, generalized terms.[8]

Discrimination may also be masked by how forms of capital are accumulated or valuated within organizations. For example, white males may be more successful in building social capital—that is, establishing ties with instrumental authority figures—especially in organizations overseen by other white males.[9] Even when institutions are deliberately designed to operate meritocratically, divisions nevertheless hinder social capital accumulation. According to sociologist Dierdre Royster, institutions thereby "create and maintain racially segregated (nonoverlapping) networks among whites and blacks."[10] Demographic features can shape access to other forms of capital as well. Employers may rely on perceptions of race as a proxy for skill or as a more general indicator of a worker's desirability or quality, shaping evaluations of cultural capital.[11] These factors interact to generate imbalances in access to vital work opportunities and resources. Furthermore, when lower-status workers *do* manage to acquire desirable jobs, they may still be consigned to less respectable stations or tasks, generating within-job inequality as well.[12]

In these ways, institutions and organizations act as sites of racialization. They are, according to ethnic studies scholar Marta Maria Maldonado, spaces in which "the everyday production, reproduction, and contest over racialized meanings and structures" occurs.[13] Moreover, as sociologist Victor Ray notes, "Organizations are racial structures that reproduce (and challenge) racialization processes."[14] Prisons are no exception. In some cases, racialization behind bars occurs in explicit ways. For instance, Philip Goodman's ethnography of prisoner intake procedures reveals how staffers and incoming prisoners are each involved in the process of officially designating racial or ethnic classifications for the purpose of segregating groups in housing assignments and elsewhere.[15] In this manner, segregation and racial categorization are built upon (imbalanced) negotiations between prisoners, officers, and administrators, each of whom act on differing motivations and possess grossly divergent levels of power. Classification and ethnoracial divisions are here embedded in daily routines, which help to construct race in carceral spaces.

Inequality is maintained not only through macro processes, but via meso- and micro-level organizational structures and practice.[16] Work is often central to these processes.[17] Inspired by the framework outlined by Victor Ray,[18] this chapter examines how formal policies aimed to limit the use of race or ethnicity in hiring decisions may be decoupled from actual practice. As one SSP officer would insist, "Policy is like a guideline. Beyond the policy, we also rely on *common sense*." In the racially charged space of the contemporary prison, common sense often includes adherence to racialized norms and "racial politics." Informal processes, which in practice often overtake formal procedure, can implicitly or explicitly privilege ethnoracial group membership in how people are treated, or decisions are made. The agency of workers of color may be severely diminished by these phenomena and their work prospects and opportunities for advancement within sites may be directly constrained. Inequities in this arena are often legitimated in discourses of staff as well as many incarcerated individuals themselves.

The Role of Formal Policy and Practice in Getting a Prison Job

Like many U.S. prisons, SSP formally prohibited discrimination in work assignments along the lines of race, ethnicity, nationality, and other demographic features. Policy dictated that work and education participation should reflect the demographic composition of the prison unit writ large whenever possible. In other words, each of the primary racial cliques in the prison should be proportionally represented at each site. These primary groups were designated by the institution as white, black, Native American, Chicano or Mexican American, and foreign national or "Paisa." The prison term "Paisa" is short for "paisano" or "countryman" in Spanish and was the name by which foreign nationals commonly self-identified. Most were citizens of Mexico, Guatemala, Cuba, or other Latin American nations. The distinction between Chicano and Paisa was salient; at times, however, they were lumped together by staffers and prisoners under the more general label of Latino.

Keeping worksites "racially balanced" between these groups was a priority for security staff. As one high-ranking officer was quick to assert, "Work isn't segregated. The work crews are *racially balanced*. So, if the yard is, say, X-percent black, a certain percent Mexican, certain percent white, we'll pull from those applications and say, 'Okay, let's hire that percentage blacks, Latinos—like, either one Paisa and one Mexican American, or two Mexican Americans—whites, et cetera." While the demographics of each site rarely mirrored the general population exactly, racial balancing remained a key feature of the work assignment process behind-the-scenes.

To track the racial and ethnic makeup of each site, the officer who oversaw program assignments relied on a massive magnetic "program board." This board, which covered an entire office wall, contained a grid of square spaces representing each work and education program. Every program's respective space on the board was populated by a set of smaller rectangular magnets, each bearing an individual prisoner's name, DOC identification number, and a small photo. These hundreds of magnetic prisoner markers were color-coded to denote racial group affiliations that individuals declared upon entry to the prison.[19] White prisoners had a white border; black prisoners had a blue border; Chicano prisoners had a pink border; foreign nationals had a purple border; Native Americans had a green border. Everyone else—officially labeled "others"—received a yellow border. "Those are mostly Asians," the programming officer asserted. With a glance at this board, officers could roughly ascertain the makeup of each worksite by the arrangement of colors in each square.[20]

When necessary, this knowledge was used to guide hiring or transfer decisions to maintain racial balancing. Still, exceptions to this policy were openly made in certain cases. The programming officer typically allowed the overseers of programs categorized as skilled worksites, such as the sign shop, fleet garage, or call center, to employ their own procedures to select or vet applicants. Certain sites like the call center and fleet garage exhibited more obvious patterns of imbalanced hiring, confirming the survey findings of criminal justice scholar Courtney Crittenden and colleagues that skilled penal labor assignments are inequitably awarded along racial lines.[21] Sites like the sign shop and food factory, however, demonstrated less clear-cut displays of hiring discrimination at this level. Yet, extended ethnographic observations revealed that disparities along racial and ethnic lines were nevertheless evident at these workplaces in the form of station or task discrimination *within* sites.

Conflicts of formal policy: Prisoner nationality

Even though one policy prohibited the use of ethnicity—which encompasses regional territorial identities or nationality[22]—in the assignment of prison jobs, another policy decreed that foreign nationals at SSP were ineligible for several choice work programs. In particular, the two "best" prison jobs, the sign shop and the call center, officially could not accept applications from non-citizens. The manager of the sign shop, Mr. Edwards, confirmed that this sometimes interfered in his hiring process: "Non-American citizens *cannot* work for [the sign shop]. I hired one gentleman once— he was from Cuba. I don't know *how* he made it through the system, but he was here three weeks. They [officers] came in and took him out."

Indeed, many Latin American nationals found themselves relegated to food factory or other undesirable workplaces. (Recall, for instance, Raul's lament that, "If you're born here . . . you get a good job.") For some foreign nationals, formal restrictions contributed to feelings of animosity towards Mexican American prisoners, whom they perceived as not facing the same limitations in their job searches or life in general. "Chicanos get everything free because they speak English well," said Armando, an incarcerated Mexican citizen. "They get a job, get a license, get a green card. *Pshh*—for a Mexican, life is hard. It's *hard* to be a fucking Mexican in this country."

Foreign nationals were also formally barred from assignments that took prisoners beyond facility walls, including highway cleanup, parks maintenance, and other crews operating in the outside world. While I could find no official written justification for the exclusion of these workers from such positions, many staffers drew on the heuristic of "the headline test" to explain it. This occupational colloquialism referred to a brief thought experiment that COs relied on when making or justifying on-the-ground decisions. Essentially, it entailed rhetorically asking: *If I make this decision and it goes wrong, will it result in negative newspaper headlines for the prison?* When I inquired into the lack of foreign nationals employed in certain jobs, one staffer insisted that, "It *must* be a regulation. There's no Paisas in the sign shop. And they can't work the [outside] crews because that doesn't pass the headline test. So, they get the food factory. Lot of 'em work the yard—porters, grounds crews." When describing the "headline test," CO Bush would tell me, "We always start with that. 'Cause even if it's just absconding from parole, if they escape related to *work*, the media—you know how they stretch things. It could blow up on us."

The Role of Racial Politics in Getting a Prison Job

Whereas some skilled worksites were formally permitted to forgo racial balancing procedures (whether because they used their own hiring processes, or because the entire Paisa population was barred from applying), other, informal factors also led to demographic imbalances at certain sites. Formal policies designed to combat workplace segregation were further weakened by the institution's willingness to allow so-called "racial politics" to influence behaviors and decisions.

Racial classification remains a principal feature of the prison social order. Upon initial processing, individuals must declare an affiliation with one of "the races" (in institutional parlance), which are officially logged and drawn on in job allocations, housing assignments, and other operations. Racial classifications also carry social weight on the prison yard. As political scientist David Skarbek notes, "All inmates are expected to affiliate with their racial or ethnic group . . . and one's race and ethnicity play a major role in determining one's place in the prison social system."[23] The rules of racial politics established boundaries between racial cliques in this social space. These codes limited, for instance, interactions between members of different racial cliques. "We don't *smoke* after another race, you don't *eat* after another race, you don't sit at the *table* with another race," one man declared. Even childhood friends of different races or ethnicities would refrain from spending one-on-one time, lest they risk potentially violent enforcement from those who were actively "political" and sought to impose these norms.

These rules originated from the top of the hierarchy from the mouths of the "heads of the different races" (sometimes also referred to as "shot callers," the "politicals," or, in official DOC lingo, the "high profiles"). These "heads" oftentimes resided in higher security prison yards but used various representatives to spread and enforce their directives in medium security units. According to one incarcerated foreign national, this could sometimes cause frustrations. "These guys serving life, twenty-five, fifty years, they never mix with me. I never see them. But they make *rules* for me?"

Beyond interactional limitations, the heads also decreed that prisoners below a certain age (typically those under either twenty-five or thirty-five years old, depending on the unit) were required to exercise on a regular basis. Prisoners contended that this was so each race would have access to strong "soldiers" in the event that violence "popped off" on the yard. Newcomers were taught these expectations early on. "I was lazy at first," one man shared. "I was like, 'Fuck that. I don't want to work out. Who are *you* guys?' You know what I mean? But it's like, 'No, you *have* to.'" Political rules also dictated how groups arranged themselves in the chow line or when queuing up for counts. Nacho, a young man who identified as Paisa and briefly worked in the car wash alongside Raul before getting fired for a disciplinary infraction back on the yard, pointed this out to me. We spotted a group of men lining up on the other side of a nearby razor wire fence between car washes one day. "See how they line up? Blacks in the back," he noted, pointing toward the orange assemblage. "There's political rules about how to line up?" I asked. "*Yeah*," he instructed me, "Blacks in the back, then us [Paisas]."

"Who's in the front?" I asked. "The *whites!*" he exclaimed, as if the answer were self-evident. "Then who?" Shaking his head, he said, "Then the Natives [Native Americans], then the Chicanos, then us, then the blacks."

Some white prisoners openly supported this white supremacist hierarchy. "I have political ink [tattoos] on my body," Franklin, a white sign shop worker, proclaimed as he indicated several images symbolizing white power. "That's just how I *am* and what I *believe*. And that's my right as an American." Others expressed disdain for the rules of the prison yard but felt too vulnerable to actively rebel against them. Lonnie, a younger black man working in the food factory, disavowed the racism that he said permeated prison, but admitted feeling helpless in the face of racial politics and feared risking the wrath of enforcers. "I'm in *their* house. The rules they have in here—I don't like 'em, but I follow 'em." His coworker, Joe, a gray-mustachioed white man, similarly stated that, "It wouldn't *bother* me eating with the black people or the Mexicans . . . . I don't [understand why] when we go to chow, we should sit with the 'right people.'" Still, when asked whether he adheres to these mealtime seating rules, he affirmed, "I *have* to because if I don't, they'll body check [assault me], and I'm not gonna take shit from nobody."

Some remained hopeful that racist structures would fade with new generations. Bobby, a middle-aged black man who had been at SSP for over a decade, shared that he was starting to see changes. "I'm noticing now, opposed to when I first came to prison in [the early 2000s], it's different," he shared. "Because, yeah, we have more younger people that are more, I guess, diverse—grew up with different cultures or whatever. And so, they're more or less more comfortable with dealing with other races and it's harder for them to conform to the prison politics."

Jake, from the call center, expressed a similar view. "To me, that's our grandparents—that's shit from the fifties," he said. "On the streets it's 2016! Welcome to the melting pot! I got friends and family who are Latino. What, I'm gonna come in here and all of a sudden be racist? *No*." Still, despite these optimistic forecasts of change, the rules and hierarchies of this system directly impacted the daily experiences of these men. In several cases, this included interventions shaping where they could or could not work.

Racial politics and work

In addition to the various rules of interaction, the heads of the different races dictated that members of their respective groups were not allowed to hold certain jobs. Although prison administrators possessed authority to compel prisoners to work, they often allowed these self-imposed restrictions to stand, thereby letting racial politics influence formal procedure.[24] Jobs commonly rejected by different racial cliques included those entailing directly "serving" staff members in a deferential capacity, repairing or strengthening carceral architecture, or frequently interacting one-on-one with overseers. For instance, I learned early that white prisoners at SSP had been instructed not to accept the job of shoeshine. When I encountered a white prisoner lounging near the shoeshine chair one morning, I asked if he worked there. He responded with shock: "White guys aren't *allowed* to be shoeshines! That's what the heads on the yard decided," he said. "Any other races can, though?" I asked. "Yeah," came his curt reply.

Later, at the fleet auto garage, I discussed my shoeshine interaction with Seth and Gael, who identified as white and Chicano, respectively. "White boys won't do shoeshine," Seth affirmed, "'cause it's degrading to polish up an officer's boots." They would also inform me that multiple groups refused to work positions like staff barber, fence repair crew, and lock welding crew. Tasks that entailed repairing the "means of captivity" were evaluated especially negatively.

There were some seemingly contradictory exceptions to these prohibitions. The heavy equipment operators, for instance, regularly dragged the prison perimeter for security purposes, but this work was not forbidden by the heads. Nor was the labor of the auto garage workers themselves, who spent their days maintaining and repairing the very vehicles with which COs policed the prisoner population. When I inquired into these apparent discrepancies, asking whether repairing staff members' vehicles perhaps also served the institution in its own way, Seth replied, "Yeah, I see what you're sayin'—because we're fixin' *their* vehicles." After pausing to think about it for another moment, he continued:

> But these [vehicles] are also used to transport *us* around. When we fix 'em, we can make sure *our people* are safe, you know? Anything to do with security—fences, razor wire, locks—we don't fix that because that's what's keeping us locked in. Why would a man build his own *prison*? But here, a bus taking a load of 50 guys statewide? We can make sure they're gonna be safe. I dunno, that's how I think of it.

They would also reveal that differences in politicized work proscriptions sometimes emerged along the intersection of national and racial lines. Seth asserted that, "We're not gonna build up the walls and fences and the razor wire that keeps us in. The white boys and the blacks and the, uh, Chicano Mexicans—the Mexican Americans—we won't do it. Only the Paisas—the Mexican nationals—will do it 'cause they don't give a fuck. They do their own thing." Gael confirmed this, "Yeah, like the welders—they [white, black, and Chicano workers] won't weld locks, you know, to lock us in. They refuse. But the Mexican nationals don't give a fuck what anybody else does. It's basically the Americans who won't do it, pretty much."

The fence crew represented another example of political rules intersecting with nationality. According to one high-ranking officer, "That's a real touchy one. Most of the guys, they get real *political* about putting up the fences to keep them in . . . . It's only the Mexican nationals that will agree to put them up. They're like: 'You have work, I'll work.' But that's just the politics of the yards." When discussing why Paisas were willing to work on the fence or lock crews when other groups refused, CO Peña proffered another view: "It's because they're not from this country . . . [so] they don't have to follow the heads' rules as much because their leadership isn't based in the U.S."

Political dynamics surrounding work were actively racializing. The (sanctioned) refusal of whites to perform the work of a shoeshine because it was "degrading," for instance, acted to label "degrading" work as strictly within the purview of workers of color. Fence and lock repair was disdained even more vehemently—not only as work not suited for whites, but as work not suited for any self-respecting man. As Seth had so passionately exclaimed, "Why would a man build his own *prison?*" Yet, being formally barred from many positions, including top-tier skilled jobs, foreign nationals perhaps could not afford to decline such work. As a result of their acceptance of seemingly profane jobs that others collectively refused, however, they became even more "othered"—not only as "minorities," but as non-citizens evidently out of step with broader prison society.

As a result of these national divides in racially influenced job searches, foreign nationals often faced "racial triangulation" vis-à-vis other ethnoracial groups.[25] They were, on the one hand, valorized for their willingness to do "hard work," making them ideal laborers from the perspective of the institution. On the other hand, however, these individuals were simultaneously construed as immutably "foreign and essentially unassimilable" as a result of these differences.[26] Paralleling the experiences of free Mexican nationals working in the U.S., this contributed to compounded forms of ostracism faced by Paisas on the prison yard. Jobs like the fence crew came to be regarded as "Mexican jobs" that no American would apparently dare perform.

These race and ethnicity-based work norms were largely taken for granted by participants. If any did knowingly or accidentally defy the directives of the racial hierarchy and accept assignment to a forbidden position, the "head" of their racial clique or their representatives on the yard could be fast to intervene. "They might get a quick *talking to*," said CO Peña, raising his eyebrows and miming air quotes as if to signal that such interventions could be more severe than just harsh words. For this reason, "They typically quit [those jobs] after a month, tops," he suggested. A defiant worker might "catch a hot one" (be punched), get "hit" (more thoroughly assaulted), or worse at the hands of designated enforcers. As Peña would go on to say, "The next thing you know, they'll come in telling me, 'Hey, that head's telling me I've got to get off [this crew].' And when your heads tell you to get off, it's—I don't care if you're six-foot-two, 240 pounds, and in the best shape in the world. When these guys come [to enforce political rules], they *don't* come one at a time. They come five, six people deep." The incarcerated remained acutely aware of these possibilities. "There's *rules* in prison," said one long-time ward of the state. "[Violating them] will put my life in jeopardy." To avoid such violence themselves, officers were typically disinclined to personally interfere with racial political mandates.

Diminishing Agency: Racialized Barriers to Within-Job Mobility

Despite its direct role in shaping interactions on the yard as well as job assignment processes, staff members and prisoners alike frequently insisted that racial politics did not influence dynamics *within* carceral workplaces. According to many, racial tensions "get left on the yard." Edwards, the sign shop boss, frequently maintained that work in his shop offered an escape from racial politics. "In the housing units, the blacks won't talk to the whites, the whites won't talk to the Mexicans, the Mexicans won't talk with the blacks. But here, in the shop, everybody works together. They have to. But when they go back to their units, they're completely different," he said. "They won't talk to each other—other races. They *have* to change completely. To survive. They have to live by this double standard. The first question I ask them—ask any new applicant—is: 'Can you work with all the races? Can you take orders from a black man? Can you *give* orders to a black man?' They'll tell you." To be sure, interactions and friendships across racial lines were observable in many sites. It was not out of the ordinary to see men of different races chatting or sitting together in the fleet garage or playing card games during slow periods in the sign shop. Nevertheless, race, ethnicity, and nationality were not without power in these contexts.

Although staffers sought to racially "balance" captive workforces, racial imbalances nevertheless frequently factored into the assignment of prisoners to different stations or jobs *within* worksites. Many expressed concerns over task segregation directly. "It's *very* cliquish on the yard—the different races," said Jared, a white prisoner, after settling into his position at the sign shop. Referring to the dominant narrative that the races "all work together" and that racial differences were not a factor at work, I asked, "Is it tough to go from that environment—the racial cliquishness [of the yard]—to here?" A slight smirk appeared on his face. "Oh, in here I'd say it's even *more* cliquish," came his reply. "How so?" I asked. "Well," he began, thinking over his words carefully, "everyone's been here so *long*. Like those guys over there?" He gestured towards the vinyl layout station where four white prisoners were hard at work. "[All] white. It's so cliquish. The black dudes," he continued, gesturing towards the screen-printing station where five black prisoners had just completed a large sign order, "they treat me more like a human than anyone else in prison. That's why I roll with the blacks over there when I can, at work."

Jared's allusion to the "cliquish" nature of the shop along racial lines, as well as his explanation that "everyone's been here so long," highlighted recurring patterns in station assignment. Just as workers drew on their social connections to "recruit" new workers when a position opened, they also had a say in who got assigned to different stations inside the shop. In most instances, new hires began in the screen-printing station. From there, they learned the basics of how the shop operated. Then, when a spot opened in another area, like vinyl layout or metal fabrication, the more senior prisoners once again recruited, this time from amongst recent hires. Typically, workers sought to promote friends. Maurice, a black worker in the shop, put it explicitly: "*We're* in charge of that [workstation assignments]. Let's say you worked in screens and you wanted to work over on computers. But you *can't* because it's full up. When there *is* an opening, they already got somebody lined up for the position. You see. So maybe you get *frustrated* 'cause you wanna learn the computers! . . . You see who's working on the computers, don't ya?" He nodded slightly toward the all-white crew at that station, "They keep they *own*."

Like Jared, Maurice noted that white prisoners tended to dominate the vinyl layout station, where they designed signage on computers and produced their creations using a large vinyl printer. This station relied on digital design techniques that are in use in the outside world today. The screen-printing station, on the other hand, relied on an outmoded process—mixing and spreading colored ink over large screen stencils to transfer images. While once the dominant method in the industry, screen-printing is no longer a common technique in outside shops. Many workers expressed interest in working with vinyl so that they could develop these more marketable skills.

However, black workers often faced difficultly transferring out of screens, leaving many stuck working only with outdated techniques. In this manner, their agency—already severely limited as an aspect of penal punishment—was further restricted relative to others in the same workplace.

Tensions sometimes rose in response to these restrictions on upward mobility. D.S., an older black prisoner, was hired onto the crew during my time there. Like most, he was first stationed in screen-printing. Recognizing that this was where new workers often began, he was hopeful that he would soon transfer to more modern tasks once he had mastered the traditional screen-printing process. During his first week on the job, he shared his plan: "See, this shit we doin' with the ink? It's obsolete. It's all computers now." Pointing to the vinyl station, he said, "That's why I'm trying to get over *there*, to design."

After a month or so had passed in the shop, D.S. had still not managed to transfer, despite seeing other recent hires get recruited into different stations. Visibly frustrated one day, he waived me over and asked, "Hey, Mr. G? When you're doing your interviews, have you learned about the criteria for working out here? Like, they ask us, 'Are you okay working with everyone—different races? You gotta be okay with everyone!' Okay? Well, you see how it is for *real*—you pick up on that?" Pointing to each respective station as he spoke, he continued, "How the Europeans all over *there* [vinyl], Mexicans over *there* [metal fabrication], and we're over *here* [screen-printing]? Now ain't that some shit?"

* * *

While the sorting of workers into different stations within the sign shop was driven by prisoners themselves—as a result of the relatively greater degree of autonomy that some were afforded—task segregation was not unique to "good jobs." For instance, the food factory, which was commonly derided as the "worst prison job" and a "prison-within-the-prison," also stifled the agency and mobility of many workers of color. However, workers there had no input into the job assignment process.

The three largest stations within the food factory were the warehouse, where prisoners shelved and inventoried dry food goods; the sandwich shop, where workers compiled sandwich ingredients; and the meat prep station, where men wrapped slices of lunch meat in plastic. Staff members who worked for the private firm managing food operations in the facility—colloquially called "white shirts" because of the white polos that their uniform required—oversaw each station with a strictness not seen in top-tier positions. Barba, a Mexican American white shirt, oversaw the meat prep station. It was accepted knowledge that Barba populated his crew almost exclusively with foreign nationals. Some working prisoners did not appreciate this. One white worker, frustrated at not being able to secure a job as a meat slicer on the crew, angrily referred to the overseer as a "racist bastard" who "only hires Mexicans." Barba, however, would defend his actions as the result of a "colorblind" approach to hiring. When a DOC representative insisted that food factory stations be "mixed" —that is, desegregated—Barba ignored it. He informed me that he did not "pay attention to the race." Instead, he refused to alter the composition of his station because he claimed to see all prisoners as the same: "I only see orange."

Not all staffers agreed with Barba's practices. The more recently hired white shirt, Davis, grew angry when Barba's entire crew skipped work to watch a soccer match one day. He shouted, "This is what happens when you hire only one race to a job, dude!" Barba shrugged it off. Davis later vented to me that, "He only hired Mexican guys to work meat. They decided to skip work yesterday, so—*tsk.*" With a shrug he added, "That's what happens when you don't mix it up!"

Months later, the food service team was rotated, and Davis was assigned as the new overseer of meat prep. Despite his earlier protestations over Barba's hiring practices, he surprisingly refused to "mix it up" when the time came. Acquiescing to this practice that he came to see as standard, Davis continued to maintain a primarily Mexican crew. He justified the continuation of primarily hiring foreign nationals as "being consistent." This, he said, was key, "because you don't want to start anything new in there [since it might] make them work less hard than they are." The fact that the other major food factory stations remained largely "racially balanced" only served to bolster his dedication. "Everybody starts in the sandwich shop—it's mixed race all in there. It's black, white," he said. "It's just [not mixed] in *my* area—it can kind of be the Mexican area."

Legitimizing Unequal Prospects

Individuals at SSP justified apparent inequities in hiring practices and within-site mobility in many ways. Some white prisoners recognized their privileged positions in the penal labor system but took no issue with the power that it accorded them. For example, an older white man working in the sign shop exhibited no hesitation in noting, matter-of-factly, "The whites work in the sign shop and good jobs, and the blacks work picking up trash." Any critiques of such trends were nothing more than "just whining," he insisted. "*One* black complains, 'Well, we can't work *here*, man! This [is] bull-shit!'" Shaking his head in annoyance, he repeated, "Just *whining*."

Others eschewed overtly racist ideologies, proffering their own explanations for divisions between groups. For example, Jake, the white call center salesman who insisted that racial political friction was "shit from the fifties," would go on to remark, "You got some guys been in here so long, bud, that they're stuck in that state of mind. And the cops, too. Their training teaches them that we're all bad guys, that there's race politics to be followed." The notion that carceral administrators and staffers played an active role in racial politics was common. Some, like Jake, regarded it as a now taken-for-granted outcome of a long tradition of racial tensions and officers' attempts to mitigate violence. As the food factory staff member Davis revealed, many institutional overseers considered it vital to remain "consistent" above all else, apparently even if that entailed enabling segregation.

Some were more overtly suspicious of staffers' motivations. One middle-aged Chicano prisoner theorized that the system of racial politics and all its consequences functioned to undermine the power of the prisoner population as a whole. "In the eighties, it wasn't like that," he said. "Everybody was together, and inmates had more power. Now, everybody's in groups, so the prison has more power. The prison *benefits*. They *want* us separated." Another worker, a black man in his thirites, echoed this rhetoric. "They don't want us all together," he told me. "That's too much power. All the blacks, all the whites, all the Mexicans—they got this whole *system* to keep us separated, 'cause we too powerful together. The way they got it set up right now, we police each other. I feel that was created by them, putting us separated by race like that." It is telling that this perspective was espoused by individuals from across ethnoracial groups, each frustrated by the ways that they had been separated by prison politics and critical of the institution's role in maintaining these divides.

Cultural justifications

A key feature of racialization within many organizations is the legitimation of inequalities along cultural, rather than explicitly racial, lines.[27] According to some SSP staffers, it was not just that certain men lacked (or had been systematically denied opportunities to develop) valuable skills or resources that explained their apparent exclusion from top-tier jobs. Instead, some believed that the possession of *other* flaws informed their supposedly limited capabilities. As one CO would claim, so-called skilled workers exhibited dedication to learning, whereas others were presumed to be unskilled or unmotivated. "I think some of these guys, they have more *integrity*," he insisted:

> A place like the food factory—that's used as like a punishment. Who wants to wrap sandwiches all day? Or grounds crews—most of those guys don't *want* to work. They hide their rake under their bed and go watch TV all day. You gotta chase 'em down. They say, "Oh, yeah, I'm sorry, I'll go work now," then do the same thing tomorrow. Some people just—I hate to say it this way—they just come in here more *ghetto*. They want to go exploit the system, to get over on somebody. But if you come

in with no skills except pushing a *rake*, then that's what you *do*! Whereas these guys [holding skilled jobs], they grew up working. They like coming here and working.

The imprisoned disproportionately hail from backgrounds of poverty and disadvantage. By the above logic, however, those lacking work skills that are in high demand are to be blamed for lacking "integrity." Such statements were often couched in unmistakably racialized rhetoric. Those who attempted to resist coercion in deskilled captive labor were regarded as "more ghetto." This was linked to assumptions of integrity so as to legitimate beliefs about why certain groups were "undeserving" of desirable work. Purportedly colorblind practices rewarding certain skillsets belied the maintenance of ethnoracial labor hierarchy behind bars.

Such patterns were apparent throughout the institution. Recall, for instance, the way Dennis, the manager of the call center, admitted to excluding applicants on account of sounding "like they're from the ghetto" or possessing particular accents. This underscores the extent to which applicants' ability to adhere to valued language norms was deeply racialized. While few black respondents managed to secure positions on the sales team despite these discriminatory criteria, Latino prisoners remained virtually absent from the site.

Following my conversation with Dennis about hiring, I decided to ask others within the call center why *they* thought people of color, and Latinos in particular, were underrepresented on the crew. One respondent was Eduardo, a Chicano civilian employee who had been hired by Dennis to help oversee the call center from the window-lined "bubble" in the middle of the sales floor. After contemplating the question, he replied, "I think it's the *accent*. They just don't do well. Everything today seems like a scam, so when people hear a Mexican accent [over the phone], they get worried: 'Oh, some dude in Mexico is scamming me!'" Paralleling his boss, Eduardo chalked demographic discrepancies largely up to accent. Yet, unlike Dennis, he did not contend that this made men ineligible for hire. On the contrary, it was the discriminatory and distrusting culture of the free world, by his logic, that made it difficult for Latin American workers to *stay* hired, even though they were rarely given the opportunity to attempt the job.

I also discussed this issue with Jake, the incarcerated white salesman tasked with training new hires. He drew on a different sort of cultural explanation for inequities in hiring. In his view, differences in the attitudes and outlooks of Hispanic and white workers explained the failings of the former while the latter thrived in the prison call center. Specifically, he emphasized racialized perceptions of personality styles to explain the lack of diversity. "I been trying to get some *éses* in here for forever," he exclaimed. "But, I think, traditionally, Mexican guys are more stoic. While us white dudes are more, uh, outgoing, you know? We'll bullshit [with] ya all day. So, they don't have as much success on the phone." Here again, perceived cultural distances were mobilized to justify a lack of compositional diversity on-the-ground.

The Misrecognition of Whiteness

The prison is a racializing institution. Black, Hispanic, and Native American individuals are disproportionately more likely to become ensnared in the criminal justice system, leading to greater rates of imprisonment among these populations and, in turn, a growing association between penal sanctions and minoritized groups.[28] Members of affected communities are more likely to be permanently burdened with the "mark" of a criminal record, which diminishes prospects.[29] Even people of color who have not had contact with the U.S. criminal justice system are often presumed to possess a criminal record, leading to racialized assumptions of criminality which breed inequalities for entire populations for generations.[30]

Ethnographic analysis of the internal workings of the carceral system—and penal labor in particular—revealed a damning reality: In addition to the harm wrought to minoritized communities by mere contact with the criminal justice apparatus generally, formal and informal internal practices reflect and aggravate inequalities at the organizational level. As the imprisoned are sorted into different labor tracts as a facet of punishment, black and brown workers are disadvantaged in the search for higher-paying, potentially rewarding jobs that many hope will ameliorate the pains of imprisonment and potentially ensure success in reentering the free world. (Further outcomes of these processes will be examined in the following chapters.)

Relative to other groups, whites were more likely to be presumed to possess skills and work ethics behind bars—just as they may be less likely to be met with assumptions of a criminal record in the free world market. Put another way, while blackness remains linked to racialized perceptions of criminality and labor market value, whiteness inversely acted as a "positive credential" disproportionately associated with job applicant desirability. These benefits are compounded as individuals pass through different organizations or institutions.[31] At SSP, the credentialing of whiteness was apparent, for instance, in how administrators and staffers permitted whites to refuse jobs like shoeshine, which were deemed too "degrading" for them yet were apparently suited for members of other groups. Those evaluating potential workers made assumptions about skills or resources shaped by beliefs tied to race, following which, black and brown prisoners were at times overtly labeled as "too ghetto" to possess valued characteristics.

More pervasive were situations in which the role of whiteness in shaping other forms of capital was "misrecognized." Simply put, misrecognition refers to processes through which the true importance of one thing—for instance, a certain characteristic, outlook, understanding, or action—is not openly recognized, but is instead attributed to something else entirely. Inequalities related to the misrecognized feature are able to be maintained precisely because they are concealed.[32] While race, ethnicity, or nationality shaped job sorting chances behind bars in key ways, it remained uncommon for many of the men caught in this system to directly note the importance of these features. To be sure, workers like Jared, Maurice, and D.S. in the sign shop openly referenced and even critiqued this system. However, many others—most frequently white workers in high profile positions—were reluctant to acknowledge the influence of race on these processes. Instead, it was far more common for individuals to point to much vaguer concepts such as "integrity" or "work ethic" in describing what mattered in getting a good job.

Various forms of capital—such as work skills, social ties, or knowledge of particular hiring norms and expectations—were highlighted in place of discussions of race, in spite of the fact that they were often intimately intertwined.[33] Even though, on the surface, valued capitals were not inherently tied to the race or ethnicity of their holder, they were often not distributed justly along demographic lines. For instance, whites at SSP often appeared better positioned to mobilize valuable social capital to secure referrals from other whites who held positions of influence. Although race shapes personal and professional networks in the free world,[34] social capital appeared even more overtly racialized in the carceral context, in alignment with racial politics.

This was also exemplified *within* sites. Many workers, such as Slim, a white computer designer in the sign shop's vinyl station, contended that station assignments came down not to race, but other factors like sociability: "Yeah, it's *kind* of racial, but then again, it's not," he said. "It's not necessarily races, [but] more or less who we can work with. It kind of *looks* racial, but . . . I mean, not everybody can work with everybody." Being able to "work with" someone, in this sense, was highly racialized (even if workers like Slim did not recognize it as so) because developing friendly ties on the yard was limited by the group boundaries of racial politics. Here again, men of color in this carceral setting—as in the free world and historically[35]—appeared to more clearly recognize white supremacy and its forces and to indicate them more readily than their white counterparts.

This extends our understanding of the prison as a racialized organization by highlighting patterns of racialization embedded in the carceral employment system. This system of labor, which is commonly, if contradictorily, framed as integral to rehabilitative and punitive functions, relies on formal and informal procedures that intersect to reproduce inequalities along racial and ethnic lines. Racial politics and institutional structures together limit the opportunities of workers of color just as they shape the misrecognition of the credentialing of whiteness. Moving forward, the next chapter turns to outcomes of these phenomena by examining disparities in working prisoners' material resources and power within prison economies that result from uneven footing in the penal labor hierarchy.

5

I Owe My Soul to the Commissary Store

Economic Stratification on the Inside

> This chewing tobacco was the coin of the realm. Two or three rations of bread for a plug was the way we exchanged, and they traded, not because they loved tobacco less, but because they loved bread more.
>
> —Jack London (1907)

Research into the impacts of incarceration on the everyday lives of the imprisoned, their families, and the broader communities from which they come and to which they will return reveals a long list of negative outcomes of doing time. From reduced job search prospects to slashed earnings, volatile family formation to stifled civic engagement, and a variety of physical and mental health challenges, the reverberations of incarceration haunt those touched by carceral institutions.[1] However, for many currently doing time, prison is a long and grueling experience, with reentry a far-off hope. In Sunbelt State Penitentiary (SSP), many had years or decades remaining in their sentences. For them, conditions behind bars often eclipsed planning for their future lives outside.[2]

At SSP, prisoner wage disparities found some men earning close to $0.10 hourly while others receive over $2, differentially shaping the lives of the incarcerated. As cost-shifting practices continue to expand,[3] prisoners themselves have grown more reliant on wages to supplement core prison services through the formal and informal economies. Labor market outcomes limit access to goods and services through these channels.

The formal prison economy refers to official institutional outlets where workers make many purchases. This chapter will describe the organization of this market and the ways in which the imprisoned spend their wages here. One's job and rate of pay determines one's ability to acquire vital foods, hygiene products, or "nonessential" entertainment goods through the prison commissary. Like the company stores of some isolated mining towns in the early twentieth century,[4] the prison commissary represents the only store where workers can spend hard-earned wages. Prisoners' families may also be impacted by these disparities as wages are also necessary to afford access to the telephone and mail services that facilitate communication with loved ones and support networks in the free world.

The quality of a prison work assignment also shapes outcomes in the informal prison economy. This includes various unsanctioned outlets administered by enterprising incarcerated salesmen and service providers. These black-market stores rely on informal currency. Today, the de facto informal currency behind bars is cheap food items, like ramen noodles. Prisoners able to acquire the necessary amount of these "soups" can purchase smuggled goods not available through formal channels. They may also employ others to do their laundry, clean their bunk, repair personal belongings, act as private security, and more. Official Department of Corrections (DOC) directives outlaw these informal transactions, making participation in the illicit economy risky. Still, those who were less able to afford necessary goods in the formal economy were often driven to this illegal marketplace.

Another Day, Another Dollar: Prisoner Pay

Despite attempts to increase prisoner pay at the national level over the years,[5] most state and federal prisoners make less than $1 per hour.[6] In states where prisoners are paid for their labors, wages may range from under $0.05 to (in rare cases) over $5 hourly, with regular jobs paying up to an average of $0.63.[7] At SSP, hourly wages were distributed via an institutional pay system sometimes referred to as an "inmate checking account." To have funds in one's account was to "have money on the books" that could be used in the formal prison economy. Most started their carceral labor careers earning around $0.09 per hour in positions like the food factory or grounds crew. For all but two work programs, pay was capped at approximately $0.50. The two exceptions to this rule were the sign shop, which offered up to approximately $1 hourly, and the call center, which offered up to approximately $2.34.[8]

Although low, an individual's wages were not necessarily static. In most positions, workers were eligible for pay raises every six months or so following regular performance evaluations. Supervising staff members assessed each worker qualitatively, often with an emphasis on compliance and subjective dedication to the job. These evaluations typically operated on a four-point scale. A worker may be graded E for "exceeds expectations," S for "satisfactory," U for "unsatisfactory," or N for "no rating." The latter was usually reserved for those who failed to attend work assignments and often brought additional sanctions like disciplinary tickets or termination.

No money, more problems: Prisoners' economic concerns

In general, access to money is vital for navigating a prison sentence in the United States. As one man, Alexey, stated matter-of-factly, "You *need* money in prison." Only a small subset of participants reported receiving at least semi-regular financial assistance from family or friends in the free world. Jim, a middle-aged warehouseman in the food factory stock room, shared that his mother put money on his books monthly. With these steady funds from the outside, he had little problem making ends meet. Few of his incarcerated counterparts could claim similar support, however. Jim remained cognizant of the advantages this offered: "I'm a *rare* inmate," he told me. "I don't need to work—I don't need to do *anything*. I just do this [work] to pass the time."

Jim's situation was indeed rare. According to Eli, "Jobs are important in here because money is scarce. A lot of people don't have family on the outside supporting them." To be sure, the incarcerated are disproportionately drawn from working class or impoverished communities and external support is far from guaranteed for the overwhelming majority.[9] As such, wages from penal labor were truly vital for most to afford basic needs and wants. One man outlined the potential severity of the issue: "If you don't have store [money], you go hungry." Another was similarly blunt: "If you're on that yard [not working], you're gonna *starve*."

The state of pay was a common source of anxiety. For the lowest paid, a full day's work might yield just enough to purchase one pack of ramen from the commissary. As one food factory meat roller stressed with a scoff, "A full day's work might get you a *soup*." When asked about his experiences with carceral labor in general, Rich immediately brought up wages. "Of course, I'm not happy about the pay," he uttered. "If anything, I barely get by. I'm not talking about *wants*; I'm talking about *needs*! I'm completely on my own in here and it's not enough."

The highest paid—those in the sign shop and call center—had notably different experiences with money. Room and board fees were automatically deducted from their wages, but even after these charges, they still took home notably higher pay than most. Many referred to them as "prison CEOs" in response to the evident disparity between their earnings and those of the general prisoner population. Their ability to purchase goods that many could only dream of—like special prison televisions made of clear plastic— only added to this perception. "The assumption on the yard is that call center workers are rich," one salesman shared. Another conceded that, "In here, we're the lucky ones. We're rich in here compared to everyone else. [Over two dollars] an hour might as *well* be CEOs in here."

The Formal Prison Economy

Few items or services are provided to the incarcerated without charge. Contemporary state prisons like SSP place strong emphasis on neoliberal agendas of fiscal responsibility, which often means high prisoner fees for things that were once provided by the state. In addition, numerous private firms operate things like the commissary store, medical care, telephone services, and more within these public institutions. Prisoners at SSP were required to pay from their institutional accounts to make use of many of these offerings.

The commissary store

The commissary was the main site of prisoner spending. This was the only official place to purchase food, hygiene products, and other goods. Estimates suggest that commissary sales nationwide amount to over $1.6 billion annually, if not more.[10] According to one study, the prisoner population spends more in the commissary than they typically earn through prison jobs, with food or hygiene products making up most of those purchases.[11]

Wednesday was "commissary day" at SSP, the day when individuals could pick up the items that they had ordered the previous week. For most, this was the highlight of the week. Even the most morose men that I met were likely to perk up on Wednesday afternoons. While crossing the yard one day, for instance, I spotted a group of familiar faces from the sign shop. They were arranged in a loosely structured line leading up to an open door and small window. Several of them waved as I approached. Felix pointed excitedly to the commissary and gave me a thumbs up. Lemmy, the self-described "Mr. Negative" of the crew, even offered a slight smile toward the open door. He was next in line.

The walls of the small, plain white room were lined with metal shelving units crowded with clear plastic trash bags. Each was filled with varieties of ramen, chips, toothpaste, and other goods. Some bulged with items; others appeared deflated, holding only a few things. Customers' names were scrawled prominently on each bag. A plainclothes staff member that worked for the private firm running the store leaned on a counter, closely inspecting a slip of paper that Denaun, the sign shop porter, had just handed her. Without fully turning her head, she called out his last name to her assistant, a tall prisoner adorned in a long-sleeve orange shirt with neck tattoos creeping up from the collar. The man spun on one foot, quickly scanned the shelves, and pulled one of the larger bags, which had Denaun's name on it. Before leaving, Denaun inspected its contents through the transparent plastic, carefully parting his goods to count each item. With a satisfied smile, he told me, "Got all my stuff this week." When he exited, Lemmy entered and said, "What's up?" After handing over his slip and receiving his large bag, he glanced inside (with much less intent than Denaun) and nodded. Hiking it over his shoulder victoriously, he exclaimed, "*This* is what we work for!" As he marched out, Sammy entered, grinning at the sight of the bag-lined shelves.

Most commissary bags were filled primarily with food items. According to prisoners and correctional staff alike, the chow provided by the state was not enough on its own to sustain an adult. Regular complaints contended that the meals were comprised of too many starches, too little protein, and shrinking portion sizes—mirroring complaints lodged against prisons throughout the nation.[12] As one food factory worker put it, "The chow is really bad. They give you little kid meals, like *that's* enough calories for a grown man." D.S., who had once worked as a server on the chow line, reported that, "The white shirts [staff overseers] encourage you to stay low on portions. It's not enough for a man to eat."

A standard lunch, called a "bag nasty," contained four slices of bread, two slices of lunchmeat, a small bag of corn chips or crackers, a mustard packet, a ranch dressing packet, a tiny packet of flavored drink powder, and a cookie. Sporadically, it might contain a slice of cheese. On many days, an opaque viscous layer coated the meat. To supplement these sparse and unappetizing offerings, those who could afford it relied heavily on food from the commissary. During lunch in the sign shop one day, Clegg added some extra chips that he had purchased to the inside of his state-provided bologna sandwich to bulk it up and mask the taste. As he brought it to his mouth he uttered, "You pretty much—if you don't have store [commissary credit], you go hungry." Snorting, his coworker, the young Bryson, added: "Or you learn to love *bread*."

Securing more satisfying sustenance in the face of deprivation was easier from a top-tier job. "In order for us to eat healthy, you have to have a job. Otherwise, it's *not* good," one man said. Another attested that work was vital, "Otherwise you're relying on the *state*." A man's financial standing could often be assessed by whether he ate purely state chow or enjoyed commissary foods. The most financially secure subsisted entirely on purchased goods.

Jimmy, for instance, concocted what he called the "perfect lunch" in terms of price as well as calorie and protein contents: prison quesadillas. Each meal break, he could be found setting up his items meticulously beside the microwave. In a small bowl, he mixed a portion of powdered refried beans in water and microwaved them. This bean mix was thickly spread onto a single flour tortilla, which was then topped with a zig-zag squeeze from a packet of spicy cheese spread and folded in half. In total, Jimmy assessed his lunch at $0.49 per meal—$1.45 for a bag of powdered beans, which made seven servings at $0.21 each; $0.30 for a packet of jalapeno squeeze cheese, which provided two servings at $0.15 each; and a pack of six tortillas for $0.78, or $0.13 each. With his above-average hourly wage from the sign shop, Jimmy assured me that he could afford these supplies and still have enough left to purchase other items for dinner and snacks.

The incarcerated could also purchase other goods, such as much needed hygiene products. The institution provided each man a small roll of thin toilet paper on a semi-regular basis; however, many reported that their roll ran out well before the next one arrived, leading them to the commissary to replenish. "You get a roll that's supposed to last you ten days," one man shared, "but it doesn't ever work that way." Other items, like denture cream, were a necessity for some but were not generally provided and had to be purchased. Expensive personal entertainment goods, such as a CD player or television, were also available but were prohibitively expensive for most at approximately $40 and $200, respectively. What's more, in addition to the commissary cost, possession of electronic appliances also brought with it a $2 monthly electricity fee. Only those with steady incomes could afford such "luxuries."

Clothing items were especially popular at the store. Although the state provided newly admitted prisoners with an orange shirt, pants, undergarments, and boots upon admission, the men of SSP were expected to purchase their own replacements or upgrades as needed. This was a source of frustration for many, especially those occupying low-paying jobs. According to the white-haired Samuél when we first met in the food factory, "We ruin our clothes working, but yet they won't replace 'em and we can't afford new ones." Indeed, the conditions of many prison jobs did result in clothing being quickly worn down. Many a warehouse worker sported stained sweatshirts with tattered sleeves or fabric hanging from the waist like fringe. Working in the food factory one day, the always-mirthful Dean pulled me aside and said, "Hey, hey, check this out." Lifting his left foot, he revealed that the sole of his state-issued boot had nearly completely peeled off. He kicked his foot slightly and the hanging sole flapped like a gaping mouth. Unable to afford sturdier boots, he had been stuck with these ones for some time. With an exaggerated shrug he pointed down and sighed, "I mean, *really?*"

Often, even when the imprisoned could afford them, supplies of new goods were quickly depleted. Jon expressed frustrations in the sign shop one day after being unable to purchase a new pair of underwear. He told his coworkers that the only thing available to him, according to the commissary store clerk, were used "shitty drawers." Visibly upset at being denied fresh products, he shouted, "Where's the money goin'? The tax money that's s'posed to be paying for [necessities like] these clothes—where's *that* goin'?"

Formal prison services

The men of SSP were also expected to pay for numerous services. Chief among these was the mandatory fee for visiting the doctor's office. Most states charge prisoners for medical care. The national average is $3.47 per trip.[13] Visiting the doctor at SSP cost approximately $4.00. Many saw this cost as unacceptable, especially considering the other expenses with which they had been saddled. The calculation of whether to visit the doctor or use one's money for food was unfortunately commonplace. On one occasion, I witnessed one man castigating another for having visited the nurse instead of purchasing additional food. "That's *four* dollars!" he shouted in frustration. "Four dollars could'a bought *two* packets of squeeze cheese, a can of chili with beans, *and* tortillas. That's a burrito—three burritos each! We could'a been eating good, but instead, you decided to go to the doctor. We could be *eatin'*, but you blew it on the doc! Don't be goin' to the doctor."

Beyond the costs, the quality of medical care was infamous amongst the imprisoned and many staff. One CO, for instance, openly derided prison medical services. "The company that does the medical is—" he paused for a moment and shook his head, "—*bad.*" A group of nearby prisoners affirmed almost in unison: "Yup." For those in poor health or with more serious conditions or injuries, this was particularly troubling. After missing a day of work in the food factory, the sturdy Armando stomped off the bus the next morning clutching his hand. One of his fingernails was completely blackened, the result of a heavy metal meat pan falling on it earlier that week. While setting up his workstation, he told me that his entire arm was sore the night after the accident, resulting in a restless night. He overslept the next morning, missed the bus to work, and was put on formal report for failure to appear. Although his injury remained painful, he said that he could not afford to visit the doctor. "Four dollars is half my check for fifteen days," the man lamented. "Plus," he continued, "they don't do nothing anyways. The only thing they do is they say to us, 'Drink a lot of water,' and that's it."

Samuél shared a similar experience. Clutching his back one afternoon between rounds of dishwashing in the food factory, he shared
that he suffered from chronic back pain. Water dripped down the
front of his red rubber apron as he stretched weakly. Before prison,
he had received disability benefits. Inside, however, he was required
to work and risked disciplinary tickets if he skipped a day to rest his
body. After his last four-dollar doctor's visit, he was prescribed Advil,
which he had to purchase from the commissary. He often struggled
to afford the painkiller on his food factory wages and expressed that
he had no plans to scrape together the money for another examination. Men who were required to make recurring or follow-up visits
were often still charged the fee. As one man complained, "They got
me listed down in *Chronic Care* and everything else. But when they
call [me for] my medical, they charge me four dollars! So, you figure
you get twenty cents an hour—that's six dollars a week? You know
what I mean? But then they take that out . . . . What do you have
left—if you have anything left?"

Another regular expense was the use of telephones to call home.
The prices of use had increased steadily, as has become the norm in
U.S. penal facilities.[14] At SSP, callers were charged over $0.10 per mi-
nute (as much as some made for an hour of work) for local calls via
the contracted phone services provider. The price for long-distance
calls was nearly double this. Although the FCC has capped the rate
that prisoners can be charged for out-of-state calls, they remain prohibitively costly for poor individuals.[15] The money that the institution earned from telephone charges was said to contribute to the
development and support of new programs. "But," claimed Maurice,
"nobody ever sees that money." Instead, he complained, more
programs seemed to have been cut than introduced in recent years.
Despite the expense, as the primary means of maintaining contact
with family and others in the free world, the phones saw constant
use. For many, this was an integral way of maintaining sanity and
morale during trying stints. Every time I visited the yard, I observed
a tight cluster of men standing around each wall-mounted phone.
Others could be seen posted in a row beside it, awaiting their turn.

Telephone access was often leveraged as a means of disciplining the prisoner population. If one received enough infractions, phone privileges could be revoked. This sanction often appeared to be issued arbitrarily from the perspective of the incarcerated. One man recounted getting punished for stepping his foot too far onto a yellow boundary line painted around the periphery of the recreational yard: "You have one *foot* over that thing . . . *bam*, you get a ticket. They take your store [access] away for two weeks. No phone calls, no nothing—for *that*." Losing phone privileges could test personal relationships with those in the free world. The man continued, "I mean, that's two weeks not calling your wife or your girlfriend. Imagine if you just got cut off? Your cell phone—your family, your work, everything, for two weeks. And then you're waiting, like, 'Damn, man, I've got five more days. Four more days left.' And then when you [finally] call, it's just like they just took two weeks of your freedom . . . . Your outside life."

For some, maintaining an "outside life" through the phones was a primary motivation to work. According to one food factory worker, his wages, though minimal, helped him access the phones during periods when his mother was unable to help him financially. "I wanted a job *quick* because I don't have any outside money. My mom wasn't helping me. After a couple months she started putting money on my books. I'd buy phone time with it mostly." Prisoners in higher-paying positions were better able to afford "putting money on their phones." According to one call center salesman, one of the biggest perks of his higher pay was "being able to put money on the phone *ourselves* so that they [family] don't have to pay for it. You know what I mean? I remember whenever I first put money on the phone and my old lady answered, and [the recording] said, 'You have a call at no expense to you.' She felt *tripped*. 'What the hell? I ain't paying for this?' And this makes them feel good."

Phone use was especially critical for those approaching release, who relied on it to arrange housing and other amenities after prison. It was important to schedule transportation as well. "I mean, we *need* to make phone calls," one man shared during the weeks leading up to his freedom. "Like, I'm thirty days to the gate [to release] and I need to get some things lined up, and if I don't have that . . . they're going to drop me off at a bus station."[16]

Savings and preparations

In addition to reentry planning via the phones, many also attempted to save a portion of their wages in the lead-up to release. For some, these concerns emerged some time before their exit date. Franklin told me matter-of-factly that, "Once you've got two years left, that's important [the pay]." For most, setting funds aside was difficult at best. Seth, working in the fleet auto garage, expressed frustrations to this end. To him, willingly participating in work was something that ought to be better rewarded. Instead, he said, "They don't make it easy for us in here. I mean, I know it's not s'posed to be [easy], but the guys out there doing jobs that they *would* have to pay ten, twenty dollars an hour for? They could at *least* pay us a *dollar* an hour so we can get by—actually have some money to get started when we're released."

Those with the highest-paying jobs were better able to amass savings. As a result, they sometimes framed their high-status assignments as a means of reentry preparedness. When asked about the qualities of his job in general terms, the newly hired call center worker Rico said, "The pay's alright. I'm doing it for my old lady. To have something for when I get out." Sign shop crewmen were similarly well-positioned, relative to those in the lower tiers, to accumulate savings. Ocho, who had worked in the shop for nearly two years, expressed excitement about his return home in thirty days (referred to as "twenty-nine and a wakeup"). "I might get out of here with over about fifteen-fifty [$1,550 in savings]," he shared, "and that's going to help me out just fine." Still, despite his ability to save, he remained cognizant of how much the institution had deducted from his checks throughout the years. "I did the math on my pay. They took over 891 *dollars* from me for room and board. And they *still* charged me two dollars [monthly] for electricity!" With a sideways glance and a chuckle, he added, "The bastards."

Not all savings were held until release. Some of the highest-paid workers reported sending remittances home throughout their prison terms. This rare level of financial stability enabled them to maintain a form of "breadwinner" status, helping preserve some degree of household normalcy to which they might return after incarceration. This was also significant for their families. According to a call center worker named Clay, "We've got our families out there. Still have mortgages. Still have car payments . . . . So, having that money [means] being able to send it out to buy our kids school supplies or Christmas presents, maybe help with the mortgage each month."

The Informal Prison Economy

While the incarcerated could purchase key goods and services through the formal prison economy, many other exchanges occurred off the books. A diverse economy and labor market operated in the shadows of the formal system. This underground market even relied on its own currency.

Informal currencies behind bars

With access to cash prohibited, special forms of money evolve within penal settings. A prison monetary token is typically an item in high demand that is readily available, durable, and easily reducible to a common scale.[17] Even though their value as money is restricted to carceral institutions, informal currencies are nevertheless treated as "the prison equivalent of cash providing exchange for goods (such as food and drugs) and to pay debts," according to public health scholar Robyn Richmond and colleagues.[18] An otherwise commonplace item may thus take on a new life as a valued black-market token to be used to buy goods, hire services, or even gamble in the subterranean prison economy.

Traditionally, cigarettes have reined in this role behind bars, but this has changed in recent years. Today, the *de facto* informal prison currency of choice is cheap, durable food items. At SSP and many other prisons, ramen noodle soup had emerged as the black-market money of choice.[19] A single ramen packet cost $0.59 through the prison commissary but could be used to make a wide variety of unauthorized purchases. Even those who disliked the salty treat regularly stocked up for use as currency.

Ramen packets, or "soups," represent an ideal medium of exchange in the prison context. They possess inherent value as affordable, easily prepared, and tasty meals. Because the imprisoned are commonly denied filling food through the chow hall, many subsist on these noodles. Additionally, ramen fulfils a powerful social role. It is a staple of large group meals, called "spreads," which are integral to community building behind bars.[20] Eating ramen instead of state-provided chow also provides an opportunity to reclaim some degree of autonomy in the face of strict limitations. The seemingly mundane effort to control what and when one eats actively defies penal structures designed to repress identity and agency.[21] Finally, soups exhibit certain standard characteristics of money. A ramen packet, much like cash, can store value for some time, act as a standardized unit of account, and be easily exchanged between buyers and sellers.[22]

The structure of the ramen market and "inmate stores"

Nearly anything at SSP could be paid for with ramen. This included items ranging from smuggled vegetables to toothpaste, as well as services like bunk cleaning and laundry. Many stated that they purchased most or all of their essential goods with ramen in the black market. It was even used for gambling in card games or sports betting.

"Soup is money in here. It's sad but true," said one man. According to another participant, Alec, "Ramen is the best money in here because it can be traded for anything else. I can go next door and trade ramen for a bag of coffee or whatever." Jose would state that "a soup is everything," suggesting that many would trade whatever they owned to get one. "It's 'cause people are hungry," he said. "You can tell how good a man's doing [financially] by how many soups he's got in his locker. '20 soups? Oh, that guy's doing good!' . . . Prison is like the streets—you use currency for everything. In here, it's soups."

Figure 5.1 depicts black-market prices of several popular goods alongside their commissary costs.[23] Fresh produce was particularly sought-after. "Fresh veggies are like lobster in here," said one man, biting into what he called a "black-market zucchini" on his lunch break. A fresh piece of pilfered produce was valued at one or two packets of ramen in the underground market, depending on the type. Onions and bell peppers were popular staples in prisoners' homemade cuisine and cost two soups. Only higher-paid individuals could afford such products on a regular basis. As one staffer overseeing the call center said with a grin, "These fools make enough money that they can buy *all* the food coming [smuggled] out of the kitchens." Additionally, caffeine was prized. Four soups could be traded for a bag of coffee. Clothing could also be purchased. For instance, two soups bought a sweatshirt. Maurice shared that one could buy a complete pair of thermal undershirt and bottoms for six soups—"a pretty good deal," he said. Hygiene products could also be acquired. A tube of denture adhesive, for example, cost one soup.

Items that have historically functioned as informal prison monies, like tobacco or envelopes, also remained available to the prisoners of SSP. A single packet of ramen could buy one envelope. This was notably different from the commissary price of two cents. Jose explained that the black-market price was driven in part by other demands: "People will pay more for an envelope when they need to write home to get more soups!"

Tobacco also remained popular. "Tailor-made" (i.e., packaged) cigarettes were readily available to those who favored and could afford them. A single soup could be traded for five cigarettes. A full pack of one popular brand cost approximately $8 ($0.40 per cigarette) at the commissary, meaning that a $0.59 soup could fetch $2 worth of cigarettes, speaking to the value of cheap food over once-dominant tobacco in the informal economy. Finally, although

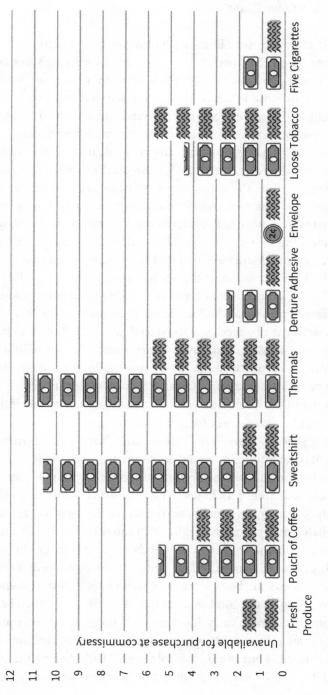

Figure 5.1 The prices of commonly traded goods in the prison black market at SSP.
Credit: Author, redrawn by Chelsea Nicolas.

hand-rolled smokes (or "loosies") had never been relied on as informal money in SSP (because quality and quantity was not consistent enough per roll to act as reliable currency), six soups could buy a pouch of loose tobacco. The commissary offered two brands, each fetching the same black-market rate. Most seemed to prefer buying loose tobacco over more expensive name brand packs.

To acquire these goods, the imprisoned turned to "inmate stores": illicit shops operated out of the bunks of entrepreneurial individuals.[24] While the commissary only opened one day weekly, black-market stores were nearly constantly accessible. Moreover, goods that were notoriously understocked in the commissary, such as new clothing items, were readily available through the underground economy. Maurice illustrated this when he showed off his thermals: "I bought my new thermals—top and bottom—[for] six soups!" Some ran specialized stores that sold only tobacco products. They offered individual "tailor-made" cigarettes taken from full packs as well as the bagged pipe tobacco that most relied on to hand roll their own smokes. Additionally, they stocked up on rolling papers, which were sometimes hard to come by. As one man insisted, "Rolling papers are like *gold!*" Cigarette stores were especially profitable earlier in the week, when addicted men grew desperate if their tobacco supplies went dry before commissary day.

Another potential benefit of "inmate stores" over the commissary was that they sometimes operated on systems of credit. This was vital for those low on funds. However, it was common for prisoners reliant on black-market purchases to rack up debts. Many owed back payments of ramen to various store operators. Those who paid their debts reliably and promptly might be granted higher credit limits. Some even refinanced debt with goods acquired on credit from competing shops. One man, Jon, described how this worked: "[When a prisoner] owes somebody store, he'll go and get it from somebody *else's* store. Then he got good *credit* at that [first] store. So, then he get more from that store. It's a cycle—that bill keep going up and up!"

Paying one's prison debts was crucial, lest one risk reprisal. "We *men*—our word is our bond," Jon told me. "That's the *one* thing we gotta hold on to in here. But some people, they word *ain't* bond.

Come to find out, they ain't *shit*." Another man revealed the potential severity of reneging on debts: "I've seen fights over ramen. Who the fuck gonna fight about ramen noodles? That's fifteen *cents* on the outs!" Another attested that, "People get killed over soup, y'know 'mean?" Despite occasional aggressions on the prison yard, the ramen economy tended to operate with limited friction day-to-day. Sociologist and criminologist John Irwin attests that in the nation's many massive carceral facilities, "there is still considerable intergroup hostility, but overall, there is a general détente among hostile groups."[25] SSP was no exception to this.

Finally, not just anyone could operate one of these "inmate stores." To do so required being endorsed by the "head" of their respective racial clique (discussed in Chapter 4). In exchange for authorization, store runners were expected to pay "tax" on all sales to this racialized hierarchy. Amounts varied but could be the equivalent of fifteen percent of earnings. Failing to pay or operating without approval was to risk violent sanction. Even with taxation, however, many shopkeepers earned more than they might from prison jobs. Some even actively sought to avoid work placements—or aimed to get fired upon assignment—so they could focus on operating stores twenty-four hours a day, seven days a week. For instance, Larry, who had been fired from the fleet auto garage during my fieldwork, operated a store out of his bunk. As his release date drew nearer, I spotted him on the yard one day and asked about his plans for the final months of his sentence. "I'll just try to keep out of the food factory," he replied. "I run my own store here, so I can make more if I stay around here."

Black-market services and shadow labor

Most men earned too little from penal labor to maintain steady flows of soups from the commissary. Furthermore, while the price of noodles had increased over the last decade, prisoner wages had not kept pace with ramen inflation. "They're *sixty* cents in here," one man exclaimed. "They were twenty, thirty cents ten years ago. And we're still getting the same pay. So, every time I look at the price sheet I have, it goes up a penny here, three cents there, where it's been accumulating throughout these years and *no* pay has been going up."

To account for inflation and supplement wages, many turned to what sociologists David Snow and Leon Anderson label "shadow work," or "compensatory subsistence strategies that are fashioned or pursued in the shadow of more conventional work . . . because participation in those markets fails to provide a living wage."[26] At SSP, engaging in shadow work was referred to as having a "hustle." Many attested that, "you gotta have a hustle to survive." Unless one could boast of financial support from outside networks, illicit trade was often vital to acquiring necessary goods. For those who had maintained informal hustles before prison, this was second nature. According to the sagacious Alberto, "I learned both ways [to work]—legal and illegal. The illegal is *survival*. Put it this way: if a nuclear bomb dropped today, the people who know survival are the ones who will make it." One food factory worker outlined several prison hustles:

> Some people clean houses . . . . If you know how to draw, you draw. If all you know how to do is sell drugs, then you sell drugs. That simple. Me, when I don't have enough money? I don't go clean houses or none of that. Sometimes I'll make a phone call for somebody [who lost phone privileges] or whatever. That's some money right there, but I don't do that that much. But people gamble and all that stuff. I mean, there's all *kinds* of things you could do.

One readily apparent hustle was stealing food to exchange in the black-market. This form of "smuggling" or "boosting" was a common feature of food service jobs. Some even regarded it as a standard perk of these positions. One man said, "I don't make enough to *buy* food from this job." In a sarcastic tone, Dean from the food factory justified food thefts as retribution for poor conditions. "They pay us twenty cents an hour, don't feed us enough at meals, and jack up the prices of everything in commissary. *Big* surprise that people are stealing fresh vegetables," he said. A man called Santos working in the meat prep station of the food factory was particularly proud of his past pilfering accomplishments. "I know what it takes to be a booster," he proclaimed. When asked to clarify, he said, "I can get away with certain things that people always [ask], 'How'd you do that?' 'I don't know.' . . . I surprise myself sometimes."

"Can you give me an example?" I asked. "Yeah," he said, "I can give an example. When we were doing turkey, I took twenty-five pounds back to the yard," he boasted. "But they pat you down," I said in disbelief. "Yeah, they do pat us down," Santos confirmed. "You always have to be on your Ps and Qs. You have to learn how to do it. And I was successful. I was one of the lucky ones that got away [that day]. Some people got caught."

"When they [staffers] catch you doing that, what do they do?"

"When you get caught doing that, it's a major [offense]. You get a ticket, you get sent to the yard, you're fired here from the food factory, depending on what it is. And then you get restitution—you got to pay back whatever you took."

For men like Santos, boosting food provided a thrill as well as an economic boon. Despite the risk, stealing items like the desirable turkey meat was a reliable way to make money on the yard. "So, when you get things like [that turkey] back to the yard, how much can you trade it for?" I asked. "It all depends," Santos mused. "On that, I made thirty-five bucks on what I took."

Aside from food smuggling, prisoners sold various services. Some cleaned others' bunks for one soup per week. Some washed others' laundry for one to two soups, depending on the amount of clothes and linens. Others gambled. Some relied on winnings from games of chance for their day-to-day sustenance. According to one such man, Rogers, "One way or another, everything in prison is about money. People will wash your clothes, hustle—anything to make money. I got it figured out. If I only spend twenty dollars a week, I'll have twenty-three hundred saved when I get out." Noting the size of this sum, I inquired, "Do you make enough working here to spend twenty a week?"

"No way," he quickly replied. Instead, to generate these savings, he shared that, "I play [the card game] pinochle every week. Make about twenty-five bucks."

Others hustled in small trades, such as operating as handymen, repairing others' possessions for a small fee. If a pair of eyeglasses broke, visiting the optometrist could entail long waits and potentially missing work; however, one with the proper skill and access to helpful materials (often acquired through smuggling) could be commissioned to make the repair. When Delroy, an older man working in the food factory, appeared with a broken pair of glasses one morning, I asked how he planned to get them fixed. He informed me, "If I went through and waited for the, uh, optometrist, they'd tell me I can't come in for work [until it's fixed]. I got a friend—they got some special strong tape. He's gonna fix 'em up for me." The "special tape," I would later learn, was smuggled from one of the industrial worksites. "What do you pay for something like that?" I asked. "Well," he began, leaning back as he recalled his experiences, "the *first* time they broke, another guy fixed it for me, and I gave him a— uh, well—a dollar." I asked if "dollar" actually meant "soup," to which he quickly nodded and flashed an amused grin. "That's right!"

Individuals with steadier flows of income could even employ others to work as their "private security" around the yard. It was not uncommon to see a call center salesman, for instance, closely accompanied by one or two other men while traversing the prison yard at the end of the workday. "These guys have more money, so they have more power on the yard," said one staffer. Gesturing toward one top seller who was closely flanked on either side, he added, "They *hire* people."

Another common hustle was producing artistic "hobbycraft." This was the practice of selling drawings, small sculptures, or other artworks. Alec, a new addition to the sign shop crew at the time of my fieldwork, was a renowned artist around the institution. He took commissions for portraits, holiday cards, and tattoo designs from those willing and able to pay. Showing me an intricate webbed design that he had sketched for a tattoo, he shared that he received the equivalent of fifteen dollars in soups for the image. This was lower than his normal fee "because the guy is a friend." Typically, Alec would expect twenty or thirty dollars for tattoo designs like this.

While artists like Alec profited from creating these designs, others did the actual tattooing. Many were proud to show off their illicit ink. Twisting his arm to reveal a fading image of a heavyset, bikini-clad woman tattooed on the back of his forearm, a worker called BB proudly exclaimed, "This is my fat lady!" Joining in, his coworker, Franklin, rolled up his sleeve to reveal a detailed brick wall on his shoulder. "Here's my prison wall, see?" Pointing to a list of names, he noted, "I got my kids here, down my arm. The bad thing is when you start out with children and you end up with grandchildren! [When] you start running out of canvas, it's time to go home," he added. "Amen," BB called back. Franklin went on, gesturing to tattooed calendar pages floating beneath the brick wall. "And here's my dates . . . People on the outside will say your calendar is your badge of honor. No, it's not. It's a reminder of how long you took yourself away from what *matters* to you." Nodding solemnly, BB added: "That's right. People on the outside get tattoos for no reason. In here, *every* inmate tattoo means something. *None* of them are without meaning."

The Risks of Informal Market Participation

Mirroring policies of the Federal Bureau of Prisons,[27] formal protocols at SSP prohibited unauthorized prisoner sales and exchanges. Nevertheless, participants reported a growing reliance on illicit trade and labor, sometimes culminating in debt, fear of physical violence, or risk of formal punishments via work demotion, expulsion, disciplinary tickets, and more. Stagnant wages contributed to dependence on underground trade as workers who had been sorted into the bottom reaches of the penal labor hierarchy were less able to afford formal market outlets.

Often, rules against illicit trade were only selectively enforced; simple exchanges were frequently overlooked as inevitable facets of prison life. One staffer shared, "I'm okay with letting little shit slide. I see it, *but—*," he shrugged, as if to indicate *what can you do*. Nevertheless, when overseers decided that a prisoner's participation in the black-market was excessive or problematic in some way, they could be quick to act. Men who operated "inmate stores," for example, were at constant risk of being "rolled up" if their entrepreneurship came to be seen as disruptive to standard operations. To be rolled up was to have correctional officers arrive at your bunk unannounced in the middle of the night, wake you up, order you to collect your belongings and roll them up into your bedroll, and lead you to a bus to an unknown destination. Often, rolled-up individuals were transported to different units within the same prison; sometimes, however, they were driven to new facilities somewhere across the state.

One day in the sign shop, for example, a worker called Luisito failed to show. He rarely if ever missed a shift, but I learned from shop chatter that he had been rolled up the night before. It turned out that Luisito had been operating a cigarette store out of his bunk on the side. No one had yet heard to where he had been moved. Mr. Edwards shared that he had heard rumors about the incident. "Some of these guys run what you might call black-market stores, which is illegal. I've been told that Luisito buys cigarettes and sells them individually. That's illegal." Taking a long drag of his own cigarette, Edwards shared that it was uncommon for higher-paid workers like his crew to run such stores; however, "for a lot of these guys, that sort of business . . . is commonplace. It's about *survival.*" Another civilian staffer in the shop, Dempsey, agreed that "It's *rare* for guys from in here to get rolled up. *Something* happened."

Although jarring for an outsider, the experience of suddenly losing a friend to institutional operations had become normalized for these men. A few days after Luisito was disappeared, another shop worker, Willie, moved into his workstation. Labor continued as usual, without further reference to the former colleague.

Roll-ups were even more common in the middle and bottom tiers of the employment system. Those unable to secure top-tier work typically remained financially needier and were forced to rely more heavily on black-market channels. For them, the informal economy truly was central to survival. As a result, they faced increased risk of sanctions from COs or administrators unhappy with their underground dealings. "The cops [COs]—they don't like if you're selling stuff," one man shared, adding, "and [if] they *see* you selling stuff, you're going to get in trouble for it. You know what I mean? But sometimes if you're hungry, you just got to do what you got to do." The soft-spoken Josh relayed that he and other food factory workers stole food because they lacked other options. "But it's risky," he said, "it's a risk-versus-reward type thing." For many, smuggling, hustling, and heavy reliance on underground purchases often seemed the only viable alternatives to hunger and need. "People that are broke, [or] that can't work, or don't," said Josh, "they're pretty much S.O.L."

Aside from rare cases like Luisito's, the highest-paid prisoners at SSP were largely buffered from much of this risk. They could purchase more commissary items and avoid unappetizing state meals, buy TVs and other entertainment items to help pass the time of long sentences, upgrade to better quality boots or replenish other worn-down clothing, visit the doctor as needed, call family on a regular basis, and even send money home in some cases. Those who were able to save for reentry were able to leave prison in much more stable positions than those forced to exit with nothing. Further, not being driven to the black-market helped these men avoid the risks of being sent to higher security yards, having time added to their sentences, or similar punishments.

High-status prisoners who nevertheless opted to participate in the underground economy were privileged in this sphere as well, for they were better able to stockpile ramen noodles to pay others to complete menial services on their behalf and acquire fresh produce or other healthier (yet expensive) foods. All the while, they avoided amassing debts to the operators of "inmate stores." In these ways, the sorting of incarcerated workers not only affected day-to-day experiences of punishment, but differentially exposed the disadvantaged to greater risks. The next chapter examines another way that labor classification shaped time behind bars: by enabling some to pursue dignity and self-worth through the carceral employment system while others remained preoccupied with enduring mounting insecurities.

6

The Dignity of Working Prisoners

Overcoming the Pains of Penal Labor

> Every prisoner knows . . . the distance which separates him from his superiors; but neither the branding irons nor chains will make him forget that he is a man. He must, therefore, be treated with humanity.
>
> —Fyodor Dostoevsky (1914)

Each new hire in the call center was required to undergo a day of training before being allowed to don their telephone headset. Jake, the so-called "inmate manager" of the sales team, was tasked with overseeing these sessions. Typically, training occurred in a small, windowless classroom around the corner from the sales floor. As trainees jotted notes or nervously shuffled through a stack of papers outlining workplace rules and instructions, Jake would calmly read from his own printed packet. Often, he punctuated the formal language of the training literature with informal insights in a more "down-to-earth" tone for which he was known and respected. For instance, during one training, he underscored the rigid guidelines for telephone use and office etiquette by adding: "The new phones . . . they won't pick up any background noise. But *still*," he cautioned, "no cursing or dirty jokes in the office." Gesturing to the areas beyond the call center, he continued, "Out here is one thing, but in *there* [at work], act like we're in the real world. Cause we *are*, far as I'm concerned. It's a business, okay." The trainees nodded solemnly and Jake, satisfied with this response, moved on.

In addition to teaching incoming salesmen the standard workplace rules and onboarding them to day-to-day procedures, these training sessions offered many new hires their first encounter with one of the key distinctions between top-tier sites and most other workplaces at Sunbelt State Penitentiary (SSP). Namely, unlike other positions they might have held, this should not be seen as a "prison job," but as a "real job" or, indeed, a "business." This was not merely a euphemism for a less stressful workplace. Rather, it highlighted concrete differences in how labor was overseen and carried out—differences that in turn helped workers like Jake to find new meaning in and through their time behind bars. If sites like the call center could be reframed as places of business rather than purely punishment, then laborers might recast themselves as employees rather than prisoners. This distinguished them from the lower rungs of the penal labor hierarchy, where workers were often unable to cultivate positive work-based identities, being preoccupied with overcoming the added indignities of their own stations.

* * *

As previous chapters have outlined, prison work conditions shape how incarcerated individuals experience life behind bars. The capabilities and resources they possess interact with their racial or ethnic identities to impact job mobility and thereby economic wellbeing, which further stratifies groups already plagued by countless hardships associated with imprisonment. Building on this, the present chapter examines how different workplaces shape the ways that prisoners understand not only their time but their own selves. At SSP, a sense of pride in one's work was central to conceptions of personal dignity.[1] As sociologist Randy Hodson writes, "life demands dignity and meaningful work is essential for dignity."[2] This is as true for the prisoner as for the free citizen. Yet, while all strive to have their humanity recognized, penal laborers face especially unequal prospects to this end. As a result, in addition to the economic outcomes of unequal job sorting discussed in the last chapter, many suffer significant non-material consequences of labor stratification as well.

The structure of the prison is fraught with hurdles to the acquisition of dignity; nevertheless, participants strategized against these forces in creative ways. In the tradition of the labor process perspective—which emphasizes how worksite organization and the relations of individuals within it intersect to shape forms of domination, resistance, and coordination in the workplace—this chapter will explore strategies that workers employed as they sought to navigate and endure carceral labor settings.

Different work environments enabled distinct forms of worker action. First, coping strategies took the shape of ritualized distractions from work routines through which the men of SSP aimed to break up the "long day's grind"[3] and *tolerate* various indignities. Next, friction strategies entailed assertions of agency that sometimes clashed with official rules or procedures. At times, these included acts of outright resistance, although often they were subtler—though no less agentic—acts of rule breaking or foot-dragging[4] to *defy* indignity. Lastly, through professionalization strategies, higher-status individuals sought distinction from others by emulating professional status and reframing workplaces as something other than standard prison jobs (like Jake did in his call center training sessions) to reclaim or *reinject* dignity into daily lives and labors.

The Pursuit of Dignity at (and through) Work

In a general sense, we may define dignity as a basic sense of selfhood and belonging in the social world.[5] Within punishment settings specifically, conceptions of dignity are commonly tied to individuals' ability to maintain a sense of humanity and the right to grow as an individual—and to have claims to this effect recognized by state actors.[6] Yet, this approach to human dignity often conflicts with the agendas of penal bureaucracies, which increasingly prioritize budgetary concerns and incapacitation over identity (re)formation.[7] To be sure, depriving the incarcerated of the basics of personhood has long been a central feature of American punishment. As prison scholar Gresham Sykes noted in 1958, upon entering such institutions, "the individual's picture of himself as a person of value . . . begins to waver and grow dim."[8]

Lacking reasonable access to resources and outlets for personal expression, incarcerated people may turn instead to "economies of dignity," or local meaning systems through which individuals may determine what characteristics are privileged, assert their own value along these lines, and preserve positive self-images.[9] Labor skills and experiences can carry considerable weight. The nature of one's work identity (often intimately tied to one's "outside life") is often central to perceptions of worth behind bars.[10] In this light, work provides a fruitful arena in which the imprisoned may actively engage in the pursuit of dignity.

The labor process perspective is valuable for examining expressions of worker agency, including dignity pursuits. Building on the insights of Marxian theorist Antonio Gramsci,[11] labor scholar Michael Burawoy popularized this perspective through examining the ways in which workers under advanced capitalism seek to fulfill material and psychological desires through shared strategies or practices on the factory floor.[12] Through such action, workers seek to alter, maneuver, or otherwise endure the labor process by drawing "from a repertoire of skills and accumulated knowledge" to achieve an array of outcomes.[13] Often, the rewards that workers seek map on to markers of dignity. For instance, workplace action may help to raise status, improve earnings, fight boredom or feelings of futility, assert shared demands, challenge inequities, demonstrate or reproduce shared values and expectations, or establish and reify group boundaries. It is through such strategies that laborers the world over endure the rigors of work. According to sociologist Ofer Sharone, worker action of this sort "may arise in virtually any area of social life where social structures generate uncertainty over obtaining a desired outcome and where agents have some discretion to engage in strategic actions in an attempt to achieve this outcome."[14]

For the nation's many working prisoners, addressing issues of restricted autonomy, poor treatment, marginal remuneration, and other prison work-related concerns—which I refer to as the pains of penal labor—is often a priority. Like their counterparts on the outside, captive laborers at SSP engaged in what Burawoy refers to as the "ubiquitous resistance of everyday life"[15] through strategic action on the prison shop floor in response to strain and uncertainty. Although their daily lives were strictly regimented, these agentic prisoners frequently exercised small degrees of autonomy or "secondary adjustments"[16] against these features of the prison labor system.

Still, the structure of carceral labor relationships establishes clear limits on expressions of agency. At the end of the day, overseers set underlying workplace rules and norms. In this way, collective practices designed to alleviate workplace challenges may indirectly entail a degree of acquiescence to broader conditions of punishment and control.[17]

The Pains of Penal Labor at Sunbelt State Penitentiary

All prisoners face the pains of imprisonment: the numerous deprivations of liberty, property, and personhood that define life behind bars.[18] The conditions of many penal labor assignments may exacerbate these challenges, introducing new hardships to the carceral experience. Nationwide, working prisoners are denied guarantees and protections that free world workers enjoy. Certain deprivations are legally allowable because these workers are not formally categorized as employees.[19] For example, prisons need not observe many state and federal worksite standards like the Fair Standards Labor Act.[20] Carceral laborers may also be denied wages or receive compensation far below wage minimums. If injured on the job or ill, they lack guaranteed time off or workers' compensation. As one worker protested, "We get no workman's comp. If we get hurt on the job, we have to go to medical in the yard—and we *still* get charged the *four*-dollar medical fee just for the visit. That's several days' pay right there! Plus, to go to medical, you have to miss work and you don't get paid for that. So that's at least a week's wages right there just for getting injured at your own damn job."

Another challenge was the lack of reliable grievance systems. As Kitty Calavita and Valerie Jenness reveal, these systems are often convoluted, slow, and outmoded, leading many to feel powerless and frustrated when attempting to make their voices heard.[21] At SSP, low-tier workers reported particularly little certainty along these lines. Responding to the suggestion that he approach his food factory managers with concerns about work conditions, one man scoffed: "One of *them*? No way! . . . They don't care about grievances unless it comes from the warden." When asked if anyone ever successfully reached the warden with concerns, he shrugged: "Not that I've ever seen." Writing a letter to the warden's office was a slow process, reliant on the internal mail system. What's more, appealing to higher-ranking officials entailed risk because it required prisoners to link their names to criticisms in writing. Instead of dependable outlets to champion concerns, many instead encountered overt disrespect and dehumanization from overseers. When failing to recall one worker's name, for instance, a food factory manager remarked with a laugh: "There's only one of me, but I don't know how many of *you* I've seen in the past twenty-four hours!"

Working prisoners also described indignities in their daily commutes. All who worked beyond the immediate prison yard had to pass through the "strip shack" before and after each workday. This captured workers from each tier of the employment system, from the food factory to the sign shop. In the strip shack, everyone, regardless of job status, was stripped naked in groups to be inspected for hidden contraband. Lemmy, from the sign shop, described it: "They strip you butt-ass naked, seven guys at a time. 'Spread your cheeks, lift your sack'—that sort of thing. That's for anybody that leaves the yard. Lotta guys don't like leaving the yard and dealing with that. Once you master that hurdle though, you can start looking for better jobs outside the yard. But it's a pain in the ass." After a pause, he added, "Sometimes literally." Apart from the call center, most jobs located on the yard (and thus free from the strip shack) were lower paying and undesirable. This included positions like trash collector, "rake pusher," or "cigarette butt collector." Seeking a decent job, then, often required submitting to the daily mortification of the strip search.

These and other factors culminated in a general sense of indignity for incarcerated workers. Many dreaded work. According to one man, "I feel better as soon as I get home. But when I'm here I don't *feel* well." With a distressed look on his face, he added, "As soon as the bus pulls up to take me here—*ugh*. It wears me down." Many staffers regarded work as merely a facet of punishment, outright rejecting workers' labor-based assertions of legitimacy. Work, according to one CO, was important solely for population management: "Otherwise, they sit in the yard all day, getting in trouble."[22] The imprisoned openly resented such treatment, insisting that, "There's no *appreciation* for what we do in here." Another said, "They're just trying to punish us. They show authority instead of showing gratitude for us working here."

Coping Strategies

When subjected to harsh expressions of authority from overseers, or in the face of long hours and boredom, captive laborers drew on coping strategies to better tolerate undignified work and break up periods of monotony.[23] In the prison setting, many workplace challenges are magnified, as are the potential stakes of worker action. Control and surveillance are heightened behind bars, where institutional architecture has been honed to increasingly monitor and restrict.[24] What's more, punishments for perceived insubordination are often severe. The slightest perceived misstep could result not only in termination but loss of privileges, extended sentencing, or transfer to a higher custody unit. Knowing the risks and working around surveillance and oversight structures, penal laborers strategically engaged in collective attempts to endure the pains of penal labor.

Coping strategies were readily apparent in the food factory, where workers were subject to intense oversight as they performed deskilled, monotonous tasks. The tactics they employed were often ostensibly simple acts that nevertheless had notable effects on morale. These took forms like group impersonations of the gruff shouts of the CO when he bellowed commands like "*Lunch!*" or "*Count time!*" through the window of his central security post. The men would mimic his gravelly voice, yelling out "*Count tiiiiiime!*" or grunting harshly in no particular direction, gradually increasing in volume in a sort of vocal "hot potato" game.

Other call-and-response activities arose when men grew restless. Slick, a sharp-eyed white prisoner in his early thirties, was notorious for initiating such moments. During a lull in bologna rolling one day, he began hopping up and down briskly. Suddenly, he yelled out in a high pitch, "Can I get a whoop, whoop!" A few scattered "whoops" came in response from different stations throughout the food factory. Unsatisfied, he continued, "I said: Whoop! *Whoop!*" The calls came back with mounting volume until CO Byrne emerged from his security office to quell the noise. When the authority figure appeared, the instigator swiftly spun on his heels with a guilty grin on his face. Slick was also known to spontaneously blurt out freestyle rap verses to lighten the mood. His compatriots would frequently join in. One rhyme that scored an especially positive reaction from the crowd was: "Ain't no studio / This here's a prison cell / Ask who I'm rollin' with / But I won't *never* tell!"

The outcome of shouting and noisy rap battles was collective amusement at the CO's frustration when he inevitably yelled "Be *quiet*," eliciting snickering from the crew. CO Byrne maintained awareness of these and other playful coping techniques. "Whenever I walk around a corner, they fuck around," he told me. "I know that." As long as his wards did not get too "rowdy," however, he often chose not to hand out formal sanctions. Still, he sought to make sure that they knew he was alert. "Sometimes I stop and watch and they freak out. 'Shit! Did he see me? Did he *see me*?' It's a big game we play here." It was common to see him halt abruptly and stare down a group of workers. "They're staring right back at me," he quietly muttered to me in one instance before speeding away down the hall once again, keys clattering.

Other staffers actively facilitated certain minor distractions toward more productive ends. In the meat prep station, where men spent their days standing in place, rolling slices of bologna or ham into cellophane-wrapped bundles, many grumbled about the monotony of the work. To keep them on task, managers in this station sometimes encouraged "meat rolling races." One of the few white men in this station, Slick was also recognized as its informal "inmate manager," in part because of his motivational skills. He was usually open to a race. One afternoon, the meat prep station overseer, Barba, stood at the end of the long steel table and attempted to goad Slick into a contest. Another worker, the heavyset Latino man called Pun, was also known to be a particularly fast roller when he wanted to be. "Uh-oh," Barba said to Slick, gesturing toward Pun, "Your competition is picking up speed." Slick, continuing to roll, shot a sideways glance toward Pun. "He's feeling the pressure," another man chimed in. "Okay," Slick conceded, "Let's go, *son!*" With a half grin, Pun accepted: "Let's do this shit."

Almost in sync, each man grabbed two pieces of bologna from the towers of sliced meat positioned between them, slapped them down, spun them up in a section of plastic wrap, and began anew. They slammed finished rolls into a nearby bin with force, as if to signal with each thud: *Done! Done again!* To speed his wrapping, Slick clutched a plastic spork that he used to quickly rip off each plastic sheet. When his gloves began to slip from the spread of meat grease, he swiftly tore off a small bit of cardboard from the plastic wrap box, put it in the loose band around his wrist, and rolled it up like a t-shirt sleeve around a pack of cigarettes. The competitors shot furtive glances at each other's technique. The other rollers and I joined in as well, trying to keep pace with Slick and Pun, although most fell short. The race continued for nearly ten minutes as Barba looked on. The unexpected end-of-game buzzer came as CO Byrne shouted, "*Count time!*" The two piles of rolled meats were too close to declare a clear winner. The men quickly nodded a silent commendation of *good game* to one another and shuffled toward the CO station to be accounted for.

The racial politics of the prison barred these men—one white, one Latino—from engaging in many activities together, such as sharing food or shaking hands (discussed in Chapter 4). Yet, the restrictive norms that limited interactions across racial lines, it would seem, did not prohibit Slick and Pun from participating in strategic play together. Like the monotony and indignity to which they offered brief reprieve, coping strategies like this spanned racial and ethnic boundaries. Although clearly orchestrated by management, the meat race functioned to override boundaries at least temporarily between racial cliques, highlighting their shared status as captive laborers.

* * *

Strategies to tolerate the pains of penal labor were not exclusive to the food factory. In the call center, prisoners worked in a very different environment, yet nevertheless relied on collective practices to cope with challenges. Much like the meat races described above, workers here sometimes turned their work duties into a form of competition to liven up the often boring or demoralizing task of making repeated, unsolicited sales calls to peddle advertising packages. The steady surveillance of civilian staff members did not ease the difficulty of these labors.

Each salesman remained acutely aware of their own and others' current sales totals. Successful sales were publicly tallied. Two dry erase boards in opposite corners of the long room tracked weekly progress. On the windows of the plexiglass-walled circular "bubble" from which the on-site staffer maintained sight of the entire workforce were scrawled the current totals of each month's top seller. A high total jotted alongside one's name was regarded as a measure of effort and skill. Whenever a new sale was made, the towering, tattooed Jake would update the totals in dry erase marker, often loudly announcing the update and offering words of encouragement to the room.

As "inmate manager," Jake was also known to issue challenges or initiate sales contests to bolster morale and spur productivity. Noticing that his coworker Taxi had been having a slow sales day one afternoon, Jake challenged him to a race. "Yo, Taxi," he called across the floor, "You and me—sell-off!" Half-turning in his chair, Taxi asked, "What? Now?"

"Yup. I'm going for the title of 'best salesman ever—between me and you!'" As Taxi chuckled, Jake continued, "Hey, how 'bout first one to make a sale, the other one does a *'pretty princess'*?" This wager was common at SSP. To "do a pretty princess" meant to stand on one leg, put a pointed finger atop one's head, and spin around like a ballet dancer while shouting "I'm a pretty princess! I'm a pretty princess!" A similar performance with which prisoners sometimes challenged one another was to "do a dead dog." This entailed dropping onto one's back, raising hands and feet to resemble paws, and rolling back and forth while howling like a dog. Both involved the voluntary mortification of the loser of the bet, challenging prisoner norms of masculinity.[25]

Sealing the bet with a nod, the men turned back to their computer terminals and got to work. They each made repeated calls for some time. After nearly two tiring hours of persistence in the face of hang ups and other failed calls, Taxi's arms finally shot into the air, victorious. Knowing immediately that he had lost, Jake leaned dramatically back in his seat and exhaled. "*Ahhh*, no!" With a shake of his head, he stood up and held his arms aloft to signal that he was preparing to make an announcement: "Hey, everyone. I'm a pretty princess." As the crew looked on, he spun around on one foot, raised his voice, and sang out: "I'm a pretty *princess!* Taxi is the best salesman *ever!*" Men at nearby cubicles chuckled. Grinning, Jake took his seat and pointed to his opponent, saying, "Nice job, Taxi. You earned it!"

Another way that incarcerated call center workers coped with their work was through a form of cathartic joking. Sales work could be demoralizing, especially when one hit a "slow streak" or encountered hostility on the other end of the line. After completing a call with a particularly challenging individual or being hung up on, the men would often pretend that the call was ongoing, spouting quiet insults into the dead phone line. When one man experienced an abrupt disconnection, he proceeded to close an imaginary sale, modifying the wording of the sales script: "So, just to confirm, sir, you wear girdles and dresses and high-heeled shoes? *Okay*, sir." Another salesman maintained decorum while struggling through a call with an apparently rude individual, but shifted dramatically once they had hung up. "Okay, ma'am," he said spitefully to the dead line, "well *thank* you for your time and enjoy the rest of your day. Okay. Go *shit* yourself, bitch."

The heart of this practice was meeting disappointments head on with humor. The men maintained professional-sounding tones even through the harshest of insults so that staff members would be less likely to note the quip, but nearby coworkers might overhear and collude in the frustration and release. Fulfilling these small acts of revenge operated as an inside joke amongst prisoners. Smoking cigarettes during breaks elicited open venting about these irritations. At such times, they coped with the challenges of the job by sharing horror stories and laughing over insults as a means to persist in the face of long hours, heavy surveillance, and other stresses of sales work amplified by the prison context.

Friction Strategies

Many individuals' social identity is tied to work status.[26] Maintaining such identities while incarcerated is especially difficult as one's standing as a "worker" is challenged or revoked. Beyond merely tolerating workplace and prison challenges through coping strategies, some laborers actively pushed back against indignities. Yet not all rule violations amount to full blown resistance. Many subtler expressions of opposition abound. To capture both explicit and subtle tactics of defiance, I frame such collective action as friction strategies. Drawing on the punishment and society scholarship of Ashley Rubin, "friction" here refers to naturally reactive responses to controlled environments through which the incarcerated express social and physical needs or desires, although not necessarily with the intent to openly challenge the prison regime writ large.[27] Some of these tactics share features with coping strategies in that they contributed to the melioration of conditions of confinement and forced labor. However, friction strategies go beyond this to include opposition to dehumanizing effects of specific workplace regulations or expressions of authority behind bars.

According to Randy Hodson, "Resistance occurs across a wide range of workplaces, but it can be expected to be most common in workplaces where anomic conditions prevail," as well as "in situations characterized by overwork and exploitation."[28] Amongst the diverse worksites of the prison employment system, the food factory most exhibited these characteristics. Workers here sometimes responded with collective violation of institutional regulations, rendering transgressions into assertions of autonomy amidst arbitrary authority. Snacking was often principal in friction between laborers and overseers. In the contemporary prison, the incarcerated commonly express autonomy and power through food activities and practices, or "foodways."[29] Secreting, hoarding, or preparing food against institutional regulations are central to these struggles.[30] In the food factory, workers were forbidden from partaking in the foods they prepared, a policy which many regarded as a denial of a basic "perk" of the job. Risking expulsion or demotion, many nonetheless tucked away bundles of bread, bologna, cookies, and other snacks while on the job, frequently in close proximity to overseers. Men from different stations made "hand-offs" of slices of lunch meat in exchange for baggies of peanut butter. Coconspirators monitored the comings and goings of staff to sneak bites or squirrel away items for later. A smiling worker with cheeks full of food was a common sight. Often, these smiles were aimed directly at staff, highlighting the current of defiance underlying these practices.

Given the shortage of nutritious or satisfying food options, fruits and vegetables were natural targets of snackers and thieves. The events of what came to be known as the "blueberry incident" revealed how readily prisoners sought out these items and how determined penal authority was to protect these less common, more expensive foods. While the warehouse crew stacked boxes of dry goods onto towering metal shelves, a man from the freezer section approached to spread the word that the site manager, Dolores, was "already asking who ate the blueberries." An order of frozen blueberries had arrived for use in cakes for a special occasion of some sort and someone promptly dipped into the box and devoured several fistfuls. Dolores rushed up and down the halls, asking nearby prisoners if they had any information. One man bluntly replied, "I got twelve years in the system and I never *once* saw a blueberry." With a confused expression, the baker named Baxter asked, "What the fuck is a blue *berry*?" It was not clear if he was serious.

Leaning on a box of dried beans, an imprisoned warehouseman named Travis shouted down the hallway to Dolores: "Just look for whoever has blue hands! Hahaha, blue fucking *teeth!* That shit stains." Dolores furrowed her brow and disappeared into the meat prep station to conduct further inquiries. Noticing a few berries scattered down the hallway, Travis called out, "Hey! Just follow the trail!" Several tiny blue treats could be spotted along the walkway leading from the freezer section where they had been held. As we followed the trail down the hallway with our eyes, the jocular Dean appeared with a push broom, sweeping with urgency. As he passed, he flashed a quick smile to reveal what appeared to be a row of blue-stained teeth. Closing his lips in a tight grin, he continued down the hall, taking a sharp turn into the sandwich shop away from Dolores. He pushed the berries off with his broom as he went. Some rolled wildly, creating a new trail. The identity of the blueberry bandit was never conclusively ascertained.

The staffers overseeing the food factory occasionally expressed frustrations regarding workers' illicit eating habits. Still, the formal rules prohibiting snacking on the job were not consistently enforced. When one staff member spotted a prisoner stuffing a small stack of cookies into his pockets, she uttered with a shrug, "That's okay, it isn't *my* station you're stealing from." As other work scholars have pointed out, "Sometimes managers *expect* workers to ignore official rules, despite public pronouncements to the contrary."[31] Nevertheless, such violations reveal dissatisfactions on the part of workers. Many prisoners were aware of this selective enforcement. According to one man, "They gotta expect we're gonna *eat*. I don't make enough to *buy* food from this job."

Overseers often facilitated friction to preclude acts of outright rebellion. If one did decide to reprimand someone for snacking, the offending party and their compatriots often responded with new obstructions. This included soldiering or goldbricking—that is, collective foot-dragging to slow down production. In some instances, they outright sabotaged the labor process. When a newly hired manager started tenaciously checking prisoners for extra food before lunch one morning, the entire workforce seemed to grow agitated. Gloves and other tools and materials suddenly began to go missing that afternoon, slowing down work considerably. According to a long-time white shirt, these setbacks could have been avoided by allowing smaller insubordinations to persist. "These guys—they're used to certain things . . . . When you take that *away*, they're gonna kick your ass. They're *pissed* and they're gonna rob us blind. They're going to sabotage us. Throw things away." To avoid this, he shared that he simply "looked the other way."

* * *

Similar friction strategies were observed at the auto garage. Although this was formally a skilled position, as a mid-tier worksite at SSP it still shared certain features with low-tier sites like the food factory. These included pay below that of top jobs as well as constant scrutiny from a permanently on-site correctional officer. Incarcerated mechanics often attempted to secure contraband food from the nearby food factory. The officer stationed in the garage, CO Peña, remained vigilant to snacking attempts. Yet, like his counterparts in the food factory, he was often selective in enforcement, allowing auto workers to consume cookies, so long as they had been provided directly from a staff member. Unsatisfied workers, however, sometimes attempted to sneak over to the food factory to score larger supplies of different snacks from food factory friends.

One day during a smoke break, a man in orange shouted over from a gated area outside the food factory: "Hey, Larry, here it is!" With a wave, he hurled a plastic trash bag over a tall razor-wired fence. It landed with a thud in the back of a nearby dump truck. Larry, who worked as a car washer at the fleet garage, waved back but left the prize secured in the rear of the truck until he could safely retrieve it when the correctional officer was away. After an hour, CO Peña finally left to perform his regular checks of the surrounding grounds. Larry hurried out to secure his prize, only to find the entire truck gone. "Where the *fuck* is the *dump truck!?*" he cried. A short while later, we heard the familiar rumble of the vehicle returning. Larry and a coworker jogged toward it. The others chuckled at their hustle across the dirt road. The tone changed, however, when CO Peña unexpectedly returned. "Oh shit, it's Peña. He sees 'em! He caught 'em," whispered one worker, turning to avoid eye contact with the officer. Seeing the CO approach, Larry's shoulders slumped. After Peña seized the bag of food from his hands, he shuffled, defeated, back toward the garage.

After several hours had passed, Larry approached the officer to dispute the confiscation of the food. Clearly agitated, Larry blurted out, "So, what, like, are we just *not* allowed to get any food anymore or *what?*" Taking a quick step toward the man, the officer responded firmly: "*Look*, if you're going to ask again about that, don't waste your breath. It has to stop."

"It's not *stealing* food. It's extra! It's stuff that's getting thrown away!"

"It don't matter. You get food from the white shirts, that's okay. Otherwise, no more. That's it. Okay, that's all!" For the time being, the issue was closed. In the coming weeks, however, Larry would once again be caught smuggling food into the garage. This time, he was promptly fired.

As prisoners engaged in friction through illicit snacking, they generated discourses regarding work and prison conditions surrounding these practices. According to their narratives, snacking represented a natural response to the withholding of perks, often bound to more general complaints of despotism and disrespect. "I don't look at it as stealing," one man said, "I look at it as making the pay right." Declarations that "they should pay us more and treat us better" were germane to such behaviors and revealed deeper resentments on the part of working prisoners. "*We're* human beings *too*. We need to be treated like we're supposed to be treated." Or, as another man said, "You can make more money just sitting at home [in your bunk] playing cards . . . . But for those of us who are out here trying to improve our lives—out here *working*—we get treated like *shit*. It ain't right. It's *supposed* to be 'corrections'! They're supposed to be teaching us ways to *improve* ourselves for the outside!" Motivated by these concerns, friction strategies responded to and fostered collective attitudes of defiance against overseers whom prisoners deemed unjust or domineering. Through seemingly simple acts like snacking, they defied restrictive environments.

Work conditions, the dynamics of the labor process, and worker and managerial practices intertwine to shape patterns of resistance, transforming grievances into collective action. In the absence of skill training, equitable pay, interesting or engaging work tasks, and regular breaks, workers in low-status positions faced compounded difficulties. Indeed, most acts of friction that I observed during my time at SSP took place within the less-desirable worksites. They were also often related to food. Although men in top-tier worksites faced numerous challenges behind bars, their work environments differed greatly. For the most part, any desire to overtly resist managerial authority that they possessed appeared overridden by other agendas.

Professionalization Strategies

At the top of the hierarchical employment system at SSP, the sign shop and call center offered higher pay, classification as skilled work, greater autonomy, and more input into the labor process. Workers in these sites still faced many indignities of prison life and labor. Yet, whereas their counterparts in low- or mid-tier prison jobs primarily pursued strategies to tolerate or defy indignity, these men sought to *inject* dignity into and through their work. They aimed to reframe the workplace as a "business" or "company" in which they held stake—in essence seeking to "transform jobs with insufficient meaning into jobs that are more worthy of their personal stature, time and effort."[32] I refer to worker tactics along these lines as professionalization strategies.

In firms or fields across contexts, managers often contribute to the reframing of employees as professionals in their fields. This occurs even in instances when workers cannot officially be categorized as such.[33] At SSP, overseers often promoted images of the "professional" and "dedicated" penal laborer. The imprisoned cannot possess formal employee classification, nor control over the knowledge base of their trades.[34] Nevertheless, the ideal of professional status retains value in the world of prison work, speaking to the perseverance of quests for legitimacy. By identifying as professional, prisoners could hope to secure self-worth in the present and establish trajectories for the future. This was tied to outlooks that valued qualities like work ethic and discipline. The importance of building skills was also stressed, such as when one call center worker attested that his job allowed him to "hone a skill that felons can use for work," so that "when I get out, I've got something set up for me." The fact that high-status workers received higher wages was alleged to reflect the very value of their skills, demonstrating that they could rely on their capabilities to subsist.

Those engaging in professionalization strategies reframed themselves as professionals in their respective fields—as the contemporaries of pro craftsmen in sign shops or pro salesmen in call centers. According to Javi, a call center worker, "It feels like a *real job*. A professional atmosphere . . . . You're representing your *company*." Jake revealed the extent to which professionalization strategies shaped outlooks: "When we're in here—[despite] wearing orange—working in a telemarketing place, *we're* telemarketers in our mind." As such, men in these sites regarded the quality of their products or services as central to the "company's success." They in turn behaved as beneficiaries of efficiency and profit. In addition to the often-muted praise of managers (usually a quick grunt or a mumbled "That's good."), these men sought to affirm self-worth and identity through embodying roles of disciplined, dedicated workers.

Engaging in professionalization strategies offered a temporary reprieve from standard prison experiences. "We know we're locked up, but it feels like a business," said Luther of the sign shop. "You feel like you're at a company, in society. Until you hear that [officer's] radio!

But it's peaceful—not like on the yard, in those [housing] bays." Dedication to labor also played a role in boundary work and distinction processes. By asserting the identity of professional, these men differentiated themselves from other workers and non-workers. Doing so also helped justify the higher pay and other perks that they received. According to Franklin, "We're professional men. *We* appreciate our job. Not like these 'street thugs.'" He would later say, "There are some of us—the more mature men—we *want* to work. We don't want the drama of the yard. It gives you something to do, gives you integrity. That's what we strive for." One man insisted that "Most motherfuckers don't wanna work. They just want to sit on the yard all day. Fucking *bums*." Men holding such views sometimes expressed that others "must *like* prison or think it's a joke."

Professionalization strategies were often encouraged by management and facilitated by the structure of top-tier worksites. In the call center, for instance, regular training sessions helped foster the imagery of the professional. Each month, a civilian salesman named Maguire entered the prison to instruct the men in the techniques and rhetoric of the field. In wingtip shoes and a power tie, he evoked the quintessential image of a professional salesman from film or television. As he spouted sales tips and lingo, prisoners took feverish notes. "'Going for the no,' as a selling strategy," Maguire instructed one day, "is: if I do *everything* I can and do everything right and they don't say '*no*' outright, then I may actually have a sale! Now, the 'law of large numbers' says there's going to be a lot of calls, a lot of sells, a lot of hang-ups—to the point that the phone starts to weigh *three hundred* pounds," he said, playacting as if he was exhausted from holding a great weight in his hand. "But, following the 'fertile market,' you keep making those calls. You keep going!"

Prisoners were energized by these sessions. When I asked the young salesman Marshall his thoughts after training one afternoon, he exclaimed, "It was bad ass! You can tell he's good—he's made a good business out of it." The sales jargon acquired in these meetings—"going for the no," the "law of large numbers," the "fertile market"—would be recited by salesmen when discussing work with one another or coaching new hires in the tricks of the trade. A stack of sales manuals in the office further reinforced this knowledge and the professional images that each sought to craft.

Overseers reinforced the idea of the prison call center as "business" or "company," generating enthusiasm among workers. Dennis, the businessman who had introduced the call center to the prison and oversaw the firm, did just this in a "company meeting" one morning. Standing in the center of the office, he chastised certain unnamed workers for their techniques in pursuing payment from customers: "We need more consistency with how the collectors are going about it. This isn't the wild, wild West. If we got someone who's coming in too aggressive, that person needs to be *gone*. Because that's not consistent with our *company*, with the company that we're trying to build here." His allusion to firing the uncooperative to advance a shared company interest framed workers as integral and trusted team members. One civilian staff member, a young man named Eduardo, shared that this rhetoric was useful for managing the incarcerated salesmen under his supervision. He explained, "If you treat 'em good, they'll work for you. If you don't make 'em feel like they're in prison, they'll work hard. They come to work to be treated different."

Many top-tier workers truly did seem to embody the interests of their managers. Assertions of dedication to quality were constant. New hires were closely trained in proper procedures and expectations by veteran workers. They were also quickly socialized into normative self-policing. Those who demonstrated work ethic, self-discipline, and dedication to the quality of the work, upon which professionalization strategies were hinged, were openly lauded by their coworkers. For instance, during a particularly slow day in the sign shop with no new orders, Lemmy used his spare time to practice his screen-printing skills. Eli, a veteran of the shop, walked over. "This sort of stuff [working during down time], the boss likes seeing this," he said. "He'll remember this when an *important* job comes through, y'know 'mean?"

Even though high-status workers offered praise to others who demonstrated professionalism, those perceived as failing to engage in ideals of professionalism were often met with disdain. Working in the sign shop one day I observed as several men discussed concerns about an apparently uncooperative coworker. As we prepared the screen-printing setup for a new run of street signs, Willie came around to collect waste from a nearby hazardous materials bin. Noticing a rag placed in the wrong spot, he shook his head and said, "It was probably Alec." Alec had recently joined the crew but had reportedly failed to embrace certain norms. Briskly stirring fresh red ink with a paint stirrer, Lemmy replied, "It probably was. He's lazy, man. Lazy and stubborn—he wants to do it his own way. I saw that from day two." Jon agreed, "He's gonna fuck around and get himself asked to not come back."

"He's never run a real order, too—no ten-sign order," Lemmy continued. "He'll have to conform if he's going to be able to do that." Nodding, Jon added. "He *have* to conform." Several weeks later, Alec would be fired from the sign shop. Upon hearing the news, one man commented, "He simply doesn't want to work. He has absolutely no ambition! It's why he didn't last here."

When men like Alec were fired from top-tier sites, their supposed lack of discipline or dedication was often mobilized to motivate others. In a different case, after another individual had been let go, Eli educated the man's replacement on why his predecessor had failed: "He would rather talk—he wanted to walk around, talk about women, talk about football," Eli warned. "'Okay,' I told him, 'when you come in here off that bus, you put your hard hat on, holding your lunch pail.' You see, he needs to come in a work mentality . . . . Good work habits lead to professionalism. I don't care if you breaking rocks or cleaning shitters, developing positive work habits has—hm, how you say it?—it has *dividends*. It'll pay off for you once you're out there looking for work."

By acting together to reframe their work and themselves, top-tier laborers attained a degree of status otherwise out of reach behind bars. According to Franklin, this was why sign shop work was more humanizing than other jobs: "It makes you feel like a regular person." Indeed, because prisoners are denied formal protections like wage minimums, economic measurements of success may be more difficult to attain. Instead, these individuals established self-worth through forging identities as disciplined, dedicated workers.[35] And, as these prisoners-as-employees came to extract personal value by approaching the worksite as a business in which they held emotional (if not material) stake, site managers benefited from improved productivity and efficiency.

Dignity and Consent

The strategies outlined in this chapter represent expressions of agency in the face of indignity, molded by prison work environments. As in free world workplaces, however, worker strategies did not only reward those engaging in them. Prison administrators and worksite overseers dictated overarching policies with which prisoners had little choice but to comply, in effect establishing the "rules of the game." By selectively enforcing policy and encouraging certain practices, institutional actors drew on these strategies to advance production or service goals and manage the workforce. Prisons are free to compel the incarcerated to work as a facet of punishment following the 13th Amendment to the Constitution. Yet, by facilitating (even cultivating) certain forms of action, overseers ensured that they not only worked, but continued to work *hard*.[36]

Through coping strategies, captive laborers discerned ways to make work more engaging, tolerating the undignified nature of disagreeable tasks or despotic oversight. Yet, many of their approaches rewarded labor efficiency, which overseers encouraged. Meat races and sales competitions, for instance, encouraged increased productivity in the food factory and call center, respectively. Similarly, through friction strategies, laborers actively defied institutional regulations. By engaging in illicit snacking, for instance, prisoners helped one another secrete and smuggle small stashes of food—often flaunting it to staff members. Many managers turned the other way in the face of these violations, however, allowing prisoners this outlet in place of more obstructive forms of resistance like sabotage (all the while maintaining authority to impose restrictions as desired). Finally, through professionalization strategies, prisoners reframed prison worksites as "businesses" and themselves as "professionals." Benefiting from increases in efficiency and quality resulting from this practice, management encouraged it by employing the same rhetorics. They further reinforced these outlooks through regular training sessions.

The distribution of these strategies across the tiers of the hierarchical carceral employment system illuminates contours in how work may function as a mechanism of control. The fact that workers in top-tier positions did not regularly engage in friction strategies, for instance, does not necessarily signal that they were free from the pains of penal labor. Rather, it may imply that the stakes of reactive practices—even in mild forms—were perhaps higher for those who had in many cases struggled for years to land top jobs. As sociologist Erving Goffman notes, the rewards of higher status disincentivize engagement in oppositional practices; meanwhile, "Low-placed members tend to have less commitment and emotional attachment to the organization than higher-placed members . . . . In consequence they seem more likely to make wide use of secondary adjustments."[37]

Other aspects of penal power were revealed through these strategies. For instance, by informally appointing "inmate managers," overseers imposed a hierarchical structure on work crews and helped ensure that conflicts remained directed at other prisoners. Though they held no formal authority, they helped buffer prison staff from other incarcerated workers. If grievances or concerns emerged, workers commonly turned to them to approach the bosses on their behalf; overseers, conversely, could pass instructions down through these incarcerated agents. It is notable that the two "inmate managers" discussed above—Slick, who managed the meat prep crews in the food factory, and Jake, who oversaw the sales crew in the call center—were often central to workplace tactics of their respective workforces.

Participation in many worker strategies—in the free world and in prison—can be said to represent a degree of implicit consent to the conditions surrounding them, reproducing underlying structures.[38] It is of critical importance to note that this notion of "consent" does *not* suggest that individuals voluntarily sustain pains of incarceration or forced labor. Rather, it affirms that they, like all laborers under advanced capitalism, may have little choice but to capitulate to specific forms of control or else risk exposure to potentially greater harms. In other words, although workers and overseers may engage in mutual concessions to ensure that work continues, overseers never relinquish access to techniques of coercion that they can deploy at any time.[39] Moreover, prisoner strategies must remain within the bounds of regulations set by on-site staff, institutional administrators, and penal policymakers. For this reason, engaging in them indirectly reifies broader structures of carceral labor and the local prison employment system. This often functions to dampen direct resistance to labor exploitation while transforming conflicts between workers and management into competition between workers and one another.

Professionalization strategies in particular served to reproduce divisions between prisoner groups, advancing a wedge between populations already divided along lines of race and nationality. Higher status prisoners engaged in distinction processes and boundary maintenance which often reframed others as less deserving or less motivated. Franklin illustrated this when he said, "the more mature men—we *want* to work . . . . [It] gives you integrity." Claiming dignity in this way denied it to others, instead suggesting that they must "want" drama over integrity.

By espousing the belief that some were lacking in work ethic or discipline and that these shortcomings explained their lower positions in the employment system, professionalization strategies entailed embracing outlooks often used to justify the use of penal labor in the first place. Adopting such outlooks, workers in top-tier positions misrecognized the capitals and characteristics that had enabled them to secure their increased status in the hierarchical prison employment system (seen in Chapters 3 and 4) as drive, work ethic, and professionalism.[40] This unveils another aspect of the labor stratification of carceral experiences: The most competitive in this internal employment system are rewarded with opportunities to reconstruct personal identities while those lacking valued capitals or characteristics may be preoccupied with tolerating or resisting added indignities.[41] Hence, instead of offering reprieve, bottom-tier work provides yet another facet of punishment against which they must struggle.

Having examined an array of personal and collective indignities, institutional and individual financial strains, and persistent inequities baked into carceral experiences through penal labor, we now turn toward broader political-economic phenomena that help explain the present shape of life and work behind bars. To these ends, the last chapter situates SSP in its post-recession neoliberal context before exploring several prescriptions for change advocated by incarcerated workers themselves.

7

Conclusion

Punishment and Labor under Neoliberal Penology

> Prisoners have always worked; only the State has been their exploiter, even as the individual employer has been the robber of organized labor.
>
> —**Emma Goldman (1911)**

Work is central to American penal punishment. It always has been. From the inception of the first penitentiary, federal, state, and private entities alike have extracted prisoner labor. Today, about two-thirds of the nation's prisoner population performs some type of (extremely low-) wage labor. The neoliberal carceral facility is not a paradigmatic total institution, set apart from society, but an economically embedded entity with a necessarily captive, racialized workforce laboring for subsistence in a particularly restrictive and dehumanizing company town.

Acknowledging this centrality means truly realizing that the operation of and experiences within the modern prison are oriented toward and attenuated by labor activities. Still, proponents of penal labor see this as evidence that imprisonment is ultimately rehabilitative. That is, that millions of incarcerated people are not financially contributing to and being treated as consumers by the carceral system, but working as a form of contrition, making prosocial contributions, and developing new, marketable skills and work ethics to serve them as they reenter society.[1] To them, it seems, work behind bars is a wholesome way to pass the time and become a productive citizen, deserving of their freedom, rather than a potential source of harm for those already marginalized by mainstream society.[2]

Throughout this book, I have tried to go beyond the rhetoric and rationalizations attending the expansion and evolution of American retributive justice, instead investigating how carceral structures and practices mapping onto fiscal and political imperatives may dramatically alter experiences behind bars. I have been guided by a rich tradition of critical scholarship, as well as some of the people directly impacted by continuing neoliberalization of the penal field: members of the nation's carceral workforce. Their accounts confirm that labor stratification is closely tied to the individual experience of incarceration. Prison work is now an economic necessity for the incarcerated, beset by the proliferating fees the institutions in which they are held use to pad budgets left bare by neoliberal politics. How any one person fares in the internal prison employment system is, however, frequently dependent on their existing capabilities, resources, and characteristics, thereby implicating longstanding social inequalities and stereotypes in the ways each prisoner understands punishment, prepares for release, and perceives their own worth. Prisons today continue to punish the poor,[3] even contributing to poverty via job sorting and compulsory labor justified by logics of rehabilitation and responsibilization.

Inspired by the Extended Case Method advanced by sociologist Michael Burawoy,[4] in these final pages, I hope to reorient the reader to the ways my fieldwork at Sunbelt State Penitentiary (SSP) can be used to "extend outward," taking a broader look at the form and function of punishment and the social forces shaping its on-the-ground practice. Then, again with the guidance of my thoughtful respondents on the inside, I consider some possible social responses to the issues I have uncovered at the intersection of prison life and labor. Where some might imagine the many issues faced by imprisoned workers could be remedied by producing more "good prison jobs," the empirical reality is that these problems are not isolated to individual jobs or facilities. They thread through the nation's history, social structures, and all the institutions now folded into the mission of the carceral system. Individual solutions are the pathologizing province of neoliberalism, and they are insufficient for addressing institutional- and societal-level inequities. Three ideas, ranging from incremental reforms to visions of radical transformation, emerged from my interviews with the imprisoned laborers of SSP. First, however, let's look back.

Prison Labor On-The-Ground

At SSP, where work is expected of all able prisoners (and additional punishments and deprivations are readily doled out to the recalcitrant), incarcerated men characterized the "good jobs" as those with higher pay, mentally or physically stimulating activities, and greater degrees of autonomy, stability, and mobility. Good jobs also tended to be less exposed to the institution's security apparatus. Conversely, "bad prison jobs" were unstable, with limited mobility and autonomy, lower pay, and deskilled tasks. These "prison-within-the-prison" positions were marked by repressive oversight. The structure of the prison employment system sorted incarcerated men into jobs, privileging those seen as having valued capitals, or combinations of useful characteristics, resources, and skills, in the competition for desirable work. Because these valued skills and resources were linked to perceptions wrapped up with race, ethnicity, and nationality, I found that deeply rooted patterns of ethnoracial bias shaped access to forms of capital,[5] resulting in between-group differences in group members' material wellbeing and subjective understandings of punishment and place.

With a greater than twenty-fold pay disparity between SSP's highest and lowest status incarcerated workers, prisoners' positions in the labor hierarchy acutely shaped their ability to participate in the internal economy of the prison. Higher-paid workers could better afford medical care, telephone and mail access, supplemental food, entertainment goods, and more. Lower-paid prisoners, conversely, depended more fully on the degraded care of the state.

Wages also influenced access to the underground economy, in which prisoners with the means could access additional nutritional, hygiene, and entertainment products as well as the skills of informal service providers. The most disadvantaged had few options but to *provide* services in shadow labor markets, which amplified their exposure to institutional surveillance and disciplinary structures. Work-related inequities impacted respondents' personal dignity. Participants innovated and shared strategies to evaluate and assert self-worth through labor, to cope with, resist, and/or reframe themselves within the prison context. Yet, engaging in these strategies in some ways entailed implicit consent to the structures and logics of penal labor. Where good jobs mean more dignity, strategizing to secure one is certainly a way to better self-conceptions. Nonetheless, *good* prison jobs are still prison jobs: coerced labor providing paltry wages with which to meet the most basic human needs.

These phenomena align with larger scale developments in American penal policy and practice, including the macro patterns of labor appropriation and social control through incarceration uncovered in classical critical scholarship,[6] as well as the micro arenas in which I found labor foregrounded in the contemporary prison. Imprisonment is more than removal from the outside world—a consequence in and of itself. It is, in a sense, insertion into a new world with its own consequences. Observations remind us that this institution is a workplace, linked to external social, political, and economic systems.

Penology: The Old, the New, and the Neoliberal

Punishment scholars Malcolm Feeley and Jonathan Simon write that U.S. prison policy in the first half of the twentieth century was largely "concerned with responsibility, fault, moral sensibility, diagnosis, or intervention and treatment of the individual offender."[7] This "old penology" is found in prevalent discourses emphasizing clinical assessment and retributive judgment, in punishment objectives centering on recidivism and the control of crime, and in the ostensibly more equitable and scientific techniques of incarceration used to target individuals and pathologies. According to Feeley and Simon, criminal law in this era focused on moral responsibility, the assignment of guilt, and incarceration as a route to rehabilitation.

The scholars pinpoint the arrival of a "new penology" to the rising conservatism of criminal justice policy in the 1970s and 1980s. This approach, unlike its predecessor, was more "concerned with techniques to identify, classify, and manage groupings sorted by dangerousness."[8] The new penal process again insisted upon the rational, scientific development of techniques to analyze probability and risk and, in seeking systems to more efficiently control populations, prioritized punishment aimed at aggregate groups rather than individuals. Demographic disparities in the rising prisoner population reveal that this shift in American corrections served to reinforce an ethnoracial hierarchy characterized by white supremacy through the warehousing of minoritized populations.[9]

Arguably, continued evolutions in correctional approaches have advanced the contemporary carceral system beyond the new penology and into what may be deemed "neoliberal penology." According to Loïc Wacquant, neoliberal agendas distilled the broader forms and functions of social control "around the shrill reassertion of penal fortitude . . . and the punitive containment and disciplinary supervision of the problem populations dwelling at the margins of the class and cultural order."[10] To help demonstrate the link between macro political-economic trends and carceral practice on the ground, I follow Feeley and Simon's framework to describe the emergent objectives, discourses, and techniques that map onto neoliberal penology.[11]

As neoliberalism rose as the dominant political-economic logic in the U.S.,[12] its effects and mutations in the field of punishment altered the quality of care available behind bars. The Great Recession further motivated institutional austerity and amplified citizen (including prisoner) consumerism. Carceral populations continued to outpace the growth in decades prior, while both state and private institutions worked to drive down per capita (or per prisoner) expenditures.[13]

Neoliberal penology is enacted in prisons that are overcrowded, underfunded, and offering fewer and poorer quality services. Thus, its aims shift over time to more fully encompass fiscal austerity. Today's system weaves together wider political and economic trends such that justice-involved individuals are reimagined as threats to security *and* budgets.[14] Personal responsibility, this way, justifies cost-shifting onto the imprisoned themselves; increasingly, the goods and services needed by prisoners have been privatized and currently incarcerated people are reconfigured as sites of profit.[15] In the years following my fieldwork, the stark outcomes of this nationwide trend have grown even more evident in the wake of the COVID-19 pandemic. Overstuffed carceral facilities became virus epicenters, leading to severe loss of human life while the survival of the institution itself remained a priority—with the pandemic, as other crises, seemingly regarded as the personal problem of the incarcerated, rather than of the institutional authorities entrusted with care.[16]

"Responsibilization" rhetoric, in fact, is key to the changing discourses surrounding punishment in the neoliberal era.[17] Incarcerated people are not regarded as wards of penal facilities but consumers of prison services, responsible for many facets of their own care.[18] Such framing has even been adopted by some amongst the imprisoned. At SSP, consumption-oriented individuals openly discussed their concerns over the cost of their captivity, lamenting the commissary prices and fee scales, even arguing that taxpayers were not getting their money's worth. For instance, D.S. shared how infrequently the food served in the chow hall in any way resembled the prison menus made available to the public when he exclaimed: "I be *damned* if I sit here and let you and my people on the outside— the ones that's not committing crimes—pay [taxes] for all this shit and be told it's *good!*" Prison authorities, from this man's perspective, were complicit in both the degraded conditions and extensive efforts to keep taxpaying citizens in the dark.

Men like D.S. accompanied their orientation toward consumer roles with an emphasis on self-reliance and personal responsibility that embodied neoliberalism (as well as the perception that there is a clear and consequential divide between *taxpayers* and *criminals*). Prisoners and staffers alike spoke about the value of work, strong work ethics, and dedication to labor. The work available to prisoners, however, is less and less "skilled," the pay (if you are not the one being paid) is laughable, and more and more of the costs of subsistence are being shifted onto those in custody.[19] As prisoners feel "uncared for, ignored, frustrated, and humiliated," and as the system becomes more reliant on their labor, neoliberal penology holds up an ideal, if not an imperative, of self-sufficiency.[20] The irony was dangerously apparent when, for instance, imprisoned workers were charged with the emergency production of goods like hand sanitizer and personal protective equipment for the fight against COVID-19. Despite producing them, captive producers were, in many facilities, prohibited from using these potentially lifesaving goods.[21]

Finally, the penological techniques that have emerged under contemporary neoliberal penology include, in line with objectives of fiscal restraint, the informal implementation of "punitive frugality."[22] This entails administrations scaling back the quality and number of prison services to satisfy political agendas to be sufficiently "tough on crime" *and* fiscally responsible.[23] Critical features like healthcare and psychiatric treatment have been slashed, as have "nonessential" programs like educational and vocational training, food and other services privatized, and provisions downsized and downgraded (any prisoner's food tray stands as evidence).[24] Many costs once covered by the state—from sufficient amounts of food to medical visits and electricity bills—have become the personal responsibility of the incarcerated. For prison laborers, these new pay-to-stay costs are painful, particularly for those relegated to lower-status jobs. The conditions are worse than ever for all prisoners, but the new carceral environment generates group-level disparities that conform to broader social patterns of discrimination. Focusing on the elderly behind bars, sociologist David Pyrooz and his colleagues add to calls for the restructuring of penal practice in noting that the aging prisoner population faces risks exacerbated by austerity-related changes including "restricted movement, [and] inaccessible or poor quality health care."[25] To the extent that punishment is expected to avoid cruelty, it is failing outright when elderly captives are allowed to die from medical neglect—even more so when inability to pay stands as a barrier to care.

The stratification of carceral experiences tied to competition in the internal employment system outlined in this book constitutes another novel technique of neoliberal penology. In constructing a hierarchical penal labor system, with desirable positions, pay, and perks distributed competitively yet opaquely,[26] the contemporary prison ensures its twin objectives of keeping institutional operations financially efficient and wielding multifaceted control over the prisoner body. The men I met who were incarcerated at SSP were acutely aware of their labor value, with one telling me, "You know, if they brought somebody [a non-incarcerated workforce] in here to do this, they'd pay 'em at *least* ten dollars . . . . It's a sweatshop in here, that's all."

Taken together, this set of penological objectives, discourses, and techniques constitutes the conditions and priorities of contemporary, post-recession neoliberal polity (see Table 7.1). Just as the "new penology" was based in and overlapped in many ways with the "old penology," neoliberal penology is building dialectically upon its antecedent.[27]

Critical penologists Georg Rusche and Otto Kirchheimer contend that the labor needs of a society align with and shape its penal forms, such that "every system of production tends to discover

Table 7.1 Evolving U.S. Corrections Strategies

	Objectives	Discourses	Techniques
Old Penology	Crime control; recidivism	Clinical diagnosis; retributive justice	Targeting the individual
New Penology	Efficient population control	Probability; risk mitigation	Targeting aggregate groups
Neoliberal Penology	Fiscal efficiency	Responsibilization; prisoner-as-consumer	Stratifying carceral experiences; generating competition & consent

punishments which correspond to its productive relationships."[28] As we have seen, in Gilded Age America, penal labor was deployed to fulfil the demands of large-scale industrial interests via convict leasing arrangements (themselves designed to extract and exploit black labor).[29] With the parallel advent of mass incarceration and neoliberalism, legislation once again expanded the prison's ability to mobilize and capitalize on captive labor.[30] This occurred in the midst of broader economic anxieties of the time, including rising labor precarity and worker competition, declining union representation and power, and yawning wage gaps between executives and entry-level employees. Subsequent years have witnessed not only rapid expansion in the number of working prisoners, but in the sheer variety of the types of labor they perform. This is reinforced by the high valuation placed on work ethic and responsibilization, which positions labor itself—in seemingly any form—as an appropriate form of "corrections."

Behind bars, as beyond them, overseers employ a mix of subtle and explicit strategies to limit worker options and heighten their reliance on wage labor, leaving them with little option but to implicitly consent to this arrangement. Staffers at SSP freely attested that the prison employment system provides "a great incentive" because prisoners "have to have good behavior" to remain competitive for the top positions. Although this system enables some to acquire greater status and higher pay than others, the "winners" in this competitive market nevertheless remain unable to ever fully escape the uncertainty, coercion, dehumanization, and precarity that comprise penal punishment in the United States. It is for these reasons that simply generating more—or more balanced access to—"good prison jobs" will not suffice to address inequities.

What Comes Next, in the Words of the Imprisoned

My time observing and participating in work at SSP confirmed to me that the contemporary American prison is a *workplace*. The experiences I've outlined throughout this book provided a true education and instilled a sense that, like other workplaces untouched by regulations and protections, it is, in many ways, a *dangerous* workplace. Still, the individuals confined to these institutions and consigned to these jobs remain the experts. In hopes that I might invert what sociologist Howard S. Becker calls the "hierarchy of credibility" that so often silences the insights of underrepresented groups into their own conditions,[31] I want to close with the penal policy prescriptions forwarded in my conversations with incarcerated workers. These largely fell into three categories ranging from incremental change to radical transformation: addressing problems with prisoner pay, repairing grievance reporting structures, and, most ambitiously, abolishing prison labor—if not the prison itself—as we know it.

Understandably, laborers were adamant in articulating how the requirement to perform mandatory labor to avoid punishment and receive as little as $0.10 an hour for the privilege was tantamount to slavery. Incarcerated men commonly described their work assignments as "slave work" and "forced labor," or their work sites as "sweatshops." Passionately, one man declared: "It's a sweatshop! A full day's work *might* get you a soup." Wages were stagnant, they said, but the cost of food to phone calls and everything in between were always on the way up. "Prison is supposed to be about rehabilitation, but it's too *expensive*. So, what can we do?" asked a participant.

Prisoners are not alone in these assessments. The United Nations' International Labor Organization, the AFL-CIO, and other prominent groups agree that their work is, indeed, a form of forced labor.[32] Scholars of law, economics, and other academic fields call the system America's "new slavery."[33] And journalists have written that, in many prisons, "slavery never ended . . . it was reinvented."[34] Pay is central to many of these assessments.

Murray, a prisoner working in SSP's call center, thought the solution seemed simple enough: "They should pay us minimum wage and have me pay rent and social security and take taxes from it!" He enumerated, among the potential benefits of this change, three upsides. First, it would help normalize prison life a little, perhaps easing the eventual transition back into society (adding to the purported rehabilitative aspects of prison work). Second, it might help individuals with limited experience paying regular bills to get into the habit (develop fiscal responsibility, as it were). Finally, much of the money would go right back to the prison in the form of prisoner rent payments and taxes (making the proposal more economically feasible, Murray presumed), while the balance might bring workers a fairer take-home wage.

He is not wrong about the benefits that such a plan might bring to the imprisoned. Stricter wage standards might mitigate many of the material struggles accompanying labor stratification and, because penal pay and thus carceral experiences vary greatly between states, institutions, and individual worksites, a set prison wage structure has the potential to help standardize penal punishment. Given that the paltry wages paid to prisoners are said to undercut wages in the outside world, some argue the establishment of a prison minimum might positively impact the U.S. working-class writ large.[35] Political resistance to the idea, however, returns us to Rusche and Kirchheimer's insight tying a society's productive landscape to its chosen forms of punishment. According to a federal study, the nation's penal institutions were, in the 1990s, so reliant on cheap labor that, were they "required to pay minimum wage to their inmate workers . . . without reducing the number of inmate hours worked, they would have to pay hundreds of millions of dollars more each year for inmate labor."[36] This conclusion handily underscores the true value of penal labor as well as the sheer unwieldiness (financially and otherwise) of mass incarceration. The neoliberal economic and political philosophy embraced by the nation's powerful in this moment, some thirty years later, is, in other words, likely too laser-focused on cost-savings and cost-recovery to alter this aspect of punishment.

A second issue that incarcerated workers believed deserves immediate attention is reform to the ineffective and risk-laden grievance and claim structures available to prisoners. Their accounts were permeated by feelings of helplessness and frustration. The prison's limited standards of care went unenforced, and prisoners did not trust staff (individually or as a group) to address their concerns. Samuél was sanguine about complaints: "*We* suffer for problems in the kitchen, problems on the yard, unsanitary conditions . . . . They don't care, 'cause they don't eat the food we eat, use the bathrooms we use. They don't *care*." Recall that, when I asked about the effectiveness of formal prisoner complaint mechanisms, one respondent set me straight: "They [staff] don't care about grievances," he told me, "unless it comes from the warden."

Law and society scholars Kitty Calavita and Valerie Jenness reveal that feelings of powerlessness in the face of outdated grievance systems are common to the American prison experience.[37] Even interventions from the highest level on prisoners' behalf have not eased these distresses in many instances. Numerous court cases in recent years highlight continued failures to prevent or correct dramatic degrees of service degradation suffered by the vulnerable prisoner population—problems against which formal complaints from *inside* the institutions have seemed ineffectual.[38] Such issues are pervasive and appear likely to continue if not worsen in the absence of public oversight.

Unlike with issues regarding pay, my respondents did not offer up concrete alternatives to address these failings. This perhaps reflects the depth of their disbelief in institutional staffers: Changes to policy or daily procedure are unlikely to easily counteract underlying mistrust. Nevertheless, their concerns, bolstered by scholarly and journalistic investigations, underscore the need for change. Prisoner apprehensions centered on a lack of "care" from overseers that made them disinclined to respond to anxieties or objections. Herein may lie the basis of a proper response. The imprisoned distrust correctional staff to communicate their stated grievances, protect and respect those who initiate them, or address them to a suitable degree (unless they are backed by an authority such as that of the warden). Addressing the faults in prisoner grievance reporting thus requires ensuring a stable and consistent outlet for making complaints, guarding the anonymity of incarcerated whistleblowers, and adding weight to the reporting process and transparency in how the DOC responds to such reports. This might be carried out, for instance, through civilian oversight committees or another sanctioned authority freer of conflicting interest and endowed with the power to monitor grievance reports and truly enforce standards of care.

Finally, A.S., a man incarcerated at SSP, was among this study's participants who dared to broach the biggest vision for change, however cautiously. Pointing to my notebook, he asked, "So, what's the story here? Prison labor? And what a *rotten* thing it is?" Without awaiting a response, he took a small step closer and continued, "History shows, whenever you use prisoners for labor—indentured servitude, forced labor, call it what you will—historically, it never works out. [But] that's the basis of capitalism: labor, as cheap as you can get it, regardless of who it affects. The lobbyists push for it, subtly or otherwise, to keep things how they are." A.S. leaned in close. "We incarcerate more people than anywhere else in the world. And we use these people—they use *us*—to do *this*." He pointed to his workplace, concluding, "All of this? *Profit*."

"So," I asked, "what's the solution to all of these issues?" A.S. shook his head grimly. "I mean, how do you change *any* caste system? Any *slavery* system?" He raised his eyebrows, letting the rhetorical question hang for a moment. Then, giving a straight-faced nod, he swiped his hand in a horizontal slashing motion to signal: *Do away with it.*

Reforming pay or grievance structures, men like A.S. insist, is meaningless if exploitation persists. Logically, we cannot discuss how to combat the harms of the criminal justice system and its prisons without at least considering abolition theory.[39] In the not-too-distant past, in fact, widespread decarceration seemed imminent. In the 1970s, the National Advisory Commission on Criminal Justice Standards and Goals, sponsored by the Department of Justice, concluded that the nation's penal facilities overwhelmingly failed at their stated goals.[40] The committee proposed a moratorium on the construction of new penal institutions and received broad support. Yet this small step toward abolition was overtaken by other agendas; instead of the path to decarceration, the nation charted its course toward mass incarceration. The abolitionist ideal has never disappeared. Dedicated and newly inspired activists in national and global protest movements have recently brought these transformative possibilities back into the mainstream. So, too, have the moral implications of mass deaths resulting from COVID-19's deadly march through overcrowded prisons.[41]

The idea of abolishing individual *components* of the prison, such as the death penalty or solitary confinement, is far less controversial as a serious consideration, and it is backed by what seems to be an exponential growth in social movements in the U.S. and abroad.[42] A national wave of prison strikes and work stoppages in the mid-2010s raised the issue in recent political consciousness,[43] and the abolition of penal labor, you will remember from Chapter 1, has historical precedent in the U.S.[44] Like the prison itself, prison labor is not a natural fixture. It is a social institution that, like any such institution, may be expected to justify its own existence. Given the problems surrounding carceral labor—including its role in the reproduction of inequality and its inability to significantly reduce recidivism, demonstrate rehabilitative achievements, or make communities safer[45]—it is high time to ask, paraphrasing punishment scholars Dario Melossi and Massimo Pavarini, *Why prison labor?*[46]

A.S. wasn't far off when he gestured to his worksite and summarized the situation ("All of this? *Profit.*"). Like he said, this system is not divorced from other social institutions, but is in fact tied to the very "basis of capitalism." A.S. was not necessarily advocating tearing down the prison walls tomorrow—that's unlikely to solve the issues underlying mass incarceration anyway—just pointing out, in his way, that prison is just part of an interconnected patchwork resulting in—if not predicated on—inequality between social strata. Foundational social theorist W.E.B. Du Bois, writing about the ideal form that the abolition of chattel slavery *might* have taken, assessed the ways reality fell far short of the movement's promise, in which "the abolition of slavery meant not simply abolition of legal ownership of the slave; it meant the uplift of slaves and their eventual incorporation into the body civil, politic, and social, of the United States."[47] Adopting a similar vision, penal abolitionists today note that this endeavor would require not simply razing the buildings, but a society-wide commitment to a "positive project" of decarceration coupled with major institutional, economic, political, and social advances to redress the harms of mass incarceration in the communities most impacted; here, abolitionist thought warns against those who would seek "better" ways to imprison rather than rendering the prison obsolete.[48] "A more complicated framework," writes abolitionist and academic Angela Davis, "may yield more options than if we simply attempt to discover a single substitute for the prison system."[49]

In place of retributive criminal justice institutions that demonstrably contribute to race, ethnicity, class, and gender inequalities, the current abolitionist movement calls us to question our responses to the social problems that precipitate the practices we collectively deem criminal. Again, this project is hopeful, proactive, and positive: It is about "building the kind of society that does not need prisons."[50] To be sure, the abolitionist project is as diverse and complex as the political, economic, and social forces that have coalesced in this moment in carceral and labor history. Yet it cannot be forgotten that today's prison empirically fails at the objective of reducing recidivism,[51] while systematically and disproportionately disrupting the lives and livelihoods of minoritized and lower-class communities.[52]

We also know that, whatever the historical era, rehabilitation, penance, and other abstract notions deployed to frame and validate prison work have often—and simultaneously—been wielded to support various systems of targeted predation. As researcher Philip Goodman explains, "that some imprisoned workers speak positively about their jobs ought not to distract us from the simultaneous, overarching reality that coercing prisoners and others to work is . . . a way of punishing, controlling, and exploiting those who labor; making the institution run smoother and cheaper; and enriching the state and/or private actors."[53] At SSP, the perks of a good job were not enough to blind many in the most privileged positions to the harsh realities of the carceral institution.

Jake, the call center's "informal manager," introduced in the opening paragraphs of this book, is one such worker. To be sure, Jake was no abolitionist. He saw prison as necessary for society: "Don't get me wrong," he said, "we need this box. There's plenty of guys in here who I wouldn't want living on my grandma's block. I'd be the one in front of her house telling 'em to boot-scoot. And I'm from the *other* side of the tracks, you know. I lived as a criminal—on *purpose!*" Even so, Jake was quick to weigh the few benefits of incapacitation against its institutional harms. "I been in here my whole life—thirteen years total—and I know that we got plenty of guys in here who *shouldn't* be. They're not criminals, they're *addicts*. They're not predators, they're *prey*." The system keeping his grandma safe was also targeting the vulnerable by offering arrest rather than assistance:

> They round up poor people. Even though these white-collar types are more likely to fuck you over, they treat *us* like demons. They do it to whole neighborhoods. They do it to whole *races!* They treat a kid like a criminal, a villain, his whole life. It's all he's ever told he is. It's the only version of himself he sees on TV. And they turn around and ask him, "Why are you like this? Why didn't you go out and get a job and work hard?" But he never gets taught that.

* * *

Beyond merely documenting policies, strategies, and behaviors, in this book I have aimed to highlight the humanity of those too often outcast and "othered." I have sought to depict the many ways that they experience the stratified system of today's prison labor apparatus—how they suffer, subsist, resist, cooperate, compete, gossip, and jest in the face of this institution's deprivations, indignities, and opportunities (sometimes simply the opportunity to fill the hours of the day). Without the contributions of men like those who so generously agreed to participate in my study, I truly could not have grasped the nuanced ways that the structure of the penal labor system amplifies the inequalities and hardships fed into, neglected by, and redoubled within American prisons.

As so many others have demonstrated, retributive and unjust penal processes do little to serve restorative or rehabilitative ends, even though they are the defining features of American punishment, today as surely as they were hundreds of years ago. Those currently confined have been ceremonially stripped of voice and vote, and so it falls to those of us currently on the outside to stand as allies and advocates, embracing their struggles to reform or even transform this system. The work of change must not become another dead-end, orange-collar job.

Conducting and Completing Prison Research

[T]his strange house, where I was to . . . endure so many emotions, and of which I could not form even an approximate idea, if I had not gone through them.

—Fyodor Dostoevsky (1914)

Prisons are daunting. These hulking stone and steel fortresses are often hidden away on remote patches of land where people seem to simply disappear for years or decades at a time. They are nearly impossible to fully fathom from the outside. Pursuing and completing this book on the inner workings of the penal labor system necessitated an approach oriented toward foregrounding the lived experiences and voices of those enduring it from within.

In this Appendix, I discuss this approach and some of the challenges that arose in the process. I first address a question that gets asked virtually any time I talk about my research: *How did you get interested in the topic?* I do my best to sketch a brief history of how the project "started," which in some ways lasted well into data collection. Then, I outline the methodologies through which I studied the dynamics of carceral labor at Sunbelt State Penitentiary (SSP). I hope that this description of my ethnographic approach will prove useful to others seeking to engage in this sort of work and interesting to readers curious to learn more about how data like these are collected.

The Multiple Beginnings of This Research

Growing up poor in St. Louis, I had a few minor brushes with the law, but thankfully never found my way into a prison cell. My first true exposure to the inside of this institution came in college as part of a sociology course. With the guidance of Professor Jody Miller, my classmates and I shuttled out to a penitentiary in central Missouri to conduct one-on-one interviews with incarcerated women working in one penal labor program. Up to this point in my life, I had alternated between wanting to pursue journalism or creative writing careers. I studied sociology in hopes of expanding my knowledge of the social inequalities that I had begun to explore in my writing. But my experience in Dr. Miller's class put me on a new path: I decided that I wanted to conduct social science research. In hindsight, this was the first "starting point" of this project.

I later found my way to graduate school and eventually decided I would continue investigating work behind bars. Trying to make that happen was not without risks. I was advised quite pragmatically that it was unlikely that I would get access to collect the observational data that I sought. It would be wise, my advisor instructed, to begin planning my "backup" dissertation idea before I lost too much time. I began another project but continued seeking entrée to a penitentiary. With luck, one state's Department of Corrections (DOC) eventually agreed to let me in to observe the dynamics of prison labor. At that moment, I felt I could finally start my work. Yet, challenges did not cease with access. In the first weeks of fieldwork at what I came to call SSP, several correctional officers (COs) would offer a snort and a sarcastic "Good *luck*." The imprisoned, they assured me, were never going to talk to an outsider like me.

The officers, thankfully, were wrong. With very few exceptions, the incarcerated workers I encountered consented to let me observe and participate in their daily work routines. Most were enthusiastic about the fact that someone had actually chosen to come from beyond prison walls to learn about their experiences.[1] With their acceptance, I once again felt like I had finally started.

Only three imprisoned men declined to participate in my ethnography. Each would tell me essentially the same thing: They had no qualms with the research; they just didn't want to be included in my fieldnotes. One gave a reason that acutely affected me. After I went over my "consent script," detailing who I was and what I hoped to do, he told me quite bluntly that he did not believe that a lone researcher could help him and he therefore felt no desire to share information with me. He suggested that perhaps a *journalist* would have something to offer, but not a sociologist. As my study progressed, he eventually changed his mind and agreed to take part, which is why I can write about him now. His only condition was that I agree to transcribe his freestyle rap routines in my field jottings, to which I happily agreed. Under his new alias, "Slick" became a key participant in my study, but our first encounter stuck with me. I could not shake the thought that maybe I had made a mistake by not pursing journalism if I wanted to have an impact.

As I progressed further into what became an eighteen-month ethnography, the largest prison labor strike in history broke out nationwide. An estimated twenty-four thousand prisoners across at least twenty-four states refused to report to work assignments on a September day in 2016, bringing operations to a halt. (Exact participation rates remain murky in part because officials are often disinclined to broadcast acts of resistance.) In many facilities, striking continued into the month. Allies in the free world circulated prisoners' demands to the media. These included pleas for fairer pay, more humane conditions, and improved educational and vocational offerings.[2]

Mainstream news reports of the unprecedented demonstration were limited, despite its scale. Those stories that did emerge often relied on second-hand accounts from outside collaborators or on furtive phone conversations with inside organizers. As a *New Yorker* report surmised, "the relative silence about the story owes as much to the difficult task of reporting across razor wire."[3] Having observed the internal dynamics of my prison fieldsite for several months by that time, I was not surprised by the difficulties of securing newsworthy information from the "black box" of the prison.

Strike activity did not reach SSP, but staffers were aware of happenings around the country. When I arrived for fieldwork around the beginning of the strike period, I found an institution on partial lockdown. Rather than checking identification at the entrance gate, as was common, two COs halted approaching vehicles farther up the road. "We're just making sure nobody who's not *supposed* to be here comes in," one informed me while scanning my ID badge. When I finally made it through and approached the gate, I passed by teams of additional officers. "Why the extra scrutiny?" I asked one CO. "Oh, just to keep everybody safe," they responded obliquely. Closer to the gate, I caught up with staffers chatting openly about the situation as they drew nearer to the concrete walls dividing the insiders and the outsiders. "They're trying to keep the *media* from sneaking in," one CO informed me, "because there might be a demonstration outside against *forced labor.*"

With the extra security, the line to enter the facility dragged. As I waited, it was difficult not to recall Slick's initial concerns about my project. In his (and surely others') eyes, a social scientist could not offer the same promise as a journalist to convey the realities of the prison world to the broadest possible public. Yet, while many reporters remained unable to reach sources on the inside to tell their stories, I had become embedded in the prison, surrounded by thousands who lived this life daily. The concerns they expressed mirrored those conveyed by strikers nationwide. "They call work a *privilege,*" one man had shared with frustration, "but we're *required* to do it. They call our pay *gratuity* so that they don't have to pay us a living wage." Many others expressed disquiet over general living conditions and an inability to express grievances. As Samuél in the food factory had stated, "We suffer for problems in the kitchen, problems on the yard, unsanitary conditions . . . . They don't care 'cause they don't eat the food we eat, use the bathroom we use." Numerous individuals—both captives and employees of this institution—had already shared such accounts and would continue to do so.

The slow-moving procession eventually reached the main gate. After the officer gestured for me to pass through, I made my way toward my worksite for the day. A cluster of orange-collared workers greeted me there. Together, we started our work.

Methodological Approach: The Ethnography of Penal Labor

I conducted this research at SSP across 2015 and 2016. I used ethnographic methods, which entail systematically observing and participating in the social world being investigated. I observed and participated in several aspects of labor at SSP over eighteen months, recording thousands of pages of notes across countless pocket notebooks to document observations and accounts of day-to-day processes and structures of prisoners' work. I was made privy to backstage operational procedures when I occasionally shadowed officers. Additionally, I recorded in-depth interviews with eighty-two prisoners and staffers regarding their experiences and outlooks towards prison life and labor.

Sunbelt State Penitentiary and its prisoners

SSP is well suited for this sort of research—it bears many features common to the U.S. penal landscape and is large enough that a broad variety of worksites and workers could be observed. It is located in the Sunbelt region (roughly, the area below the 36th Parallel[4]). Historically, the southern half of the nation was home to the rapid expansion of penal labor, particularly in the years following the abolition of slavery.[5] Today, in the face of chronic labor shortages and massive carceral populations that might be mobilized as a surplus workforce, the region remains the seat of such activity and wields growing influence over national penal policy.[6]

Conducting research in a carceral institution involves the participation of three primary entities: researcher, respondents, and the organization itself.[7] Ensuring the confidentiality of vulnerable prisoner participants, staffers, and the particular facility required the distortion of some characteristics. Anonymizing the name and certain details was a condition of access, but I will here provide what information I can to help contextualize findings within these confines.

SSP is in the top quartile of U.S. prisons in terms of average daily population size. Because providing direct demographic data might compromise confidentiality, I developed a strategy to provide slightly altered demographics that will not precisely mirror any single prison in the region. To do this, I aggregated demographic information of four comparable institutions to provide an approximate portrait of the SSP population. These four institutions are located in the Sunbelt region and possess populations and security levels relatively analogous to my site. Table A.1 provides an approximation of the racial/ethnic makeup of SSP derived from this aggregation. The demographics of individual worksites where fieldwork was conducted are also reported. These were altered in proportion to the adjusted general population figures to maintain pertinent relationships. Rounding or changing organizational statistics such as this for the purposes of confidentiality is often necessary in institutional ethnography.[8]

This was a state prison, meaning its administrative and security staff were state employees. However, many civilian staff members employed by private firms oversaw certain services like food production and medical care, or managed work programs like the call center. The privatization of penal labor in this manner is accomplished via public–private partnerships through which individual businesses remunerate the Department of Corrections for the ability to operate behind prison walls. Unlike work release programs or traditional convict leasing systems, most prisoners involved in such work do not typically leave the penitentiary and their wages and other facets of care are provided through the institution (though often following payments via the firm).

Table A.1   Racial/Ethnic Composition of SSP Worksites

	Race/Ethnicity (%)				
	White	Black	Mexican American	Foreign National	Other
General Population	35	33	17	13	2
Call Center	70	22	8	0	0
Sign Shop	39	43	11	0	7
Fleet Garage	57	0	14	29	0
Food Factory	24	24	19	32	1

Note: The percentages reported here have been adjusted to ensure the confidentiality of participants and of the institution itself.

Because of its size, SSP was subdivided into multiple units, which were largely self-contained. My research primarily took place within one of the largest units, which housed over one thousand men. Colloquially, prisoners here referred to their unit in general terms as "the yard," which was meant to capture the housing bays, recreational space, and several adjacent buildings. This was a medium security yard, which contained a large prisoner population and housed a model variety of worksites. Laborers were unable to move between units at will, meaning that this yard was home to a largely contained employment system with its own worksites, staff overseers acting as managers, and a captive workforce.

Ethnographic data collection and considerations

To secure access to this facility, I first met with the Director of the Department of Corrections under whose jurisdiction it fell. Following initial contact via post, I was invited to outline my proposed research strategy and the particulars of the project. Priorities included freely navigating the prison complex during prisoner work hours, formalizing processes of consent, accessing private spaces to conduct one-on-one interviews, ensuring that my presence would not burden departmental resources, and scheduling requisite DOC training procedures (which, it turned out, primarily consisted of video presentations from staff orientation modules detailing basic safety procedures and chains of command).

I was granted an ID badge so that I could enter and exit SSP freely and was accorded the status of "volunteer," which is typically reserved for non-employee entrants like visiting tutors or chaplains. As neither prisoners nor employees, volunteers often occupy an ambiguous standing in the social order of the prison. The relative uniqueness of their position contributes to social encounters that do not necessarily adhere to established scripts and hierarchies. This allowed me to sometimes alter my role on-site. On most days, I operated as visiting "worker" (or "intern," as one participant insisted) alongside penal laborers in different workplaces. Occasionally, I shadowed staff, observing institutional operations within and beyond prison walls. Experiencing each of these stages of programming, management, and security revealed a fuller portrait of the form and functions of prison labor. At times, navigating the various formal and informal hierarchies of the facility could be challenging. I often felt like a Simmelian "stranger": *in* but not *of* the prisoner and staffer groups in the institution, all of whom remained engaged in a tireless vertical struggle.[9]

Wearing plain clothes, my researcher status overt to all, I openly traversed the facility at different times during prisoner working hours (weekdays between approximately 4:30 am and 5:30 pm) to observe work in multiple spaces as well as outdoor recreation areas. Over time, I became a more regular fixture at SSP. I worked alongside prisoners of varying ages, racial and ethnic groups, work histories, and criminal records. To accommodate my online teaching duties, I was typically on-site between three and five workdays weekly, which aligns with strategies advocated by other prison ethnographers.[10] Sensitive to the potential for institutional accommodations to my presence, I remained alert for observable changes in operations surrounding my fieldwork. The length of data collection helped diminish the effects of any procedural alterations that might have influenced practices early on. Additionally, I developed a strategy of arriving to the facility at differing times of day and refrained from alerting penal laborers, staff members, or administrators to my schedule. This impeded the potential for behavioral or operational changes around my research schedule.

I took field jottings, which I subsequently typed to generate extensive fieldnotes, as my primary form of data collection. Initially, these prioritized descriptive accounts of the physical and social space of the prison. Over time, they became increasingly focused on what are now the themes of this book, which took fuller shape during data collection. For instance, I systematically began noting barriers between prisoner groups, different strategies participants used to overcome the challenges of prison life and labor, prisoner and staff member orientations toward different jobs and workers, and, vitally, the skills and resources that were valued in the carceral employment system. Many additional or adjacent themes were also captured in my notes, some of which are explored in print elsewhere.

To structure field visits and better focus my observations on consistent processes and themes over time, I opted to emphasize the laborers, staff, and daily occurrences of four primary worksites: the sign shop, fleet auto garage, food factory, and call center. Consent at these locations was established during "town hall" style meetings in which I read from a script detailing my project and answered questions from prisoners and staff before seeking verbal affirmation from each individual that they were willing to participate. Upon encountering new potential participants, I went through the same general process one-on-one. As noted, almost all the individuals I encountered on-site quickly consented to participate in ethnographic observations. Those who declined (initially three men, then only two after Slick consented) were omitted from written notes at their request. Many eagerly shared experiences and perspectives. Several warmly regarded me by nicknames like "Hemmingway" or "Kerouac" on account of my regular notetaking. Calls like, "Hey, put *this* in your book!" were frequent.

In-depth interviews

To supplement observational data, I conducted eighty-two semi-structured in-depth interviews—sixty-nine with imprisoned workers and thirteen with staff members. Prisoner participants were drawn from the four primary worksites where I conducted fieldwork. Questions covered topics relating to life behind bars with special interest in perceptions and practices tied to work. Interviewees discussed their labor histories in and out of prison, assessments of different jobs, experiences navigating the carceral employment system, challenges surrounding prison services, and plans and expectations for release. The nature of the dominating schedules around which prison life is organized sometimes impacted the length of these interviews. Because of this, they ranged from fifteen to eighty minutes, averaging approximately thirty minutes. Interviews were recorded using a digital recorder and transcribed later.

Although most prisoners quickly consented to inclusion in observational fieldnotes, some were initially reluctant to participate in interviews. One reason for this was that many had experienced video or audio recordings used against them in court and were apprehensive of my recorder. One man, for example, consented to talk to me without the device. I took detailed notes by hand during his interview. Several officers were similarly reticent to be recorded, citing historical instances (indirectly recounted to them) in which COs had been sanctioned for recorded statements or behaviors. Another reason that some incarcerated individuals were hesitant to consent to sit-down interviews early on was that these were conducted one-on-one. Solo encounters between prisoners and non-prisoners were often met with suspicion. For fear of attracting negative attention, a small number declined to be interviewed. In several instances, men who initially expressed concerns later consented once my presence became normalized and I had been sufficiently "vouched for" by others.

As time went on, prisoners and staffers alike grew more trusting of my motivations and consented to interviews at increasing rates. Influenced by the racial politics of the institution—informal rules governing and limiting interactions between racial/ethnic cliques, as discussed in Chapter 4—white prisoners were quicker to consent to interviews in the early weeks of collection, increasing their final participation rates. The reluctance of other groups eventually faded but nevertheless resulted in fewer interviews overall. The final prisoner interview sample was: fourteen black, twenty Hispanic (twelve Mexican American, eight foreign national), one Native American, and thirty-four white.

* * *

My ethnographic and interview-based approach positioned me to capture the organization of prison workplaces and micro-level processes and practices of labor.

This also allowed me to illustrate the meso-level composition of the various work programs constituting an internal prison employment system. As a result, these qualitative data reveal structures and processes that other methods may overlook.

In the end, I hope that Slick was wrong about the ability of researchers to document, draw attention to, and help address the plights that he and millions of others have endured behind bars. For that to be possible, however, the work cannot stop here. Continued empirical examinations of shrouded carceral institutions in the U.S. (as abroad) are vital. Indeed, the issues outlined in this book persist in large part because the American prison remains obscured from public view and oversight. Conducting research such as this is challenging—to be sure, it can be punishing in its own way—but it is a challenge that I am confident will continue finding champions.

Notes

Chapter 1

1. All names in this book—including the names of individuals, the institution itself, and certain departments or firms—are pseudonyms. Specific information about the facility, such as its location or particulars regarding the size and characteristics of its prisoner population, have also been minimized or altered to secure confidentiality. Formerly incarcerated readers may recognize many features of SSP, regardless of where they did their time. As such, the challenges that I document here should not be attributed to any particular individuals or state DOC regime but should be addressed in a more systematic way nationwide.

2. Terms like "correctional officer" refer to badged security staff within the institution. Such language is not intended to imply anything about the job, those who hold it, or what they do day-to-day; rather, it reflects modern professional preferences. For these reasons, I also avoid terms like "guard," which is often deemed unfavorable to today's staffers, when describing this occupational category. Finally, correctional staff are distinct from "civilian" prison employees, such as administrative staff, human resources, non-badged overseers of certain work programs, and others, in that their badges and titles reflect particular powers and prerogatives.

3. Careful consideration of language used to discuss people who have come into contact with the prison is essential. Labels like "inmate" or "offender" may have harmful and lasting impacts. In an effort to deindividualize and mortify the imprisoned, state and institutional actors often solely refer to currently incarcerated individuals by such terms, stripping away personal identifiers like given names. As such, I use these terms only when quoting others, including incarcerated participants, prison staff, and other scholars. I instead prioritize people-first language. I also use the terms "imprisoned" and "prisoner" as this language "conveys a physical or mental state of being rather than an identity." Akiba Solomon, "What Words We Use—and Avoid — When Covering People and Incarceration," *The Marshall Project*, April 2021, https://www.themarshallproj ect.org/2021/04/12/what-words-we-use-and-avoid-when-covering-people-and-incarceration. See also Alexandra Cox, "The Language of Incarceration," *Incarceration* 1, no. 1 (July 2020): 1–13, doi:10.1177/2632666320940859.

4. Later, I will discuss the various fines, fees, restitution, and other costs of life within the prison that will cut into this nest egg and put others in even tighter financial positions.

5. Wendy Sawyer and Peter Wagner, "Mass Incarceration: The Whole Pie 2020," *Prison Policy Initiative* (2020), https://www.prisonpolicy.org/reports/pie2 020.html; Roy Walmsley, *World Prison Population List*, 11th ed. (London, UK: Institute for Criminal Policy Research, 2010).

6. Fabrice Guilbaud, "Working in Prison: Time as Experienced by Inmate-Workers," *Revue francaise de sociologie* 51, no. 5 (July 2010): 41–68; James Stephan, "Census of State and Federal Correctional Facilities, 2005," Census of State and Federal Correctional Facilities (Washington, DC: Bureau of Justice Statistics, 2008), https://www.bjs.gov/content/pub/pdf/csfcf05.pdf.

7. Whitney Benns, "American Slavery, Reinvented," *The Atlantic* (September 2015): 5, https://www.theatlantic.com/business/archive/2015/09/prison-labor-in-america/406177/; see also, Robbie Brown and Kim Severson, "Enlisting Prison Labor to Close Budget Gaps," *The New York Times* (February 2011):, sec. U.S., https://www.nytimes.com/2011/02/25/us/25inmates.html; Laura Murphy and Jesselyn McCurdy, "ACLU Letter to the House Subcommittee on Financial Management, the Budget and International Security Expressing Concerns about S. 346, Which Prevents Offenders from Obtaining Job Skills and Benefitting from Opportunities for Rehabilitation," *American Civil Liberties Union* (2004), https://www.aclu.org/letter/aclu-letter-house-subcommittee-financial-management-budget-and-international-security.

8. "Race" is not a natural or biological category; it is a social construct that nevertheless has very real consequences for lived experience (not only in prison, but worldwide). My usage of this term occurs with this in mind.

9. Sarah Lageson and Christopher Uggen, "How Work Affects Crime—And Crime Affects Work—Over The Life Course," in *Handbook of Life-Course Criminology: Emerging Trends and Directions for Future Research*, eds. Chris L. Gibson and Marvin D. Krohn (New York: Springer, 2013), 201–212, doi:10.1007/978-1-4614-5113-6_12.

10. Jeffrey Bouffard, Doris Layton Mackenzie, and Laura J. Hickman, "Effectiveness of Vocational Education and Employment Programs for Adult Offenders," *Journal of Offender Rehabilitation* 31, no. 1–2 (2008): 1–41, doi:10.1300/J076v31n01_01; Richard P. Seiter and Karen R. Kadela, "Prisoner Reentry: What Works, What Does Not, and What Is Promising," *Crime & Delinquency* 49, no. 3 (July 2003): 360–388, doi:10.1177/0011128703049003002.

11. Sara Wakefield and Christopher Uggen, "Incarceration and Stratification," *Annual Review of Sociology* 36, no. 1 (2010): 393, doi:10.1146/annurev.soc.012809.102551.

12. Bruce Western and Becky Pettit, "Incarceration & Social Inequality," *Daedalus* 139, no. 3 (July 2010): 8, doi:10.1162/DAED_a_00019.

13. By socioeconomic class (or status), I refer to position and power within a stratified economy and labor system. A relational concept, class captures access to valuable resources as well as the degree to which agents are exploited by, or may exploit, others. Class is a powerful force underlying social inequalities. Those at the peak of class hierarchies own or control valuable resources and institutions, with which they may oppress and exploit those below. Narrower class distinctions may be observed between non-elite (or non-exploiting) members of society. This is often assessed, for example, by differences in income, occupational status, or education. Class and race often intersect to aggravate inequalities: Becky Pettit and Bruce Western, "Mass Imprisonment and the Life Course: Race and Class Inequality in U.S. Incarceration," *American Sociological Review* 69, no. 2 (April 2004): 151–169, doi:10.1177/000312240406900201. For a more detailed examination of class, see Erik Olin Wright, "Social Class," in *Encyclopedia of Social Theory*, ed. George Ritzer (Thousand Oaks, CA: SAGE Publications, 2004), 717–724. See also: Dario Melossi, "The Penal Question in 'Capital,'" *Crime and Social Justice*, no. 5 (1976): 26–33.

14. Jeffrey Morenoff, "Racial and Ethnic Disparities in Crime and Delinquency in the United States," in *Ethnicity and Causal Mechanisms*, eds. Michael Rutter and Marta Tienda (New York: Cambridge University Press, 2005), 139–173; Darren Wheelock and Christopher Uggen, "Punishment, Crime, and Poverty," in *The Colors of Poverty: Why Racial and Ethnic Disparities Persist* (New York: Russell Sage Foundation, 2008), 261–292, https://www.jstor.org/stable/10.7758/9781610447249.

15. Loïc Wacquant, *Prisons of Poverty* (Minneapolis, MN: University of Minnesota Press, 2009).

16. Wakefield and Uggen, "Incarceration and Stratification"; Robert P. Weiss, "'Repatriating' Low-Wage Work: The Political Economy of Prison Labor Reprivatization in the Postindustrial United States," *Criminology* 39, no. 2 (May 2001): 253–292, doi:10.1111/j.1745-9125.2001.tb00923.x; Bruce Western, *Punishment and Inequality in America* (New York: Russell Sage Foundation, 2006).

17. Katherine Beckett, Kris Nyrop, and Lori Pfingst, "Race, Drugs, and Policing: Understanding Disparities in Drug Delivery Arrests," *Criminology* 44, no. 1 (2006): 105–137, doi:10.1111/j.1745-9125.2006.00044.x; Alfred Blumstein and Allen J. Beck, "Population Growth in U. S. Prisons, 1980–1996," *Crime and Justice* 26 (January 1999): 17–61, doi:10.1086/449294; James Lynch and William Sabol, "Prison Use and Social Control. Policies, Processes, and Decisions of the Criminal Justice System," *Policies, Processes, and Decisions of the Criminal Justice System* 3 (2000): 7–44; Darrell Steffensmeier, Jeffery Ulmer, and John Kramer, "The Interaction of Race, Gender, and Age in Criminal Sentencing: The Punishment Cost of Being Young, Black, and Male," *Criminology* 36, no. 4 (1998): 763–798, doi:10.1111/j.1745-9125.1998.

tb01265.x; Nicole Van Cleve, *Crook County: Racism and Injustice in America's Largest Criminal Court* (Stanford, CA: Stanford Law Books, 2016).

18. Brenden Beck, "Broken Windows in the Cul-de-Sac? Race/Ethnicity and Quality-of-Life Policing in the Changing Suburbs," *Crime & Delinquency* 65, no. 2 (February 2019): 270–292, doi:10.1177/0011128717739568; Mona Lynch and Marisa Omori, "Crack as Proxy: Aggressive Federal Drug Prosecutions and the Production of Black–White Racial Inequality," *Law & Society Review* 52, no. 3 (2018): 773–809, doi:10.1111/lasr.12348; Victor M. Rios, *Punished: Policing the Lives of Black and Latino Boys* (New York: NYU Press, 2011); Wakefield and Uggen, "Incarceration and Stratification"; Western and Pettit, "Incarceration & Social Inequality."

19. For example, Jamie Fellner, "Race and Drugs," in *The Oxford Handbook of Ethnicity, Crime, and Immigration*, eds. Sandra M. Bucerius and Michael Tonry (New York: Oxford University Press, 2013), 194–223.

20. Michelle Alexander, *The New Jim Crow: Mass Incarceration in the Age of Colorblindness* (New York: The New Press, 2012); Douglas A. Blackmon, *Slavery by Another Name: The Re-Enslavement of Black Americans from the Civil War to World War II* (New York: Anchor Books, 2009); Earl Smith and Angela J. Hattery, "Incarceration: A Tool for Racial Segregation and Labor Exploitation," *Race, Gender & Class* 15, no. 1 (2008): 79–97. Researchers have promoted several theories to account for these patterns, e.g., David Garland, "Theoretical Advances and Problems in the Sociology of Punishment," *Punishment & Society* 20, no. 1 (January 2018): 8–33, doi:10.1177/1462474517737274; John Pfaff, *Locked In: The True Causes of Mass Incarceration-and How to Achieve Real Reform* (New York: Basic Books, 2017); Malcolm M. Feeley and Jonathan Simon, "The New Penology: Notes on the Emerging Strategy of Corrections and Its Implications," *Criminology* 30, no. 4 (1992): 449–474, doi:10.1111/j.1745-9125.1992.tb01112.x; Loïc Wacquant, "The New 'Peculiar Institution': On the Prison as Surrogate Ghetto," *Theoretical Criminology* 4, no. 3 (August 2000): 377–389, doi:10.1177/1362480600004003007.

21. For a critical review of the extensive body of research into collateral consequences in these areas, see: David S. Kirk and Sara Wakefield, "Collateral Consequences of Punishment: A Critical Review and Path Forward," *Annual Review of Criminology* 1, no. 1 (2018): 171–194, doi:10.1146/annurev-criminol-032317-092045.

22. For example, Andrea Cantora, "Navigating the Job Search after Incarceration: The Experiences of Work-Release Participants," *Criminal Justice Studies* 28, no. 2 (April 2015): 141–160, doi:10.1080/1478601X.2014.947032; Joe LaBriola, "Post-Prison Employment Quality and Future Criminal Justice Contact," *RSF: The Russell Sage Foundation Journal of the Social Sciences* 6, no. 1 (March 2020): 154–172, doi:10.7758/RSF.2020.6.1.07; Sandra Susan Smith and Jonathan Simon, "Exclusion and Extraction: Criminal Justice Contact and the Reallocation of Labor," *RSF: The Russell Sage Foundation Journal of*

the Social Sciences 6, no. 1 (March 2020): 1–27, doi:10.7758/RSF.2020.6.1.01; Amy Solomon et al., "From Prison to Work: The Employment Dimensions of Prisoner Reentry," Research Report, Reentry Roundtable (Washington, DC: Urban Institute, 2004), https://www.voced.edu.au/content/ngv:17453; John R. Sutton, "Imprisonment and Labor Market Outcomes: Evidence from 15 Affluent Western Democracies" (October 2002), http://www.antoniocasella. eu/nume/Sutton_2002.pdf; Cody Warner, Joshua Kaiser, and Jason N. Houle, "Locked Out of the Labor Market? State-Level Hidden Sentences and the Labor Market Outcomes of Recently Incarcerated Young Adults," *RSF: The Russell Sage Foundation Journal of the Social Sciences* 6, no. 1 (March 2020): 132–151, doi:10.7758/RSF.2020.6.1.06.

23. Richard Freeman, "Crime and the Employment of Disadvantaged Youth," in *Urban Labor Markets and Job Opportunity*, ed. George E. Peterson (Washington, DC: Urban Institute Press, 1992), 201–237; Bruce Western, *Homeward: Life in the Year After Prison: Life in the Year After Prison* (New York: Russell Sage Foundation, 2018); Bruce Western, Jeffrey R. Kling, and David F. Weiman, "The Labor Market Consequences of Incarceration," *Crime & Delinquency* 47, no. 3 (July 2001): 410–427, doi:10.1177/0011128701047003007; Western and Pettit, "Incarceration & Social Inequality."

24. Harry J. Holzer, "Collateral Costs: Effects of Incarceration on Employment and Earnings Among Young Workers," in *Do Prisons Make Us Safer? The Benefits and Costs of the Prison Boom*, eds. Steven Raphael and Michael A. Stoll (New York: Russell Sage Foundation, 2009), 239–266; Devah Pager, Bruce Western, and Bart Bonikowski, "Discrimination in a Low-Wage Labor Market: A Field Experiment," *American Sociological Review* 74, no. 5 (2009): 777–799; Becky Pettit and Christopher J. Lyons, "Incarceration and the Legitimate Labor Market: Examining Age-Graded Effects on Employment and Wages," *Law & Society Review* 43, no. 4 (2009): 725–756, doi:10.1111/j.1540-5893.2009.00387.x; Bruce Western and Katherine Beckett, "How Unregulated Is the U.S. Labor Market? The Penal System as a Labor Market Institution," *American Journal of Sociology* 104, no. 4 (January 1999): 1030–1060, doi:10.1086/210135. The formerly incarcerated may be actively discriminated against by employers during the hiring process: Roger Boshier and Derek Johnson, "Does Conviction Affect Employment Opportunities," *British Journal of Criminology* 14, no. 3 (1974): 264–268; Holzer, "Collateral Costs"; Devah Pager, *Marked: Race, Crime, and Finding Work in an Era of Mass Incarceration* (Chicago: University of Chicago Press, 2007); Monica Solinas-Saunders, Melissa J. Stacer, and Roger Guy, "Ex-Offender Barriers to Employment: Racial Disparities in Labor Markets with Asymmetric Information," *Journal of Crime and Justice* 38, no. 2 (April 2015): 249–269, doi:10.1080/0735648X.2013.870492. In many jurisdictions, ex-prisoners are even legally barred from employment in many industries: Margaret Love, Susan Kuzma, and Keith Waters, *Civil*

Disabilities of Convicted Felons: A State-by-State Survey (Washington, DC: U.S. Department of Justice, Office of the Pardon Attorney, 1996); Western, Kling, and Weiman, "The Labor Market Consequences of Incarceration." Prisoners often face limited opportunities for skill development or capital accumulation behind bars, which, when coupled with removal from formal labor market activity, may result in an erosion of marketable skills, social ties, and resources: Wakefield and Uggen, "Incarceration and Stratification"; Joel Waldfogel, "The Effect of Criminal Conviction on Income and the Trust 'Reposed in the Workmen,'" *The Journal of Human Resources* 29, no. 1 (1994): 62–81, doi:10.2307/146056; John Hagan, "The Social Embeddedness of Crime and Unemployment," *Criminology* 31, no. 4 (November 1993): 465–491, doi:10.1111/j.1745-9125.1993.tb01138.x.

25. Amanda Geller, Irwin Garfinkel, and Bruce Western, "The Effects of Incarceration on Employment and Wages: An Analysis of the Fragile Families Survey," *Center for Research on Child Wellbeing, Working Paper* 1 (2006): 2006; Pettit and Lyons, "Incarceration and the Legitimate Labor Market"; Pettit and Western, "Mass Imprisonment and the Life Course"; Wakefield and Uggen, "Incarceration and Stratification."

26. See Manuela Cunha, "The Ethnography of Prisons and Penal Confinement," *Annual Review of Anthropology* 43, no. 1 (October 2014): 217–233, doi:10.1146/annurev-anthro-102313-030349; Keramet Reiter, "Making Windows in Walls: Strategies for Prison Research," *Qualitative Inquiry* 20, no. 4 (April 2014): 417–428, doi:10.1177/1077800413515831; Loïc Wacquant, "The Curious Eclipse of Prison Ethnography in the Age of Mass Incarceration," *Ethnography* 3, no. 4 (December 2002): 371–397, doi:10.1177/1466138102003004012. As always, there remain some exceptions; c.f., Rachel Ellis, "Redemption and Reproach: Religion and Carceral Control in Action among Women in Prison," *Criminology* 58, no. 4 (2020): 747–772, doi:10.1111/1745-9125.12258; Philip Goodman, "Race in California's Prison Fire Camps for Men: Prison Politics, Space, and the Racialization of Everyday Life," *American Journal of Sociology* 120, no. 2 (September 2014): 352–394, doi:10.1086/678303; Lynne Haney, *Offending Women: Power, Punishment, and the Regulation of Desire* (Berkeley: University of California Press, 2010); John Irwin, *The Warehouse Prison: Disposal of the New Dangerous Class* (Oxford, UK: Oxford University Press, 2004); Jill McCorkel, *Breaking Women: Gender, Race, and the New Politics of Imprisonment* (New York: NYU Press, 2013).

27. Jeremy Travis, Bruce Western, and Steve Redburn, *The Growth of Incarceration in the United States: Exploring Causes and Consequences* (Washington, DC: National Academies Press, 2014), 354, https://academicworks.cuny.edu/jj_pubs/27/, emphasis added.

28. Wakefield and Uggen, "Incarceration and Stratification," 393–394. Other work reveals how the prison is shaped by a constellation of ties to outside actors and institutions: Todd Clear, *Imprisoning Communities: How Mass Incarceration*

Makes Disadvantaged Neighborhoods Worse (New York: Oxford University Press, 2007); Ben Crewe, *The Prisoner Society: Power, Adaptation and Social Life in an English Prison* (New York: Oxford University Press, 2009); Cunha, "The Ethnography of Prisons and Penal Confinement"; Loïc Wacquant, "Deadly Symbiosis: When Ghetto and Prison Meet and Mesh," *Punishment & Society* 3, no. 1 (January 2001): 95–133, doi:10.1177/14624740122228276. Here, again, labor is central, as Fabrice Guilbaud notes: "Though they [prisoners] have been removed from social life by judicial decision, they are nonetheless 'organically' linked to society by way of their productive labor." Guilbaud, "Working in Prison," 42.

29. Marie Gottschalk, "Cell Blocks & Red Ink: Mass Incarceration, the Great Recession & Penal Reform," *Daedalus* 139, no. 3 (July 2010): 62–73, doi:10.1162/DAED_a_00023; Mona Lynch, *Sunbelt Justice: Arizona and the Transformation of American Punishment* (Stanford, CA: Stanford Law Books, 2009).

30. Courtney A. Crittenden, Barbara A. Koons-Witt, and Robert J. Kaminski, "Being Assigned Work in Prison: Do Gender and Race Matter?," *Feminist Criminology* 13, no. 4 (October 2018): 359–381, doi:10.1177/1557085116668990.

31. While popular discussions of prison privatization focus largely on privately-run, for-profit facilities, these represent only a small fraction of prisons in the United States. Privatization today pervades the criminal justice system, such as through public-private contracts for services behind bars. See Jill McCorkel, "Banking on Rehab: Private Prison Vendors and the Reconfiguration of Mass Incarceration," *Studies in Law, Politics, and Society*, Studies in Law, Politics, and Society, 77 (January 2018): 49–67, doi:10.1108/S1059-433720180000077003.

32. See Arne Kalleberg, *Good Jobs, Bad Jobs: The Rise of Polarized and Precarious Employment Systems in the United States, 1970s–2000s* (New York: Russell Sage Foundation, 2011); David Marsden, *A Theory of Employment Systems: Micro-Foundations of Societal Diversity* (Oxford, UK: Oxford University Press, 1999); Paul Osterman, "Choice of Employment Systems in Internal Labor Markets," *Industrial Relations: A Journal of Economy and Society* 26, no. 1 (1987): 46–67, doi:10.1111/j.1468-232X.1987.tb00693.x.

33. Dario Melossi and Massimo Pavarini, *The Prison and the Factory: Origins of the Penitentiary System (40th Anniversary Edition)*, 2nd English Edition (Basingstoke, Hampshire: Palgrave Macmillan, 2018), 185.

34. Many policymakers throughout history have maintained that labor is useful for the "rehabilitation" of the imprisoned. Yet, the ability of labor or vocational programming to reduce recidivism (a metric of rehabilitation) has not been consistently empirically supported. See Kathleen E. Maguire, Timothy J. Flanagan, and Terence P. Thornberry, "Prison Labor and Recidivism," *Journal of Quantitative Criminology* 4, no. 1 (March 1988): 3–18, doi:10.1007/BF01066881.

35. With rare exceptions, Alabama, Arkansas, Florida, Georgia, and Texas do not pay the many prison laborers within their carceral institutions. Wendy

Sawyer, "How Much Do Incarcerated People Earn in Each State?," *Prison Policy Initiative* (2017), https://www.prisonpolicy.org/blog/2017/04/10/wages/.

36. Joshua Page and Joe Soss, "The Predatory Dimensions of Criminal Justice," *Science* 374, no. 6565 (October 2021): 291–294, doi:10.1126/science.abj7782.

37. Jonathan Simon, *Poor Discipline* (Chicago: University of Chicago Press, 1993), 39.

38. A. Roger Ekirch, *Bound for America: The Transportation of British Convicts to the Colonies, 1718–1775* (Oxford, UK: Clarendon Press, 1990); Michael Ignatieff, *A Just Measure of Pain: The Penitentiary in the Industrial Revolution, 1750–1850* (New York: Pantheon Books, 1978).

39. Michael Meranze, *Laboratories of Virtue: Punishment, Revolution, and Authority in Philadelphia, 1760–1835*, 2nd ed. (Chapel Hill, NC: University of North Carolina Press, 1996).

40. Mary Gibson, "Global Perspectives on the Birth of the Prison," *The American Historical Review* 116, no. 4 (October 2011): 1040–1063, doi:10.1086/ahr.116.4.1040; David J. Rothman, *The Discovery of the Asylum* (New Brunswick, NJ: Transaction Publishers, 1971).

41. Thomas Greenleaf, *Laws of the State of New York: Comprising the Constitution, and the Acts of the Legislature, since the Revolution, from the First to the Twentieth Session, Inclusive* (New York: Thomas Greenleaf, 1797).

42. Melossi and Pavarini, *The Prison and the Factory (40th Anniversary)*; Georg Rusche and Otto Kirchheimer, *Punishment and Social Structure*, 5th ed. (Piscataway, NJ: Transaction Publishers, 2009); Julia Floyd Smith, *Slavery and Plantation Growth in Antebellum Florida, 1821–1860* (Gainesville, FL: University Press of Florida, 1973).

43. Meranze, *Laboratories of Virtue*; Rothman, *The Discovery of the Asylum*.

44. Ashley T. Rubin, *The Deviant Prison: Philadelphia's Eastern State Penitentiary and the Origins of America's Modern Penal System, 1829–1913* (Cambridge, UK: Cambridge University Press, 2021); Judith Ryder, "Auburn State Prison," *Encyclopedia Britannica* (Springfield, MA: Merriam-Webster, 2013), https://www.britannica.com/topic/Auburn-State-Prison.

45. Rusche and Kirchheimer, *Punishment and Social Structure*.

46. Erin Hatton, "Working Behind Bars: Prison Labor in America," in *Labor and Punishment: Work in and Out of Prison* (Oakland, California: University of California Press, 2021), 17–50.

47. Michele Goodwin, "The Thirteenth Amendment: Modern Slavery, Capitalism, and Mass Incarceration," *Cornell Law Review* 104 (2018): 899–990.

48. Jennifer E. Cobbina, *Hands Up, Don't Shoot* (New York: NYU Press, 2019); Goodwin, "The Thirteenth Amendment."

49. Heather Ann Thompson, "Rethinking Working-Class Struggle through the Lens of the Carceral State: Toward a Labor History of Inmates and Guards," *Labor* 8, no. 3 (September 2011): 15–45, doi:10.1215/15476715-1275226.

50. Edward L. Ayers, *Vengeance and Justice: Crime and Punishment in the 19th Century American South* (New York: Oxford University Press, 1984); Alex Lichtenstein, *Twice the Work of Free Labor: The Political Economy of Convict Labor in the New South* (London: Verso, 1996).

51. Rebecca McLennan, *The Crisis of Imprisonment: Protest, Politics, and the Making of the American Penal State, 1776–1941* (Cambridge, UK: Cambridge University Press, 2008).

52. Blackmon, *Slavery by Another Name*.

53. Rusche and Kirchheimer, *Punishment and Social Structure*; Thompson, "Rethinking Working-Class Struggle through the Lens of the Carceral State."

54. Thompson, "Rethinking Working-Class Struggle through the Lens of the Carceral State"; Heather Ann Thompson, "The Prison Industrial Complex: A Growth Industry in a Shrinking Economy," *New Labor Forum* 21, no. 3 (October 2012): 39–47, doi:10.4179/NLF.213.0000006.

55. Mona Lynch, *Hard Bargains: The Coercive Power of Drug Laws in Federal Court* (New York: Russell Sage Foundation, 2016); Katherine Beckett and Megan Ming Francis, "The Origins of Mass Incarceration: The Racial Politics of Crime and Punishment in the Post–Civil Rights Era," *Annual Review of Law and Social Science* 16, no. 1 (2020): 433–452, doi:10.1146/annurev-lawsocsci-110819-100304.

56. U.S. Department of Justice, "Prison Industry Enhancement Certification Program" (1979); U.S. Department of Justice, "Justice Systems Improvement Act," *Pub. L. No. Public Law* 96–157 (1979), https://www.congress.gov/bill/96th-congress/senate-bill/241.

57. Dario Melossi, "Gazette of Morality and Social Whip: Punishment, Hegemony and the Case of the USA, 1970–92," *Social & Legal Studies* 2, no. 3 (September 1993): 259–279, doi:10.1177/096466399300200301.

58. Melossi, "Gazette of Morality and Social Whip." Moreover, mounting fear of so-called "street crime" spurred an emphasis on risk assessment in criminal justice. See Feeley and Simon, "The New Penology"; Jonathan Simon, *Governing Through Crime: How the War on Crime Transformed American Democracy and Created a Culture of Fear* (Oxford, UK: Oxford University Press, 2007).

59. Lawrence Mishel et al., *The State of Working America* (Ithaca, NY: Cornell University Press, 2012); Peter Gottschalk and Robert Moffitt, "The Rising Instability of U.S. Earnings," *Journal of Economic Perspectives* 23, no. 4 (December 2009): 3–24, doi:10.1257/jep.23.4.3.

60. Loïc Wacquant, "Class, Race & Hyperincarceration in Revanchist America," *Daedalus* 139, no. 3 (July 2010): 74–90, doi:10.1162/DAED_a_00024; Reuben Jonathan Miller, "Race, Hyper-Incarceration, and US Poverty Policy in Historic Perspective," *Sociology Compass* 7, no. 7 (2013): 573–589, doi:10.1111/soc4.12049.

61. Pfaff, *Locked In*.

62. Hewlett-Packard, McDonald's, Walmart, Cornell Corrections, Corrections Corporation of America, GEO Group, the American Legislative Exchange Council, and others invested heavily in these lobbying efforts. Thompson, "The Prison Industrial Complex."

63. Hadar Aviram, "The Correctional Hunger Games: Understanding Realignment in the Context of the Great Recession," *The ANNALS of the American Academy of Political and Social Science* 664, no. 1 (March 2016): 260–279, doi:10.1177/0002716215599938; Loïc Wacquant, "Crafting the Neoliberal State: Workfare, Prisonfare, and Social Insecurity," *Sociological Forum* 25, no. 2 (2010): 197–220, doi:10.1111/j.1573-7861.2010.01173.x.

64. Tracey Kyckelhahn, "State Corrections Expenditures, FY 1982–2010" (Washington, DC: Bureau of Justice Statistics, 2012); Hadar Aviram, *Cheap on Crime: Recession-Era Politics and the Transformation of American Punishment* (Berkeley, CA: University of California Press, 2015); Lynch, *Sunbelt Justice*.

65. Rachel Ellis, "Prison Labor in a Pandemic," *Contexts* 19, no. 4 (November 2020): 90–91, doi:10.1177/1536504220977950.

66. Stephan, "Census of State and Federal Correctional Facilities, 2005."

67. See Frederic L. Pryor, "Industries Behind Bars: An Economic Perspective on the Production of Goods and Services by U.S. Prison Industries," *Review of Industrial Organization* 27, no. 1 (August 2005): 1–16, doi:10.1007/s11151-005-4401-3. Although most prisoners engage in work for the carceral facility or the state, a subset engage work that falls under public-private partnerships between the state and private firms. See Kelley Davidson, "'The Insourcing of Prison Labor': Seven US Corporate Household Names Use Prison Labor to Produce Their Goods," *The Centre for Research on Globalization* (November 2015), https://www.globalresearch.ca/the-insourcing-of-prison-labor-seven-us-corporate-household-names-use-prison-labor-to-produce-their-goods/5492033?print=1.

68. Philip Goodman, "'Another Second Chance': Rethinking Rehabilitation through the Lens of California's Prison Fire Camps," *Social Problems* 59, no. 4 (2012): 437–458; Philip Goodman, "Hero and Inmate: Work, Prisons, and Punishment in California's Fire Camps," *The Journal of Labor & Society* 15, no. 3 (2012): 353–376; Haney, *Offending Women*; Erin Hatton, "When Work Is Punishment: Penal Subjectivities in Punitive Labor Regimes," *Punishment & Society* 20, no. 2 (April 2018): 174–191, doi:10.1177/1462474517690001; Solomon et al., "From Prison to Work: The Employment Dimensions of Prisoner Reentry"; Stephan, "Census of State and Federal Correctional Facilities, 2005."

69. Noah D. Zatz, "Working at the Boundaries of Markets: Prison Labor and the Economic Dimension of Employment Relationships," *Vanderbilt Law Review* 61 (2008): 857–958; Noah D. Zatz, "Prison Labor and the Paradox of Paid Nonmarket Work," in *Economic Sociology of Work*, ed. Nina Bandelj, vol. 18,

Research in the Sociology of Work (Bingley, UK: Emerald Group Publishing Limited, 2009), 369–398, doi:10.1108/S0277-2833(2009)0000018017; Erin Hatton, *Coerced: Work Under Threat of Punishment* (Berkeley, CA: University of California Press, 2020).

70. Benns, "American Slavery, Reinvented," 4.

71. Rob Atkinson and Knut A. Rostad, "Can Inmates Become an Integral Part of the U.S. Workforce?" *Research Report, Urban Institute Reentry Roundtable* (Washington, DC: Urban Institute, 2003), doi:10.1037/e717792011-001.

72. This is true regardless of benefit status upon incarceration. See Social Security Administration, "What Prisoners Need To Know" (Washington, DC: US Government Printing Office, 2010).

73. Sawyer, "How Much Do Incarcerated People Earn in Each State?"

74. Kim Shayo Buchanan, "It Could Happen to You: Pay-to-Stay Jail Upgrades," *Michigan Law Review First Impressions* 106 (2007): 60–66; Frances T. Gipson and Elizabeth A. Pierce, "Current Trends in State Inmate User Fee Programs for Health Services," *Journal of Correctional Health Care* 3, no. 2 (October 1996): 159–178, doi:10.1177/107834589600300205; Gottschalk, "Cell Blocks & Red Ink"; Steven J. Jackson, "Mapping the Prison Telephone Industry," in *Prison Profiteers: Who Makes Money from Mass Incarceration*, eds. Tara Herivel and Paul Wright (New York: The New Press, 2007), 235–248; Kirsten D. Levingston, "Making the Bad Guy Pay: Growing Use of Cost Shifting as an Economic Sanction," in *Prison Profiteers: Who Makes Money from Mass Incarceration*, eds. Tara Herivel and Paul Wright (New York: The New Press, 2007), 52–79; Lynch, *Sunbelt Justice*; Amy B. Smoyer and Giza Lopes, "Hungry on the Inside: Prison Food as Concrete and Symbolic Punishment in a Women's Prison," *Punishment & Society* 19, no. 2 (April 2017): 240–255, doi:10.1177/1462474516665605; Paul Von Zielbauer, "Private Health Care in Jails Can Be a Death Sentence," in *Prison Profiteers: Who Makes Money from Mass Incarceration*, eds. Tara Herivel and Paul Wright (New York: The New Press, 2009), 204–227.

75. Thomas Biebricher, *The Political Theory of Neoliberalism* (Redwood City, CA: Stanford University Press, 2019).

76. Aviram, "The Correctional Hunger Games"; Kyckelhahn, "State Corrections Expenditures, FY 1982–2010."

77. Hadar Aviram, "Humonetarianism: The New Correctional Discourse of Scarcity," *Hastings Race and Poverty Law Journal* 7, no. 1 (2010): 1–52; Buchanan, "It Could Happen to You"; Wacquant, "Crafting the Neoliberal State"; Weiss, " 'Repatriating' Low-Wage Work."

78. Aviram, *Cheap on Crime*.

79. Aviram; Bernard E. Harcourt, "Neoliberal Penality: A Brief Genealogy," *Theoretical Criminology* 14, no. 1 (February 2010): 74–92, doi:10.1177/1362480609352785; Loïc Wacquant, *Punishing the Poor: The Neoliberal Government of Social Insecurity* (Durham, NC: Duke University Press, 2009).

80. Wacquant, *Punishing the Poor*, 162.

81. Nicola Lacey, "Punishment, (Neo)Liberalism and Social Democracy," in *The SAGE Handbook of Punishment and Society*, eds. Jonathan Simon and Richard Sparks (London: SAGE, 2013), 260–280; Melossi and Pavarini, *The Prison and the Factory (40th Anniversary)*; Georg Rusche, "Labor Market and Penal Sanction: Thoughts on the Sociology of Criminal Justice," trans. Gerda Dinwiddie, *Crime and Social Justice*, no. 10 (1978–1933): 2–8; Rusche and Kirchheimer, *Punishment and Social Structure*.

82. Several prominent scholars emphasize the role of schools to these ends: Pierre Bourdieu and Jean-Claude Passeron, *Reproduction in Education, Society and Culture*, trans. Richard Nice, 2nd ed. (London: Sage Publications, 1990); Mitchell L. Stevens, Elizabeth A. Armstrong, and Richard Arum, "Sieve, Incubator, Temple, Hub: Empirical and Theoretical Advances in the Sociology of Higher Education," *Annual Review of Sociology* 34, no. 1 (2008): 127–151, doi:10.1146/annurev.soc.34.040507.134737; Paul Willis, *Learning to Labor: How Working Class Kids Get Working Class Jobs* (New York: Columbia University Press, 1977).

83. Pierre Bourdieu, *The Field of Cultural Production* (New York: Columbia University Press, 1993).

84. Jeffrey J. Sallaz and Jane Zavisca, "Bourdieu in American Sociology, 1980–2004," *Annual Review of Sociology* 33, no. 1 (2007): 23, doi:10.1146/annurev.soc.33.040406.131627.

85. See Pierre Bourdieu, *The Social Structures of the Economy* (Cambridge, UK: Polity, 2005).

86. Bourdieu, 195.

87. Peter M. Blau and Otis Dudley Duncan, *The American Occupational Structure* (New York: John Wiley & Sons Inc, 1967).

88. Willis, *Learning to Labor*.

89. Pierre Bourdieu, *The State Nobility: Elite Schools in the Field of Power* (Redwood City, CA: Stanford University Press, 1996).

90. Western and Beckett, "How Unregulated Is the U.S. Labor Market?"

91. In broad terms, "labor process" refers to the means by which labor power (or workers' capacity to work, commodified) is turned into actual productive activity. The labor process *perspective* focuses especially on the relational component of the labor process, or the social relations into which actors enter as part of the production process: Chris Smith, "The Short Overview of the Labour Process Perspective and History of the International Labour Process Conference," in *International Labour Process Conference, Leeds* (Leeds, UK: International Labour Process Conference, 2012). For a broader introduction to labor process theory, see Karl Marx, *Capital: Volume One*, ed. Friedrich Engels, trans. Samuel Moore and Edward Aveling (Mineola, NY: Dover Publications, Inc., 2019).

92. Michael Burawoy, *Manufacturing Consent: Changes in the Labor Process under Monopoly Capitalism* (Chicago: University of Chicago Press, 1979); Michael Burawoy, "Between the Labor Process and the State: The Changing Face of Factory Regimes under Advanced Capitalism," *American Sociological Review* 48, no. 5 (1983): 587–605; Michael Burawoy, *The Politics of Production: Factory Regimes under Capitalism and Socialism* (New York: Verso Books, 1985). Burawoy advances prior scholarship, e.g., Harry Braverman, *Labor and Monopoly Capital: The Degradation of Work in the Twentieth Century* (New York: Monthly Review Press, 1974); Donald F. Roy, "'Banana Time': Job Satisfaction and Informal Interaction," *Human Organization* 18, no. 4 (1959): 158–168. He also draws on insights from Antonio Gramsci to conceptualize the control of the laboring classes: Antonio Gramsci, *Selections from the Prison Notebooks*, trans. Quintin Hoare and Geoffrey Nowell Smith (New York: International Publishers, 1971).

93. Burawoy, *Manufacturing Consent*; Jeffrey J. Sallaz, "Permanent Pedagogy: How Post-Fordist Firms Generate Effort but Not Consent," *Work and Occupations* 42, no. 1 (February 2015): 3–34, doi:10.1177/0730888414551207; Ofer Sharone, *Flawed System/Flawed Self: Job Searching and Unemployment Experiences* (Chicago: University of Chicago Press, 2014).

94. Candace Kruttschnitt et al., "Bringing Women's Carceral Experiences into the 'New Punitiveness' Fray," *Justice Quarterly* 30, no. 1 (February 2013): 18–43, doi:10.1080/07418825.2011.603698; Candace Kruttschnitt and Rosemary Gartner, "Women's Imprisonment," *Crime and Justice* 30 (January 2003): 1–81, doi:10.1086/652228; Jill McCorkel, "Embodied Surveillance And The Gendering Of Punishment," *Journal of Contemporary Ethnography* 32, no. 1 (February 2003): 41–76, doi:10.1177/0891241602238938; Alison Liebling, "A New 'Ecology of Cruelty'? The Changing Shape of Maximum-Security Custody in England and Wales," in *Extreme Punishment*, eds. Keramet Reiter and Alexa Koenig (New York: Palgrave Macmillan, 2015), 91–114; Keramet Reiter, *23/7: Pelican Bay Prison and the Rise of Long-Term Solitary Confinement* (New Haven, CT: Yale University Press, 2016).

95. The technical functions of institutions like this "effectively disguise their social function as agents of ritual exclusion": Bourdieu, *The State Nobility*, 73.

96. Philip Goodman, "'It's Just Black, White, or Hispanic': An Observational Study of Racializing Moves in California's Segregated Prison Reception Centers," *Law & Society Review* 42, no. 4 (2008): 739, doi:10.1111/j.1540-5893.2008.00357.x; Michael L. Walker, "Race Making in a Penal Institution," *American Journal of Sociology* 121, no. 4 (January 2016): 1051–1078, doi:10.1086/684033.

97. Such phenomena can be observed across diverse organizations: Victor Ray, "A Theory of Racialized Organizations," *American Sociological Review* 84, no. 1 (February 2019): 26–53, doi:10.1177/0003122418822335.

98. As with other institutional details, reported wages have been modified for purposes of confidentiality. The lowest hourly wage ($0.09) was generated by calculating the average of the lowest-paid prison jobs of each state in the Sunbelt region (discounting states that pay no wages and wages for correctional industries jobs). The highest hourly wage ($2.34) was generated by calculating the average of the highest-paying prison jobs in each state paying over $1. I limited this calculation to only those paying over $1 hourly because I have reported in prior publications that the SSP call center pays over this; additionally, the approximated wage this produces is comparable to the actual pay scale of SSP, so that the gap between the lowest and highest paid prisoners is maintained. Data used to make these calculations were drawn from Sawyer, "How Much Do Incarcerated People Earn in Each State?"

99. Although I do not adopt the language of "games" here, the strategies of penal laborers might be conceptualized in this way. Work games "emerge historically out of struggle and bargaining, but they are played within limits" set by workplace structure. Burawoy, *Manufacturing Consent*, 80.

100. Erving Goffman, *Asylums* (New York: Anchor Books, 1961), 171.

Chapter 2

1. Kalleberg, *Good Jobs, Bad Jobs*; Marsden, *A Theory of Employment Systems*; Osterman, "Choice of Employment Systems in Internal Labor Markets."

2. Michael Gibson-Light, "Classification Struggles in Semi-Formal and Precarious Work: Lessons from Inmate Labor and Cultural Production," *Research in the Sociology of Work* 31 (2017): 61–89, https://doi.org/10.1108/S0277-283320170000031002; Zatz, "Working at the Boundaries of Markets: Prison Labor and the Economic Dimension of Employment Relationships"; Zatz, "Prison Labor and the Paradox of Paid Nonmarket Work."

3. Some were exempted from work assignments at SSP. This included those participating in education classes that took place during work hours. This was commonly remedial education and high school-equivalency instruction. The rest were largely those who had been classified as physically or mentally unfit for work or deemed too great a security threat (e.g., those labeled "flight risks" because of prior escape attempts).

4. Western and Beckett, "How Unregulated Is the U.S. Labor Market?"; Western and Pettit, "Incarceration & Social Inequality."

5. The notion of the prison as "a city" and related metaphors were common. Another staffer would say: "It's a *monster* in here! It's basically its own city." Similarly, one incarcerated worker referred to the prison as a distinct "biosphere." Another saw it as a sinister "empire." Many would refer to the institution as a "giant warehouse"—sometimes as a site of labor, other times in

the sense of storing bodies, with one going so far as to paint it as a "human cube farm."

6. John M. Eason, *Big House on the Prairie: Rise of the Rural Ghetto and Prison Proliferation* (Chicago: University of Chicago Press, 2017). For a discussion of the complex visibility of prisoners' labor, see Lindsey Raisa Feldman, "Anti-Heroes, Wildfire, and the Complex Visibility of Prison Labor," *Crime, Media, Culture* 16, no. 2 (2020), 221–238, doi:10.1177/1741659019865309.

7. Kalleberg, *Good Jobs, Bad Jobs*.

8. Benns, "American Slavery, Reinvented"; Blackmon, *Slavery by Another Name*.

9. As noted, wages reported here have been slightly altered to protect institutional anonymity.

10. See, e.g., Levingston, "Making the Bad Guy Pay."

11. My usage of these and related terms throughout reflects institutional classifications only and is not a statement on the talents and capabilities of workers themselves.

12. Gottschalk, "Cell Blocks & Red Ink"; Lynch, *Sunbelt Justice*.

13. Kate Mulholland, "Workplace Resistance in an Irish Call Centre: Slammin', Scammin' Smokin' an' Leavin'," *Work, Employment and Society* 18, no. 4 (December 2004): 709–724, doi:10.1177/0950017004048691; Jeffrey J. Sallaz, *Lives on the Line: How the Philippines Became the World's Call Center Capital* (New York: Oxford University Press, 2019).

14. For example, Tracy F. H. Chang and Douglas E. Thompkins, "Corporations Go to Prisons: The Expansion of Corporate Power in the Correctional Industry," *Labor Studies Journal* 27, no. 1 (March 2002): 45–69, doi:10.1177/0160449X0202700104; Josh Eidelson, "Are Private Prison Companies Using Forced Labor?," *Bloomberg.com* (November 8, 2017), https://www.bloomb erg.com/news/articles/2017-11-08/are-private-prisons-using-forced-labor; Annie McGrew and Angela Hanks, "It's Time to Stop Using Our Mass Incarceration System for Free Labor," *Moyers.com* (October 2017), https:// billmoyers.com/story/time-stop-using-mass-incarceration-system-free-labor/.

15. Rachel Kushner, "Is Prison Necessary? Ruth Wilson Gilmore Might Change Your Mind," *The New York Times* (April 2019): sec. Magazine, https://www.nytimes.com/2019/04/17/magazine/prison-abolition-ruth-wilson-gilmore.html; See also, McCorkel, "Banking on Rehab"; Richard Harding, *Private Prisons and Public Accountability* (New York: Routledge, 2018), doi:10.4324/9781351308045; Brad W. Lundahl et al., "Prison Privatization: A Meta-Analysis of Cost and Quality of Confinement Indicators," *Research on Social Work Practice* 19, no. 4 (July 2009): 383–394, doi:10.1177/1049731509331946; David Shichor, *Punishment for Profit: Private Prisons/Public Concerns* (Thousand Oaks, CA: SAGE Publications, Inc, 1995).

16. For example, Asatar Bair, *Prison Labor in the United States: An Economic Analysis* (Oxfordshire, UK: Routledge, 2007), doi:10.4324/9780203933985; James B. Jacobs, *Stateville: The Penitentiary in Mass Society* (Chicago: University of Chicago Press, 1977); Maguire, Flanagan, and Thornberry, "Prison Labor and Recidivism"; David B. Wilson, Catherine A. Gallagher, and Doris L. MacKenzie, "A Meta-Analysis of Corrections-Based Education, Vocation, and Work Programs for Adult Offenders," *Journal of Research in Crime and Delinquency* 37, no. 4 (2000): 347–368, doi:10.1177/0022427800037004001.
17. Stephan, "Census of State and Federal Correctional Facilities, 2005."
18. Leonardo Antenangeli and Matthew Durose, *Recidivism of Prisoners Released in 24 States in 2008: A 10-Year Follow-Up Period (2008–2018)* (Washington, DC: Bureau of Justice Statistics, 2021).
19. Shawn D. Bushway, Michael A. Stoll, and David Weiman, *Barriers to Reentry? The Labor Market for Released Prisoners in Post-Industrial America* (New York: Russell Sage Foundation, 2007); Pager, Western, and Bonikowski, "Discrimination in a Low-Wage Labor Market: A Field Experiment"; Western, *Homeward.*
20. Thompson, "The Prison Industrial Complex," 43.

Chapter 3

1. Western, *Punishment and Inequality in America*, 198.
2. Richard Arum and Gary LaFree, "Educational Attainment, Teacher-Student Ratios, and the Risk of Adult Incarceration Among U.S. Birth Cohorts Since 1910," *Sociology of Education* 81, no. 4 (October 2008): 397–421, doi:10.1177/003804070808100404; Pettit and Western, "Mass Imprisonment and the Life Course"; Western, Kling, and Weiman, "The Labor Market Consequences of Incarceration."
3. Other scholars have employed Bourdieu's concepts to examine the prison. His notion of the "bureaucratic field" has been deployed to help explain the development of the carceral state in the neoliberal era: Wacquant, "Crafting the Neoliberal State." Others draw on a Bourdieusian framework to sketch the broader "penal field": Joshua Page, *The Toughest Beat: Politics, Punishment, and the Prison Officers Union in California* (Oxford, UK: Oxford University Press, 2011); Philip Goodman, Joshua Page, and Michelle S. Phelps, *Breaking the Pendulum: The Long Struggle Over Criminal Justice* (New York: Oxford University Press, 2017). The prison's functions have similarly been situated in a "field of power," or the social space in which political or other forms of power are situated: Loïc Wacquant, "Bourdieu, Foucault, and the Penal State in the Neoliberal Era," in *Foucault and Neoliberalism*, eds. Daniel Zamora and Michael Behrent (Cambridge, UK: Polity, 2016), 124–143. Finally, Bourdieu's concept of

"doxa" has been drawn on to illuminate societal acceptance of punitive ideals as natural and valid: Jennifer A. Schlosser, "Bourdieu and Foucault: A Conceptual Integration Toward an Empirical Sociology of Prisons," *Critical Criminology* 21, no. 1 (March 2013): 31–46, doi:10.1007/s10612-012-9164-1.

4. Bourdieu, *The State Nobility*, 73. Other scholars identify related sorting processes in less elite school settings; for example, Elizabeth A. Armstrong and Laura T. Hamilton, *Paying for the Party* (Cambridge, MA: Harvard University Press, 2013); Willis, *Learning to Labor*.

5. Pierre Bourdieu, *Outline of a Theory of Practice*, trans. Richard Nice (Cambridge, UK: Cambridge University Press, 1977); Bourdieu, *The Social Structures of the Economy*. Different field positions enable different opportunities for action or mobility. Joshua Page applies this conceptual framework to map the "penal field," or "the social space in which agents struggle to accumulate and employ penal capital—that is, the legitimate authority to determine penal policies and priorities": Page, *The Toughest Beat*, 10.

6. For a summary of this and related concepts, see Sallaz and Zavisca, "Bourdieu in American Sociology, 1980–2004."

7. Sallaz and Zavisca, "Bourdieu in American Sociology, 1980–2004," 23.

8. Hatton, "When Work Is Punishment."

9. Gottschalk, "Cell Blocks & Red Ink"; Wacquant, *Punishing the Poor*.

10. For example, Annika Fredrikson, "Vocational Training in Prisons Can Fill Industry Gaps," *Christian Science Monitor* (September 2015), https://www.csmonitor.com/Business/2015/0908/Vocational-training-in-prisons-can-fill-industry-gaps; Sarah Shemkus, "Beyond Cheap Labor: Can Prison Work Programs Benefit Inmates?," *The Guardian* (December 2015): sec. Guardian Sustainable Business, https://www.theguardian.com/sustainable-business/2015/dec/09/prison-work-program-ohsa-whole-foods-inmate-labor-incarceration.

11. For example, Lucius Coulete and Daniel Kopf, "Out of Prison & Out of Work" (Northampton, MA: Prison Policy Initiative, 2018), https://www.prisonpolicy.org/reports/outofwork.html; Pager, Western, and Bonikowski, "Discrimination in a Low-Wage Labor Market: A Field Experiment." Further, empirical studies suggest that the impacts of vocational programming on recidivism—that is, prison labor's ability to reduce the likelihood of felony re-arrest—are largely insignificant: Maguire, Flanagan, and Thornberry, "Prison Labor and Recidivism." Instead, penal science suggests that imprisonment may have "iatrogenic" effects, meaning that even if its use is intended to do social good, it nevertheless has profoundly negative outcomes, worsening the very problems it seeks to solve: Francis T. Cullen, Cheryl Lero Jonson, and Daniel S. Nagin, "Prisons Do Not Reduce Recidivism: The High Cost of Ignoring Science," *The Prison Journal* 91, no. 3 suppl (September 2011): 48S–65S, doi:10.1177/0032885511415224.

12. Pierre Bourdieu, *Language and Symbolic Power* (Cambridge, UK: Blackwell Publishers, 1992); Bourdieu and Passeron, *Reproduction in Education, Society and Culture*.

13. Wakefield and Uggen, "Incarceration and Stratification."

14. H. Samy Alim, John R. Rickford, and Arnetha F. Ball, eds., *Raciolinguistics: How Language Shapes Our Ideas About Race* (New York: Oxford University Press, 2016), 27.

15. Karen Chapple, "Networks to Nerdistan: The Role of Labor Market Intermediaries in the Entry-Level IT Labor Market," *International Journal of Urban and Regional Research* 30, no. 3 (2006): 559, doi:10.1111/j.1468-2427.2006.00674.x.

16. Pierre Bourdieu and Loïc Wacquant, *An Invitation to Reflexive Sociology* (Chicago: University of Chicago Press, 1992); Ray May Hsung, Nan Lin, and Ronald L. Breiger, *Contexts of Social Capital: Social Networks in Markets, Communities and Families* (Oxfordshire, UK: Routledge Taylor & Francis Group, 2009), doi:10.4324/9780203890097.

17. Mark Granovetter, *Getting a Job: A Study of Contacts and Careers* (Chicago: University of Chicago Press, 1974).

18. For example, Gottschalk, "Cell Blocks & Red Ink"; Wacquant, *Punishing the Poor*.

19. For example, Benns, "American Slavery, Reinvented"; Brown and Severson, "Enlisting Prison Labor to Close Budget Gaps"; Fredrikson, "Vocational Training in Prisons Can Fill Industry Gaps"; Shemkus, "Beyond Cheap Labor."

20. Arum and LaFree, "Educational Attainment, Teacher–Student Ratios, and the Risk of Adult Incarceration Among U.S. Birth Cohorts Since 1910"; Pettit and Western, "Mass Imprisonment and the Life Course"; Wakefield and Uggen, "Incarceration and Stratification."

21. Bourdieu, *The State Nobility*.

22. Bourdieu, *The State Nobility*, 73.

23. Western and Pettit, "Incarceration & Social Inequality."

24. For example, Michael Rocque and Quincy Snellings, "The New Disciplinology: Research, Theory, and Remaining Puzzles on the School-to-Prison Pipeline," *Journal of Criminal Justice* 59 (November 2018): 3–11, doi:10.1016/j.jcrimjus.2017.05.002.

25. David S. Pedulla and Devah Pager, "Race and Networks in the Job Search Process," *American Sociological Review* 84, no. 6 (November 2019): 983–1012, doi:10.1177/0003122419883255.

Chapter 4

1. Goodman, "Race in California's Prison Fire Camps for Men," 354.

2. Goodman, "'It's Just Black, White, or Hispanic,'" 739. For examination of race within jails, see, Walker, "Race Making in a Penal Institution."

3. Wacquant, "The New 'Peculiar Institution,'" 385. See also: Wacquant, *Prisons of Poverty*.

4. For example, Wakefield and Uggen, "Incarceration and Stratification"; Western and Pettit, "Incarceration & Social Inequality." Disadvantages intersecting with gender are also apparent, such as in the rise of black female imprisonment: Mark G. Harmon and Breanna Boppre, "Women of Color and the War on Crime: An Explanation for the Rise in Black Female Imprisonment," *Journal of Ethnicity in Criminal Justice* 16, no. 4 (October 2018): 309–332, doi:10.1080/15377938.2015.1052173.

5. Erin Hatton, "'Either You Do It or You're Going to the Box': Coerced Labor in Contemporary America," *Critical Sociology* 45, no. 6 (September 2019): 910, doi:10.1177/0896920518763929.

6. Walker, "Race Making in a Penal Institution," 1052.

7. For example, Emilio J. Castilla, "Gender, Race, and Meritocracy in Organizational Careers," *American Journal of Sociology* 113, no. 6 (May 2008): 1479–1526, doi:10.1086/588738.

8. Joan Acker, "Hierarchies, Jobs, Bodies: A Theory of Gendered Organizations," *Gender & Society* 4, no. 2 (June 1990): 139–158, doi:10.1177/089124390004002002.

9. Deirdre A. Royster, *Race and the Invisible Hand: How White Networks Exclude Black Men from Blue-Collar Jobs* (Berkeley: University of California Press, 2003).

10. Royster, 113.

11. Marta María Maldonado, "Racial Triangulation of Latino/a Workers by Agricultural Employers," *Human Organization* 65, no. 4 (Winter 2006): 353–361, http://dx.doi.org/10.17730/humo.65.4.a84b5xykr0dvp91l.

12. Curtis K. Chan and Michel Anteby, "Task Segregation as a Mechanism for Within-Job Inequality: Women and Men of the Transportation Security Administration," *Administrative Science Quarterly* 61, no. 2 (June 2016): 184–216, doi:10.1177/0001839215611447; Barbara F. Reskin and Patricia A. Roos, *Job Queues, Gender Queues: Explaining Women's Inroads into Male Occupations* (Philadelphia: Temple University Press, 1990).

13. Maldonado, "Racial Triangulation of Latino/a Workers by Agricultural Employers," 353.

14. Ray, "A Theory of Racialized Organizations," 27.

15. See, Goodman, "'It's Just Black, White, or Hispanic.'" Michael Walker examines related race-making processes in a U.S. jail: Walker, "Race Making in a Penal Institution."

16. Barbara F. Reskin, "The Proximate Causes of Employment Discrimination," *Contemporary Sociology* 29, no. 2 (2000): 319–328, doi:10.2307/2654387.

17. Racialized and gendered segregation occurs, for instance, through how tasks are assigned amongst correctional officers: Dana M. Britton, *At Work in the Iron Cage: The Prison as Gendered Organization* (New York: NYU Press, 2003). This is also evident in how jobs are assigned amongst female prisoners: Sheryl J. Grana, *Women and Justice* (Lanham, MD: Rowman & Littlefield, 2010); Sarah Haley, *No Mercy Here: Gender, Punishment, and the Making of Jim Crow Modernity* (Chapel Hill, NC: University of North Carolina Press, 2016); Crittenden, Koons-Witt, and Kaminski, "Being Assigned Work in Prison."

18. Ray, "A Theory of Racialized Organizations."

19. As Goodman reveals, this declaration of race is an iterative process between prisoners and staffers during intake rituals. See: Goodman, "'It's Just Black, White, or Hispanic.'" I was unable to observe these proceedings at SSP firsthand.

20. Prisoners themselves almost exclusively identified by these declared ethnoracial identities. For this reason, my own "coding" of the race and ethnicity of participants mostly adhered to these declarations. Exceptions include those who self-identified by categories other than their color-coded institutional designation. The primary example of this was individuals identifying as "mixed race."

21. Crittenden, Koons-Witt, and Kaminski, "Being Assigned Work in Prison."

22. Andreas Wimmer, "The Making and Unmaking of Ethnic Boundaries: A Multilevel Process Theory," *American Journal of Sociology* 113, no. 4 (January 2008): 970–1022, doi:10.1086/522803.

23. David Skarbek, *The Social Order of the Underworld: How Prison Gangs Govern the American Penal System* (Oxford, UK: Oxford University Press, 2014), 79.

24. Such allowances are common. See Skarbek, *The Social Order of the Underworld*.

25. Claire Jean Kim, "The Racial Triangulation of Asian Americans," *Politics & Society* 27, no. 1 (1999): 105–138.

26. Maldonado, "Racial Triangulation of Latino/a Workers by Agricultural Employers," 355; see also Marta Maria Maldonado, "'It Is Their Nature to Do Menial Labour': The Racialization of 'Latino/a Workers' by Agricultural Employers," *Ethnic and Racial Studies* 32, no. 6 (July 2009): 1017–1036, doi:10.1080/01419870902802254.

27. Maldonado, "Racial Triangulation of Latino/a Workers by Agricultural Employers."

28. Smith and Hattery, "Incarceration"; Wacquant, "The New 'Peculiar Institution.'"

29. Pager, *Marked*.

30. Sarah Esther Lageson, Mike Vuolo, and Christopher Uggen, "Legal Ambiguity in Managerial Assessments of Criminal Records," *Law & Social Inquiry* 40, no. 1 (2015): 175–204, doi:10.1111/lsi.12066; Mike Vuolo, Sarah Lageson, and Christopher Uggen, "Criminal Record Questions in the Era of 'Ban the Box,'" *Criminology & Public Policy* 16, no. 1 (2017): 139–165, doi:10.1111/1745-9133.12250.

31. Ray, "A Theory of Racialized Organizations."
32. Pierre Bourdieu, *Pascalian Meditations*, trans. Richard Nice (Redwood City, CA: Stanford University Press, 2000).
33. Some have referred to whiteness as a form of "racist symbolic capital" along these lines: Anja Weiß, "Racist Symbolic Capital: A Bourdieuian Approach to the Analysis of Racism," in *Wages of Whiteness & Racist Symbolic Capital*, eds. Wulf D. Hund, Jeremy Krikler, and David R. Roediger (Berlin, Germany: Lit Verlag, 2010), 37–56.
34. For example, Royster, *Race and the Invisible Hand*.
35. See W. E. B. Du Bois, *The Souls of Black Folk* (Scotts Valley, CA: CreateSpace Independent Publishing Platform, 2014).

Chapter 5

1. Kirk and Wakefield, "Collateral Consequences of Punishment." See also Seiter and Kadela, "Prisoner Reentry"; Jeremy Travis and Christy Visher, "Prisoner Reentry and the Pathways to Adulthood: Policy Perspectives," in *On Your Own without a Net: The Transition to Adulthood for Vulnerable Populations*, eds. D. Wayne Osgood et al. (Chicago: University of Chicago Press, 2005), 145–177.
2. Josh Seim suggests that priorities may evolve as prisoners approach release dates: Josh Seim, "Short-Timing: The Carceral Experience of Soon-to-Be-Released Prisoners," *Punishment & Society* 18, no. 4 (October 2016): 442–458, doi:10.1177/1462474516641377.
3. Criminal justice predation occurs both behind and beyond bars: Laurie L. Levenson and Mary Gordon, "The Dirty Little Secrets about Pay-to-Stay," *Michigan Law Review First Impressions* 106 (2007): 67–70; Joshua Page and Joe Soss, "The Predatory Dimensions of Criminal Justice," *Science* 374, no. 6565 (October 2021): 291–294, doi:10.1126/science.abj7782.
4. Hardy Green, *The Company Town: The Industrial Edens and Satanic Mills That Shaped the American Economy* (New York: Basic Books, 2010).
5. Zatz, "Prison Labor and the Paradox of Paid Nonmarket Work."
6. Pryor, "Industries Behind Bars."
7. Sawyer, "How Much Do Incarcerated People Earn in Each State?" Most states do pay *some* prison wages. Alabama, Arkansas, Florida, Georgia, and Texas are exceptions that provide no compensation for most penal labor.
8. As previously discussed, these reported wages are approximations that have been slightly adjusted as part of confidentiality procedures designed to help protect the identity of institutional actors.
9. Wakefield and Uggen, "Incarceration and Stratification."

10. Stephen Raher, "Paging Anti-Trust Lawyers: Prison Commissary Giants Prepare to Merge," *Prison Policy Initiative* (blog) (July 2016), https://www.priso npolicy.org/blog/2016/07/05/commissary-merger/.

11. Stephen Raher, "The Company Store," *Prison Policy Initiative* (blog) (May 2018), https://www.prisonpolicy.org/reports/commissary.html.

12. Alysia Santo and Andy Rossback, "What's in a Prison Meal?," *The Marshall Project* (July 2015), https://www.themarshallproject.org/2015/07/07/what-s-in-a-prison-meal.

13. Beth Schwartzapfel, "How Bad Is Prison Health Care? Depends on Who's Watching," *The Marshall Project* (February 2018), https://www.themarshall project.org/2018/02/25/how-bad-is-prison-health-care-depends-on-who-s-watching. Much like emergency medical care in the outside world, treatment is administered regardless of ability to pay, but those unable to pay may incur debt to the institution for associated fees.

14. Jackson, "Mapping the Prison Telephone Industry."

15. Wendy Sawyer, "Why Expensive Phone Calls Can Be Life-Altering for People in Jail—and Can Derail the Justice Process," *Prisonpolicy.org* (2019), https://www.prisonpolicy.org/blog/2019/02/05/jail-phone-calls/.

16. For more on the difficulty this can cause for freshly-released individuals, see Michael Gibson-Light and Josh Seim, "Punishing Fieldwork: Penal Domination and Prison Ethnography," *Journal of Contemporary Ethnography* Online First (2020): 1–25, doi:10.1177/0891241620932982.

17. Michael P. Gray, *The Business of Captivity: Elmira and Its Civil War Prison* (Kent, OH: Kent State University Press, 2001); Polina Karpova, "Predicting Inmate Economic Conflict in Female Housing Units: Individual Factors Versus Social Climate Factors" (MS Thesis, Eastern Kentucky University, 2013); Adam Reed, "'Smuk Is King': The Action of Cigarettes in a Papua New Guinea Prison," in *Thinking Through Things*, eds. Amiria Henare, Martin Holbraad, and Sari Wastell (London: Routledge, 2007), 42–56.

18. Robyn Richmond et al., "Tobacco in Prisons: A Focus Group Study," *Tobacco Control* 18, no. 3 (June 2009): 178, doi:10.1136/tc.2008.026393. See also Stephen Lankenau, "Smoke 'Em If You Got 'Em: Cigarette Black Markets in U.S. Prisons and Jails," *The Prison Journal* 81, no. 2 (June 2001): 142–161, doi:10.1177/0032885501081002002.

19. Prisoners nationwide have adopted ramen or other cheap foods as money: Drew Harwell, "Honey Buns Sweeten Life for Florida Prisoners," *Tampa Bay Times* (2010), http://www.tampabay.com/features/humaninterest/honey-buns-swee ten-life-for-florida-prisoners/1142687; NPR Staff, "Behind Bars, Cheap Ramen Is As Good As Gold," *NPR* (November 2015), https://www.npr.org/sections/ thesalt/2015/11/04/454671629/behind-bars-cheap-ramen-is-as-good-as-gold; Ben Paynter, "Prison Economics: How Fish and Coffee Become Cash," *Wired* (January 2011), https://www.wired.com/2011/01/st_prisoncurrencies/;

Justin Scheck, "Mackerel Economics in Prison Leads to Appreciation for Oily Fillets," *Wall Street Journal* (October 2008): sec. Business, https://www.wsj. com/articles/SB122290720439096481; Matthew Yglesias, "Prison Currency," *Think Progress* (blog) (October 2008), http://thinkprogress.org/yglesias/2008/ 10/02/189810/prison_currency. For a more in-depth examination of the transition from tobacco to ramen as a leading prison currency, see Michael Gibson-Light, "Ramen Politics: Informal Money and Logics of Resistance in the Contemporary American Prison," *Qualitative Sociology* 41, no. 2 (June 2018): 199–220, doi:10.1007/s11133-018-9376-0.

20. Sandra Cate, "'Breaking Bread with a Spread' in a San Francisco County Jail," *Gastronomica* 8, no. 3 (2008): 17–24, doi:10.1525/gfc.2008.8.3.17; Clifton Collins, Jr. and Gustavo "Goose" Alvarez, *Prison Ramen: Recipes and Stories from Behind Bars* (New York: Workman Publishing Company, 2015).

21. Erika Camplin, *Prison Food in America* (London: Rowman & Littlefield Publishers, 2017); Thomas Ugelvik, "The Hidden Food: Mealtime Resistance and Identity Work in a Norwegian Prison," *Punishment & Society* 13, no. 1 (January 2011): 47–63, doi:10.1177/1462474510385630. Ramen's role as an expressive good or "ritual supply" tied to evolving insecurities further magnifies its value. See Goffman, *Asylums*.

22. Irena Asmundson and Ceyda Oner, "Back to Basics—What Is Money? Without It, Modern Economies Could Not Function," *Finance and Development* 49, no. 3 (2012): 52; Geffrey Ingham, "Money Is a Social Relation," *Review of Social Economy* 54, no. 4 (December 1996): 507–529, doi:10.1080/ 00346769600000031.

23. Black-market prices were derived from many accounts, triangulated across times and settings. Senior participants lamented increases in food costs over the years (with little or no increase in wages). Nevertheless, commissary prices did not change over my time at SSP. For sample commissary lists, see Camplin, *Prison Food in America*.

24. Irwin, *The Warehouse Prison*.

25. Irwin, *The Warehouse Prison*, 111.

26. David A. Snow and Leon Anderson, *Down on Their Luck: A Study of Homeless Street People* (Berkeley: University of California Press, 1993), 146.

27. Federal Bureau of Prisons, "Inmate Personal Property," Program Statement Number 5580.08 § (2011).

Chapter 6

1. In this regard, we may see work as central to "penal subjectivities," i.e., the ways in which individuals orient to and make meaning of punishment: Lori Sexton, "Penal Subjectivities: Developing a Theoretical Framework for Penal

Consciousness," *Punishment & Society* 17, no. 1 (January 2015): 114–136, doi:10.1177/1462474514548790.

2. Randy Hodson, *Dignity at Work* (Cambridge, UK: Cambridge University Press, 2001), 3. Seeking or safeguarding personal dignity is a key factor motivating various worker strategies and actions across settings. See, e.g., Michèle Lamont, *The Dignity of Working Men: Morality and the Boundaries of Race, Class, and Immigration* (Cambridge, Massachusetts: Harvard University Press, 2002); Paul Thompson and Kirsty Newsome, "The Dynamics of Dignity at Work," *Research in the Sociology of Work* 28 (2016): 79–100. Yet, human dignity is rarely prioritized in approaches to sentencing or punishment: Jonathan Simon, *Mass Incarceration on Trial: A Remarkable Court Decision and the Future of Prisons in America* (New York: The New Press, 2014).

3. Roy, "Banana Time."

4. Scholars have examined various obfuscations falling on this spectrum. See Ashley T. Rubin, "Resistance or Friction: Understanding the Significance of Prisoners' Secondary Adjustments," *Theoretical Criminology* 19, no. 1 (February 2015): 23–42, doi:10.1177/1362480614543320; Hatton, *Coerced*.

5. Allison J. Pugh, *Longing and Belonging: Parents, Children, and Consumer Culture* (Berkeley: University of California Press, 2009).

6. Freeden Oeur, "Recognizing Dignity: Young Black Men Growing Up in an Era of Surveillance," *Socius* 2 (January 2016): 2378023116633712, doi:10.1177/2378023116633712; Rios, *Punished*. Many international courts recognize prisoner rights to dignity: Jeremy Waldron, "How Law Protects Dignity," SSRN Scholarly Paper (Rochester, NY: Social Science Research Network, December 2011), doi:10.2139/ssrn.1973341; Dirk van Zyl Smit and Sonja Snacken, *Principles of European Prison Law and Policy: Penology and Human Rights* (New York: Oxford University Press, 2009). Nevertheless, the U.S. incarcerated population continues to be systematically stripped of such entitlements: Nora V. Demleitner, "Human Dignity, Crime Prevention, and Mass Incarceration: A Meaningful, Practical Comparison Across Borders," *Federal Sentencing Reporter* 27, no. 1 (2014): 1–6, doi:10.1525/fsr.2014.27.1.1; Sonja Snacken, "Punishment, Legitimate Policies and Values: Penal Moderation, Dignity and Human Rights," *Punishment & Society* 17, no. 3 (July 2015): 397–423, doi:10.1177/1462474515590895; James Q. Whitman, *Harsh Justice: Criminal Punishment and the Widening Divide Between America and Europe* (New York: Oxford University Press, 2003); Jonathan Simon, "The Second Coming of Dignity," in *The New Criminal Justice Thinking*, eds. Sharon Dolovich and Alexandra Natapoff (New York: NYU Press, 2017), 275–307.

7. Simon, "The Second Coming of Dignity."

8. Sykes, *The Society of Captives*, 79.

9. Pugh, *Longing and Belonging*.

10. In a rare qualitative examination of contemporary supermax facilities, Lorna Rhodes illustrates how prisoners remain driven by desire for respect and to have humanity or personal "being" recognized. In one exchange between a prisoner and his psychiatrist, the incarcerated man's work history as a carpenter and his identity as someone who "like[s] to work with my hands" provided a critical therapeutic anchor in working through trauma resulting from dehumanizing carceral experiences: Lorna Rhodes, *Total Confinement: Madness and Reason in the Maximum Security Prison* (Berkeley, CA: University of California Press, 2004), 109.

11. Particularly Gramsci's advancement of the concept of hegemony, through which consent is organized and challenges to capitalism are absorbed: Gramsci, *Selections from the Prison Notebooks*.

12. Labor process scholars often use the metaphor of "work games" to describe these forms of strategic worker action—not because they are *fun*, but because they require calculated tactics to derive worth or reward. See: Burawoy, *Manufacturing Consent*; Sharone, *Flawed System/Flawed Self*. The framework and conceptual apparatus that Michael Burawoy developed in this work has been employed by subsequent scholars adopting the "labor process paradigm" or "labor process perspective." See Smith, "The Short Overview of the Labour Process Perspective and History of the International Labour Process Conference."

13. Brian Halpin, "Game Playing," in *Sociology of Work: An Encyclopedia*, ed. Vicki Smith (Thousand Oaks, CA: SAGE Publications, 2013), 311.

14. Sharone, *Flawed System/Flawed Self*, 190.

15. Burawoy, *Manufacturing Consent*, 77.

16. Strategic action against rigid institutional directives: Goffman, *Asylums*.

17. Given the unparalleled influence of penal power, it may be that less tolerable strategies are even more likely to be quashed. For discussions of parallel processes in free world contexts, see: Michael Burawoy, "The Written and the Repressed in Gouldner's Industrial Sociology," *Theory and Society* 11, no. 6 (1982): 831–851; Bourdieu, *The State Nobility*.

18. Sykes, *The Society of Captives*.

19. Although not without efforts to the contrary throughout history: Thompson, "Rethinking Working-Class Struggle through the Lens of the Carceral State."

20. Pryor, "Industries Behind Bars," 10.

21. Kitty Calavita and Valerie Jenness, *Appealing to Justice: Prisoner Grievances, Rights, and Carceral Logic* (Oakland, CA: University of California Press, 2014).

22. James Jacobs recounts similar trends at Illinois' Stateville Penitentiary in the mid-twentieth century. While officials publicly framed labor as rehabilitative, he revealed that they relied on it to "coerce the inmate into a conformity that would ultimately produce a respect for the rules" as well as "reinforce

control by keeping inmates busy rather than providing job training." Jacobs, *Stateville*, 46–47.

23. Such responses have been demonstrated under systems of direct control in many contexts, e.g., Roy, "Banana Time"; Sallaz, "Permanent Pedagogy."

24. Foucault, *Discipline and Punish*; Irwin, *The Warehouse Prison*.

25. For an examination of masculinity behind bars, see Yvonne Jewkes, "Men Behind Bars: 'Doing' Masculinity as an Adaptation to Imprisonment," *Men and Masculinities* 8, no. 1 (July 2005): 44–63, doi:10.1177/1097184X03257452.

26. Yet, such markers of social standing are often precarious and may be regularly tested or rejected by others. See Robin Leidner, "Work Identity without Steady Work: Lessons from Stage Actors," *Research in the Sociology of Work* 29 (January 2016): 3–35, doi:10.1108/S0277-283320160000029008.

27. Rubin, "Resistance or Friction."

28. Hodson, *Dignity at Work*, 60.

29. Amy B. Smoyer, "Mapping Prison Foodways," in *Experiencing Imprisonment: Research on the Experience of Living and Working in Carceral Institutions*, ed. Carla Reeves (London: Routledge, 2016), 96–112; Ugelvik, "The Hidden Food."

30. Rod Earle and Coretta Phillips, "Digesting Men? Ethnicity, Gender and Food: Perspectives from a 'Prison Ethnography,'" *Theoretical Criminology* 16, no. 2 (May 2012): 141–156, doi:10.1177/1362480612441121; Amy B. Smoyer, "Making Fatty Girl Cakes: Food and Resistance in a Women's Prison," *The Prison Journal* 96, no. 2 (March 2016): 191–209, doi:10.1177/0032885515596520; Smoyer and Lopes, "Hungry on the Inside."

31. Steven Henry Lopez, "Efficiency and the Fix Revisited: Informal Relations and Mock Routinization in a Nonprofit Nursing Home," *Qualitative Sociology* 30, no. 3 (2007): 226.

32. Hodson, *Dignity at Work*, 45.

33. The label of "professional" has rhetorical and moral power upon which laborers and managers alike may draw. For example, nineteenth-century correctional officers sought specialized authority: Ashley T. Rubin, "Professionalizing Prison: Primitive Professionalization and the Administrative Defense of Eastern State Penitentiary, 1829–1879," *Law & Social Inquiry* 43, no. 1 (ed 2018): 182–211, doi:10.1111/lsi.12263. Employers may draw on feelings of professional competency and work-based identities to engender effort and secure loyalty: Sallaz, "Permanent Pedagogy"; Stephen R. Barley and Gideon Kunda, "Design and Devotion: Surges of Rational and Normative Ideologies of Control in Managerial Discourse," *Administrative Science Quarterly* 37, no. 3 (1992): 363–399, doi:10.2307/2393449. Workers in turn may assert distinctions between themselves and others in lower status positions or non-workers along the lines of competency, morality, and authority: Jeffrey J. Sallaz, "Service Labor

and Symbolic Power: On Putting Bourdieu to Work," *Work and Occupations* 37, no. 3 (August 2010): 295–319, doi:10.1177/0730888410373076.

34. Thompson, "Rethinking Working-Class Struggle through the Lens of the Carceral State."

35. Much like the working-class men studied by Michèle Lamont in *The Dignity of Working Men*.

36. To paraphrase Burawoy, *Manufacturing Consent*.

37. Goffman, *Asylums*, 201.

38. Pierre Bourdieu, *The Logic of Practice*, trans. Richard Nice (Cambridge, UK: Polity, 1991); Burawoy, *Manufacturing Consent*. Burawoy in particular advances this notion of consent, building on the thinking of Gramsci: Gramsci, *Selections from the Prison Notebooks*. For an examination of overlaps between Gramsci and Bourdieu (and Burawoy himself), see Michael Burawoy, *Symbolic Violence: Conversations with Bourdieu* (Durham, NC: Duke University Press Books, 2019).

39. As Burawoy and Wright note, despotism *always* underlies hegemony: Michael Burawoy and Erik Olin Wright, "Coercion and Consent in Contested Exchange," *Politics & Society* 18, no. 2 (June 1990): 251–266, doi:10.1177/003232929001800206.

40. Some may argue that those already exhibiting characteristics like self-discipline, respect for authority, or desire to work might self-select into the pursuit of top-tier work or be more likely to be hired. If this be the case, however, it merely serves to highlight the reproductive function of the prison employment system.

41. Those on the bottom rungs of the penal labor hierarchy may be stuck at the bottom of a "sandpile of dignity": Michael Gibson-Light, "Sandpiles of Dignity: Labor Status and Boundary-Making in the Contemporary American Prison," *RSF: The Russell Sage Foundation Journal of the Social Sciences* 6, no. 1 (March 2020): 198–216, doi:10.7758/RSF.2020.6.1.09.

Chapter 7

1. Researchers contest the so-called rehabilitative capabilities of incarceration in the U.S. in general. See Cullen, Jonson, and Nagin, "Prisons Do Not Reduce Recidivism"; David Roodman, "The Impacts of Incarceration on Crime," SSRN Scholarly Paper (Rochester, NY: Social Science Research Network, September 2017), doi:10.2139/ssrn.3635864. Work and vocational programming fail to significantly affect recidivism rates: Maguire, Flanagan, and Thornberry, "Prison Labor and Recidivism."

2. See Benns, "American Slavery, Reinvented"; Goodwin, "The Thirteenth Amendment"; Lichtenstein, *Twice the Work of Free Labor*.

3. Wacquant, *Punishing the Poor*.

4. Michael Burawoy, "The Extended Case Method," *Sociological Theory* 16, no. 1 (1998): 4–33, doi:10.1111/0735-2751.00040.

5. Continuing pre- and post-prison inequalities. See Simon, *Poor Discipline*; Wacquant, *Prisons of Poverty*; Wakefield and Uggen, "Incarceration and Stratification"; Pager, *Marked*; Western and Pettit, "Incarceration & Social Inequality."

6. Rusche, "Labor Market and Penal Sanction"; Rusche and Kirchheimer, *Punishment and Social Structure*.

7. Feeley and Simon, 452.

8. Feeley and Simon, 452. This reflected what John Irwin said of the U.S. jail system—that it functioned to manage risk imposed by the "underclass" or "rabble" of society: John Irwin, *The Jail: Managing the Underclass in American Society* (Berkeley, CA: University of California Press, 1985).

9. Recent research suggests that such patterns have been globalized. See Andrew P. Davis and Michael Gibson-Light, "Difference and Punishment: Ethno-Political Exclusion, Colonial Institutional Legacies, and Incarceration," *Punishment & Society* 22, no. 1 (2020), 1462474518816643, doi:10.1177/1462474518816643.

10. Wacquant, *Punishing the Poor*, xx.

11. O'Malley notes that the project of concretely linking neoliberalism and penality is incomplete: Pat O'Malley, "Rethinking Neoliberal Penality," SSRN Scholarly Paper (Rochester, NY: Social Science Research Network, August 2015), doi:10.2139/ssrn.2644010. As such, I aim to introduce greater systematicity to various aspects of neoliberal penology as experienced on-the-ground.

12. Biebricher, *The Political Theory of Neoliberalism*; see also Kathleen C. Schwartzman, *The Chicken Trail: Following Workers, Migrants, and Corporations across the Americas* (Ithaca, NY: Cornell University Press, 2013).

13. Aviram, "The Correctional Hunger Games"; Kyckelhahn, "State Corrections Expenditures, FY 1982–2010."

14. This may represent a partial reflection of aspects of an even *older* penality: In the late eighteenth century, advancements in manufacturing and technology rendered punitive labor unprofitable because it could not compete with rapidly developing industry. In this setting, "the institution came to lose its economic dimension, its existence becoming a heavy burden to the authorities; the administrators of the New World were particularly concerned with financial order" (Melossi and Pavarini, *The Prison and the Factory* (40th Anniversary), 173.).

15. Wacquant, "Crafting the Neoliberal State"; Aviram, *Cheap on Crime*; Lynch, *Sunbelt Justice*.

16. Brittany Friedman, "Toward a Critical Race Theory of Prison Order in the Wake of COVID-19 and Its Afterlives: When Disaster Collides with Institutional Death by Design," *Sociological Perspectives* (April 2021), 07311214211005485, doi:10.1177/07311214211005485.

17. For example, Ana Ballesteros-Pena, "Responsibilisation and Female Imprisonment in Contemporary Penal Policy: 'Respect Modules' ('Módulos de Respeto') in Spain," *Punishment & Society* 20, no. 4 (October 2018): 458–476, doi:10.1177/1462474517710241.

18. Aviram, *Cheap on Crime*.

19. For more thorough examinations of state and institutional developments under neoliberalism, see David Osborne, "Reinventing Government," *Public Productivity & Management Review* 16, no. 4 (1993): 349–356, doi:10.2307/3381012; Dennis A. Rondinelli and G. Shabbir Cheema, eds., *Reinventing Government for the Twenty-First Century: State Capacity in a Globalizing Society* (Bloomfield, CT: Kumarian Press, 2003); Wacquant, "Crafting the Neoliberal State."

20. Smoyer and Lopes, "Hungry on the Inside," 244.

21. Ellis, "Prison Labor in a Pandemic."

22. Lynch, *Sunbelt Justice*.

23. Marie Gottschalk, *The Prison and the Gallows: The Politics of Mass Incarceration in America* (Cambridge, UK: Cambridge University Press, 2006); Gottschalk, "Cell Blocks & Red Ink."

24. For more on the trimming of health services, see Ramsey Clark, "Prisons: Factories of Crime," in *Prisons, Protests, and Politics*, eds. Burton Atkins and Henry Glick (Upper Saddle River, NJ: Prentice-Hall, 1972), 15–24; Carl Clements, "Prison Resource Management: Working Smarter, Not Harder," *The ANNALS of the American Academy of Political and Social Science* 478, no. 1 (March 1985): 173–182, doi:10.1177/0002716285478001015; Wendy Pogorzelski et al., "Behavioral Health Problems, Ex-Offender Reentry Policies, and the 'Second Chance Act,'" *American Journal of Public Health* 95, no. 10 (October 2005): 1718–1724, doi:10.2105/AJPH.2005.065805. For more on food service and related cuts, see Gottschalk, *The Prison and the Gallows*; Smoyer and Lopes, "Hungry on the Inside." For more on vocational training and education cuts, see: Clements, "Prison Resource Management"; Gottschalk, "Cell Blocks & Red Ink"; Margo Schlanger, "Civil Rights Injunctions over Time: A Case Study of Jail and Prison Court Orders," *New York University Law Review* 81 (2006): 630.

25. David C. Pyrooz et al., "Views on COVID-19 from Inside Prison: Perspectives of High-Security Prisoners," *Justice Evaluation Journal* 3, no. 2 (July 2020): 295, doi:10.1080/24751979.2020.1777578.

26. Maintaining the employment system's "flexibility": Schwartzman, *The Chicken Trail*.

27. This is partly driven, no doubt, by ongoing struggles between bureaucratic and political actors in the penal field. See: Goodman, Page, and Phelps, *Breaking the Pendulum*.

28. Rusche and Kirchheimer, *Punishment and Social Structure*, 5. Rusche and Kirchheimer offer the epitome of this view, which David Garland sums up as: where supply of labor is low, "then the state and its penal institutions will be less ready to dispense with the valuable resources which their captives represent, and more likely to put offenders to work in some way or another." David Garland, *Punishment and Modern Society: A Study in Social Theory* (Chicago: University of Chicago Press, 1990), 93. Although some have challenged aspects of Rusche and Kirchheimer's empirical approach, this theoretical contention remains compelling. Other scholarship explores continued relationships between labor and punishment, especially within capitalist democracies. See Melossi and Pavarini, *The Prison and the Factory (40th Anniversary)*; Melossi, "Gazette of Morality and Social Whip"; Meranze, *Laboratories of Virtue*; Ignatieff, *A Just Measure of Pain*.

29. Goodwin, "The Thirteenth Amendment"; McLennan, *The Crisis of Imprisonment*.

30. McLennan, *The Crisis of Imprisonment*.

31. Howard S. Becker, "Whose Side Are We On?," *Social Problems* 14, no. 3 (1967): 239–247, doi:10.2307/799147. The voices of the incarcerated remain underrepresented in discussions of penal reform. I aim to play a small role in amplifying some of them.

32. International Labor Organization, "Convention Concerning Forced or Compulsory Labour (No. 29)" (1930), https://www.ilo.org/dyn/normlex/en/f?p=NORMLEXPUB:12100:0::NO::P12100_ILO_CODE:C029; International Labor Organization, "Abolition of Forced Labour Convention (No. 105)" (1957), https://www.ilo.org/dyn/normlex/en/f?p=NORMLEXPUB:12100:0::NO:12100:P12100_ILO_CODE:C105; International Labor Organization, "Use of Prison Labor," Document, Q&As on Business and Forced Labour, 2016, http://www.ilo.org/empent/areas/business-helpdesk/faqs/WCMS_DOC_ENT_HLP_FL_FAQ_EN/lang--en/index.htm; AFL-CIO, "The Exploitation of Prison Labor," ALF-CIO, May 1997, https://aflcio.org/about/leadership/statements/exploitation-prison-labor.

33. Bair, *Prison Labor in the United States*; Faina Milman-Sivan, "Prisoners for Hire: Towards a Normative Justification of the ILO's Prohibition of Private Forced Prisoner Labor," *Fordham International Law Journal* 36 (2013): 1619–1682.

34. Benns, "American Slavery, Reinvented"; see also Beth Schwartzapfel, "A Primer on the Nationwide Prisoners' Strike," The Marshall Project, September 2016, https://www.themarshallproject.org/2016/09/27/a-primer-on-the-nationwide-prisoners-strike.

35. Noah Smith, "Paying Inmates Minimum Wages Helps the Working Class," *Bloomberg.Com* (June 2017), https://www.bloomberg.com/opinion/articles/2017-06-02/paying-inmates-minimum-wages-helps-the-working-class.

36. United States General Accounting Office, "Prisoner Labor: Perspectives on Paying the Federal Minimum Wage" (Washington, DC: General Accounting Office, 1993), 2.

37. Calavita and Jenness, *Appealing to Justice*.

38. For example, Lauren Castle, "9th Circuit Orders Arizona to Pay $1.4M in Prison Health Care Lawsuit," *Arizona Republic* (January 2020), https://www.azcentral.com/story/news/local/arizona/2020/01/29/ninth-circuit-orders-ariz ona-pay-prison-healthcare-lawsuit/4610339002/; Schwartzapfel, "How Bad Is Prison Health Care?"; Christie Thompson, "Where Crossword Puzzles Count as Counseling," *The Marshall Project* (June 2017), https://www.themarshallproj ect.org/2017/06/12/where-crossword-puzzles-count-as-counseling.

39. The fields of sociology and criminology have been slower to adopt abolitionist platforms than other social science disciplines: Michelle Brown and Judah Schept, "New Abolition, Criminology and a Critical Carceral Studies," *Punishment & Society* 19, no. 4 (October 2017): 440–462, doi:10.1177/1462474516666281. Nevertheless, current trends in incarceration and the reemergence of debates over criminal justice transformation invite scholars to contribute to this discourse.

40. National Advisory Commission on Criminal Justice Standards and Goals, "Task Force Report on Corrections" (Washington, DC: US Government Printing Office, 1973).

41. Leola A. Abraham, Timothy C. Brown, and Shaun A. Thomas, "How COVID-19's Disruption of the U.S. Correctional System Provides an Opportunity for Decarceration," *American Journal of Criminal Justice* 45, no. 4 (August 2020): 780–792, doi:10.1007/s12103-020-09537-1.

42. Dismantling facets of the penal system may be thought of as "partial abolition": Eduardo Bautista Duran and Jonathan Simon, "Police Abolitionist Discourse? Why It Has Been Missing (and Why It Matters)," in *The Cambridge Handbook of Policing in the United States*, eds. Tamara Rice Lave and Eric Miller (Cambridge, UK: Cambridge University Press, 2019), 85–103, https://doi.org/10.1017/9781108354721; Thomas Mathiesen, *The Politics of Abolition* (London: Martin Robertson, 1974).

43. E. Tammy Kim, "A National Strike Against 'Prison Slavery,'" *The New Yorker* (October 2016), https://www.newyorker.com/news/news-desk/a-national-str ike-against-prison-slavery; Toussaint Losier, "The Movement Against 'Modern Day Slavery,'" *Jacobin* (September 2018), https://jacobinmag.com/2018/09/pri son-strike-slavery-labor-jls-abolition.

44. Thompson, "Rethinking Working-Class Struggle through the Lens of the Carceral State." Organizations such as the Incarcerated Workers Organizing Committee continue this endeavor: Incarcerated Workers Organizing Committee, "IWOC's Statement of Purpose," Incarcerated Workers Organizing Committee, 2014, https://incarceratedworkers.org/about.

45. Bair, *Prison Labor in the United States*; Jacobs, *Stateville*; Maguire, Flanagan, and Thornberry, "Prison Labor and Recidivism"; Wilson, Gallagher, and MacKenzie, "A Meta-Analysis of Corrections-Based Education, Vocation, and Work Programs for Adult Offenders."

46. Melossi and Pavarini asked, *Why prison?* in their classic text: Melossi and Pavarini, *The Prison and the Factory (40th Anniversary)*.

47. W.E.B. Du Bois, *Black Reconstruction in America: Toward a History of the Part Which Black Folk Played in the Attempt to Reconstruct Democracy in America, 1860-1880* (New York: Routledge, 1935), 170. Unfortunately, as Du Bois notes, racialized labor hierarchy continued and took new forms. Michele Goodwin maps out how slavery was not abolished, but merely transformed through the Black Codes, into Jim Crow, and onward: Goodwin, "The Thirteenth Amendment."

48. Angela Y. Davis, *Are Prisons Obsolete?* (New York: Seven Stories Press, 2003); Allegra M. McLeod, "Prison Abolition and Grounded Justice," *UCLA Law Review* 62, no. 5 (2015): 1156–1239.

49. Davis, *Are Prisons Obsolete?*, 106.

50. Waskow 1972, quoted in Davis, *Are Prisons Obsolete?* This project would indeed entail society-wide change. This may include allocating greater funding toward and restructuring educational institutions to diminish the trend of preparing some for college while leaving others for prison: James J. Heckman and Dimitriy V. Masterov, "The Productivity Argument for Investing in Young Children," *Applied Economic Perspectives and Policy* 29, no. 3 (October 2007): 446–493, doi:10.1111/j.1467-9353.2007.00359.x. It would also require bolstering mental health and rehabilitation programming outside of prison to combat the mental and emotional disorders, addiction, and dual diagnosis that contribute to "criminality": Pogorzelski et al., "Behavioral Health Problems, Ex-Offender Reentry Policies, and the 'Second Chance Act.'" Decriminalizing drug use would relieve disproportionate criminal enforcement in minoritized communities: Beckett, Nyrop, and Pfingst, "Race, Drugs, and Policing"; Wacquant, *Punishing the Poor*. Reforming or dismantling policing and surveillance structures that profile already-disadvantaged communities would also diminish disproportionate punishment: Alexander, *The New Jim Crow*; Alex S. Vitale, *The End of Policing* (New York: Verso, 2017). To confront lasting ethnoracial dominance from the ante-bellum era through today, an abolitionist future may challenge conceptions of value linked to neoliberal ideals of self-reliance through formal labor that is often precarious or unrewarding: Michelle Brown, "The Work of Abolition: Dismantling the Criminal Justice Labor Force" (June 2018). Beyond deconstructing forced labor systems on the inside, this would include walking back the criminalization of labor market under- or non-participation: Wacquant, *Prisons of Poverty*. Finally, social welfare and living wage programming may help combat socio-economic inequality linked to

higher rates of incarceration: Marie Gottschalk, "Razing the Carceral State," *Social Justice* 42, no. 2 (140) (2015): 31–51; Marie Gottschalk, *Caught: The Prison State and the Lockdown of American Politics* (Princeton, NJ: Princeton University Press, 2016).

51. Cullen, Jonson, and Nagin, "Prisons Do Not Reduce Recidivism"; Roodman, "The Impacts of Incarceration on Crime."

52. Morenoff, "Racial and Ethnic Disparities in Crime and Delinquency in the United States"; Wheelock and Uggen, "Punishment, Crime, and Poverty."

53. Philip Goodman, "Conclusion," in *Labor and Punishment: Work in and Out of Prison*, ed. Erin Hatton (Oakland, CA: University of California Press, 2021), 260.

Appendix

1. See Heith Copes, Andy Hochstetler, and Anastasia Brown, "Inmates' Perceptions of the Benefits and Harm of Prison Interviews," *Field Methods* 25, no. 2 (May 2013): 182–196, doi:10.1177/1525822X12465798.

2. Schwartzapfel, "A Primer on the Nationwide Prisoners' Strike."

3. Kim, "A National Strike Against 'Prison Slavery.'"

4. See: Clyde E. Browning and Wil Gesler, "The Sun Belt-Snow Belt: A Case of Sloppy Regionalizing," *The Professional Geographer* 31, no. 1 (1979): 66–74, doi:10.1111/j.0033-0124.1979.00066.x.

5. Blackmon, *Slavery by Another Name*; Goodwin, "The Thirteenth Amendment"; Thompson, "Rethinking Working-Class Struggle through the Lens of the Carceral State." This maps onto more general patterns of incarceration in the region, which has been a bellwether of trends in U.S. penal policy: Michael C. Campbell, Matt Vogel, and Joshua Williams, "Historical Contingencies and the Evolving Importance of Race, Violent Crime, and Region in Explaining Mass Incarceration in the United States," *Criminology* 53, no. 2 (2015): 180–203, doi:10.1111/1745-9125.12065.

6. Michael C. Campbell and Heather Schoenfeld, "The Transformation of America's Penal Order: A Historicized Political Sociology of Punishment," *American Journal of Sociology* 118, no. 5 (March 2013): 1375–1423, doi:10.1086/669506; Weiss, "'Repatriating' Low-Wage Work."

7. For example, Stephen P. Borgatti and José-Luis Molina, "Toward Ethical Guidelines for Network Research in Organizations," *Social Networks, Ethical Dilemmas in Social Network Research* 27, no. 2 (May 2005): 107–117, doi:10.1016/j.socnet.2005.01.004. Gibson-Light and Seim discuss issues related to working with penal institutions-as-participant: Gibson-Light and Seim, "Punishing Fieldwork."

8. For example, Gideon Kunda, *Engineering Culture: Control and Commitment in a High-Tech Corporation* (Philadelphia: Temple University Press, 2006).

9. Georg Simmel, "The Stranger," in *The Sociology of Georg Simmel*, ed. Kurt Wolff (New York: Simon and Schuster, 1950).

10. Roy King and Alison Liebling, "Doing Research in Prisons," in *Doing Research on Crime and Justice* (New York: Oxford University Press, 2008), 431–454.

References

Abraham, Leola A., Timothy C. Brown, and Shaun A. Thomas. "How COVID-19's Disruption of the U.S. Correctional System Provides an Opportunity for Decarceration." *American Journal of Criminal Justice* 45, no. 4 (August 2020): 780–792. https://doi.org/10.1007/s12103-020-09537-1.

Acker, Joan. "Hierarchies, Jobs, Bodies: A Theory of Gendered Organizations." *Gender & Society* 4, no. 2 (June 1990): 139–158. https://doi.org/10.1177/089124390004002002.

AFL-CIO. "The Exploitation of Prison Labor." *ALF-CIO* (May 1997). https://aflcio.org/about/leadership/statements/exploitation-prison-labor.

Alexander, Michelle. *The New Jim Crow: Mass Incarceration in the Age of Colorblindness*. New York: The New Press, 2012.

Alim, H. Samy, John R. Rickford, and Arnetha F. Ball, eds. *Raciolinguistics: How Language Shapes Our Ideas About Race*. New York: Oxford University Press, 2016.

Alvarez, Gustavo. *The Pawn*. Seattle, WA: Amazon Publishing, 2020.

Antenangeli, Leonardo, and Matthew Durose. *Recidivism of Prisoners Released in 24 States in 2008: A 10-Year Follow-Up Period (2008–2018)*. Washington, DC: Bureau of Justice Statistics, 2021.

Armstrong, Elizabeth A., and Laura T. Hamilton. *Paying for the Party*. Cambridge, MA: Harvard University Press, 2013.

Arum, Richard, and Gary LaFree. "Educational Attainment, Teacher-Student Ratios, and the Risk of Adult Incarceration Among U.S. Birth Cohorts Since 1910." *Sociology of Education* 81, no. 4 (October 2008): 397–421. https://doi.org/10.1177/003804070808100404.

Asmundson, Irena, and Ceyda Oner. "Back to Basics-What Is Money? Without It, Modern Economies Could Not Function." *Finance and Development* 49, no. 3 (2012): 52.

Atkinson, Rob, and Knut A. Rostad. "Can Inmates Become an Integral Part of the U.S. Workforce?" *Research Report Urban Institute Reentry Roundtable*. Washington, DC: Urban Institute, 2003: 1–25. https://doi.org/10.1037/e717792011-001.

Aviram, Hadar. "Are Private Prisons to Blame for Mass Incarceration and Its Evils: Prison Conditions, Neoliberalism, and Public Choice Prison Privatization: Impacts on Urban Communities." *Fordham Urban Law Journal* 42, no. 2 (2014): 411–450.

Aviram, Hadar. *Cheap on Crime: Recession-Era Politics and the Transformation of American Punishment*. Berkeley, CA: University of California Press, 2015.

Aviram, Hadar. "The Correctional Hunger Games: Understanding Realignment in the Context of the Great Recession." *The ANNALS of the American Academy of Political and Social Science* 664, no. 1 (March 2016): 260–279. https://doi.org/ 10.1177/0002716215599938.

Aviram, Hadar. "Humonetarianism: The New Correctional Discourse of Scarcity." *Hastings Race and Poverty Law Journal* 7, no. 1 (2010): 1–52.

Ayers, Edward L. *Vengeance and Justice: Crime and Punishment in the 19th Century American South.* New York: Oxford University Press, 1984.

Bair, Asatar. *Prison Labor in the United States: An Economic Analysis.* Oxfordshire, UK: Routledge, 2007. https://doi.org/10.4324/9780203933985.

Ballesteros-Pena, Ana. "Responsibilisation and Female Imprisonment in Contemporary Penal Policy: 'Respect Modules' ('Módulos de Respeto') in Spain." *Punishment & Society* 20, no. 4 (October 2018): 458–476. https://doi.org/ 10.1177/1462474517710241.

Barley, Stephen R., and Gideon Kunda. "Design and Devotion: Surges of Rational and Normative Ideologies of Control in Managerial Discourse." *Administrative Science Quarterly* 37, no. 3 (1992): 363–399. https://doi.org/10.2307/2393449.

Beaumont, Gustave de, and Alexis de Tocqueville. *On the Penitentiary System in the United States and Its Application in France*, translated by Francis Lieber. Philadelphia, PA: Carey, Lea & Blanchard, 1833. http://archive.org/details/onp enitentiarysy00beauuoft.

Beck, Brenden. "Broken Windows in the Cul-de-Sac? Race/Ethnicity and Quality-of-Life Policing in the Changing Suburbs." *Crime & Delinquency* 65, no. 2 (February 2019): 270–292. https://doi.org/10.1177/0011128717739568.

Becker, Howard S. "Whose Side Are We On?" *Social Problems* 14, no. 3 (1967): 239–247. https://doi.org/10.2307/799147.

Beckett, Katherine, and Megan Ming Francis. "The Origins of Mass Incarceration: The Racial Politics of Crime and Punishment in the Post–Civil Rights Era." *Annual Review of Law and Social Science* 16, no. 1 (2020): 433–452. https://doi. org/10.1146/annurev-lawsocsci-110819-100304.

Beckett, Katherine, Kris Nyrop, and Lori Pfingst. "Race, Drugs, and Policing: Understanding Disparities in Drug Delivery Arrests." *Criminology* 44, no. 1 (2006): 105–137. https://doi.org/10.1111/j.1745-9125.2006.00044.x.

Benns, Whitney. "American Slavery, Reinvented." *The Atlantic* (September 2015). https://www.theatlantic.com/business/archive/2015/09/prison-labor-in-amer ica/406177/.

Berkman, Alexander. *Prison Memoirs of an Anarchist.* New York: Mother Earth Publishing Association, 1912. https://www.gutenberg.org/ebooks/34406/pg34 406-images.html.utf8.

Biebricher, Thomas. *The Political Theory of Neoliberalism.* Redwood City, CA: Stanford University Press, 2019.

Blackmon, Douglas A. *Slavery by Another Name: The Re-Enslavement of Black Americans from the Civil War to World War II.* New York: Anchor Books, 2009.

Blau, Peter M., and Otis Dudley Duncan. *The American Occupational Structure.* New York: John Wiley & Sons Inc, 1967.

Blumstein, Alfred, and Allen J. Beck. "Population Growth in U. S. Prisons, 1980–1996." *Crime and Justice* 26 (January 1999): 17–61. https://doi.org/10.1086/449294.

Borgatti, Stephen P., and José-Luis Molina. "Toward Ethical Guidelines for Network Research in Organizations." *Social Networks, Ethical Dilemmas in Social Network Research* 27, no. 2 (May 2005): 107–117. https://doi.org/10.1016/j.socnet.2005.01.004.

Boshier, Roger, and Derek Johnson. "Does Conviction Affect Employment Opportunities." *British Journal of Criminology* 14, no. 3 (1974): 264–268.

Bouffard, Jeffrey, Doris Layton Mackenzie, and Laura J. Hickman. "Effectiveness of Vocational Education and Employment Programs for Adult Offenders." *Journal of Offender Rehabilitation* 31, no. 1–2 (2008): 1–41. https://doi.org/10.1300/J076v31n01_01.

Bourdieu, Pierre. *Distinction: A Social Critique of the Judgement of Taste*. Translated by Richard Nice. Cambridge, MA: Harvard University Press, 1984.

Bourdieu, Pierre. *The Field of Cultural Production*. New York: Columbia University Press, 1993.

Bourdieu, Pierre. *Language and Symbolic Power*. Cambridge, UK: Blackwell Publishers, 1992.

Bourdieu, Pierre. *Outline of a Theory of Practice*. Translated by Richard Nice. Cambridge, UK: Cambridge University Press, 1977.

Bourdieu, Pierre. *The Logic of Practice*. Translated by Richard Nice. Cambridge, UK: Polity, 1991.

Bourdieu, Pierre. *Pascalian Meditations*. Translated by Richard Nice. Redwood City, CA: Stanford University Press, 2000.

Bourdieu, Pierre. *The Social Structures of the Economy*. Cambridge, UK: Polity, 2005.

Bourdieu, Pierre. *The State Nobility: Elite Schools in the Field of Power*. Redwood City, CA: Stanford University Press, 1996.

Bourdieu, Pierre, and Jean-Claude Passeron. *Reproduction in Education, Society and Culture*. Translated by Richard Nice. 2nd edition. London: Sage Publications, 1990.

Bourdieu, Pierre, and Loïc Wacquant. *An Invitation to Reflexive Sociology*. Chicago: University of Chicago Press, 1992.

Braverman, Harry. *Labor and Monopoly Capital: The Degradation of Work in the Twentieth Century*. New York: Monthly Review Press, 1974.

Britton, Dana M. *At Work in the Iron Cage: The Prison as Gendered Organization*. New York: NYU Press, 2003.

Brown, Michelle. "The Work of Abolition: Dismantling the Criminal Justice Labor Force." Presented at the Annual Meeting on Law and Society, Toronto, Canada, June 2018.

Brown, Michelle, and Judah Schept. "New Abolition, Criminology and a Critical Carceral Studies." *Punishment & Society* 19, no. 4 (October 2017): 440–462. https://doi.org/10.1177/1462474516666281.

x

Castle, Lauren. "9th Circuit Orders Arizona to Pay $1.4M in Prison Health Care Lawsuit." *Arizona Republic* (January 2020). https://www.azcentral.com/story/news/local/arizona/2020/01/29/ninth-circuit-orders-arizona-pay-prison-healthcare-lawsuit/4610339002/.

cate, sandra. "'Breaking Bread with a Spread' in a San Francisco County Jail." *Gastronomica* 8, no. 3 (2008): 17–24. https://doi.org/10.1525/gfc.2008.8.3.17.

Chan, Curtis K., and Michel Anteby. "Task Segregation as a Mechanism for Within-Job Inequality: Women and Men of the Transportation Security Administration." *Administrative Science Quarterly* 61, no. 2 (June 2016): 184–216. https://doi.org/10.1177/0001839215611447.

Chang, Tracy F. H., and Douglas E. Thompkins. "Corporations Go to Prisons: The Expansion of Corporate Power in the Correctional Industry." *Labor Studies Journal* 27, no. 1 (March 2002): 45–69. https://doi.org/10.1177/0160449X0202700104.

Chapple, Karen. "Networks to Nerdistan: The Role of Labor Market Intermediaries in the Entry-Level IT Labor Market." *International Journal of Urban and Regional Research* 30, no. 3 (2006): 548–563. https://doi.org/10.1111/j.1468-2427.2006.00674.x.

Clark, Ramsey. "Prisons: Factories of Crime." In *Prisons, Protests, and Politics*, edited by Burton Atkins and Henry Glick, 15–24. Upper Saddle River, NJ: Prentice-Hall, 1972.

Clear, Todd. *Imprisoning Communities: How Mass Incarceration Makes Disadvantaged Neighborhoods Worse*. New York: Oxford University Press, 2007.

Clements, Carl. "Prison Resource Management: Working Smarter, Not Harder." *The ANNALS of the American Academy of Political and Social Science* 478, no. 1 (March 1985): 173–182. https://doi.org/10.1177/0002716285478001015.

Cobbina, Jennifer E. *Hands Up, Don't Shoot*. New York: NYU Press, 2019.

Collins, Jr., Clifton, and Gustavo "Goose" Alvarez. *Prison Ramen: Recipes and Stories from Behind Bars*. New York: Workman Publishing Company, 2015.

Copes, Heith, Andy Hochstetler, and Anastasia Brown. "Inmates' Perceptions of the Benefits and Harm of Prison Interviews." *Field Methods* 25, no. 2 (May 2013): 182–196. https://doi.org/10.1177/1525822X12465798.

Coulete, Lucius, and Daniel Kopf. "Out of Prison & Out of Work." Northampton, Massachusetts: Prison Policy Initiative, 2018. https://www.prisonpolicy.org/reports/outofwork.html.

Cox, Alexandra. "The Language of Incarceration." *Incarceration* 1, no. 1 (July 2020): 1–13. https://doi.org/10.1177/2632666320940859.

Crewe, Ben. *The Prisoner Society: Power, Adaptation and Social Life in an English Prison*. New York: Oxford University Press, 2009.

Crittenden, Courtney A., Barbara A. Koons-Witt, and Robert J. Kaminski. "Being Assigned Work in Prison: Do Gender and Race Matter?" *Feminist Criminology* 13, no. 4 (October 2018): 359–381. https://doi.org/10.1177/1557085116668990.

Cullen, Francis T., Cheryl Lero Jonson, and Daniel S. Nagin. "Prisons Do Not Reduce Recidivism: The High Cost of Ignoring Science." *The Prison Journal*

91, no. 3 suppl (September 2011): 48S–65S. https://doi.org/10.1177/003288551 1415224.

Cunha, Manuela. "The Ethnography of Prisons and Penal Confinement." *Annual Review of Anthropology* 43, no. 1 (October 2014): 217–233. https://doi.org/ 10.1146/annurev-anthro-102313-030349.

Davidson, Kelley. "'The Insourcing of Prison Labor': Seven US Corporate Household Names Use Prison Labor to Produce Their Goods." The Centre for Research on Globalization (November 2015). https://www.globalresearch.ca/ the-insourcing-of-prison-labor-seven-us-corporate-household-names-use-pri son-labor-to-produce-their-goods/5492033?print=1.

Davis, Andrew P., and Michael Gibson-Light. "Difference and Punishment: Ethno-Political Exclusion, Colonial Institutional Legacies, and Incarceration." *Punishment & Society* 22, no. 1 (2020), 1462474518816643. https://doi.org/ 10.1177/1462474518816643.

Davis, Angela Y. *Are Prisons Obsolete?* New York: Seven Stories Press, 2003.

Demleitner, Nora V. "Human Dignity, Crime Prevention, and Mass Incarceration: A Meaningful, Practical Comparison Across Borders." *Federal Sentencing Reporter* 27, no. 1 (2014): 1–6. https://doi.org/10.1525/fsr.2014.27.1.1.

Dostoïeffsky, Fedor [Dostoevsky, Fyodor]. *The House of The Dead, or Prison Life in Siberia*. New York: E.P. Dutton & Co, 1914. https://www.gutenberg.org/files/ 37536/37536-h/37536-h.htm.

Du Bois, W.E.B. *Black Reconstruction in America: Toward a History of the Part Which Black Folk Played in the Attempt to Reconstruct Democracy in America, 1860–1880*. New York: Routledge, 1935.

Du Bois, W.E.B. *The Souls of Black Folk*. Scotts Valley, CA: CreateSpace Independent Publishing Platform, 2014.

Duran, Eduardo Bautista, and Jonathan Simon. "Police Abolitionist Discourse? Why It Has Been Missing (and Why It Matters)." In *The Cambridge Handbook of Policing in the United States*, edited by Tamara Rice Lave and Eric Miller, 85–103. Cambridge, UK: Cambridge University Press, 2019. https://doi.org/10.1017/ 9781108354721.

Earle, Rod, and Coretta Phillips. "Digesting Men? Ethnicity, Gender and Food: Perspectives from a 'Prison Ethnography.'" *Theoretical Criminology* 16, no. 2 (May 2012): 141–156. https://doi.org/10.1177/1362480612441121.

Eason, John M. *Big House on the Prairie: Rise of the Rural Ghetto and Prison Proliferation*. Chicago: University of Chicago Press, 2017.

Eidelson, Josh. "Are Private Prison Companies Using Forced Labor?" *Bloomberg. com* (November 2017). https://www.bloomberg.com/news/articles/2017-11-08/ are-private-prisons-using-forced-labor.

Ekirch, A. Roger. *Bound for America: The Transportation of British Convicts to the Colonies, 1718–1775*. Oxford, UK: Clarendon Press, 1990.

Ellis, Rachel. "Prison Labor in a Pandemic." *Contexts* 19, no. 4 (November 2020): 90–91. https://doi.org/10.1177/1536504220977950.

Ellis, Rachel. "Redemption and Reproach: Religion and Carceral Control in Action among Women in Prison." *Criminology* 58, no. 4 (2020): 747–772. https://doi.org/10.1111/1745-9125.12258.

Federal Bureau of Prisons. Inmate Personal Property, Program Statement Number 5580.08 § (2011).

Feeley, Malcolm M., and Jonathan Simon. "The New Penology: Notes on the Emerging Strategy of Corrections and Its Implications." *Criminology* 30, no. 4 (1992): 449–474. https://doi.org/10.1111/j.1745-9125.1992.tb01112.x.

Feldman, Lindsey Raisa. "Anti-Heroes, Wildfire, and the Complex Visibility of Prison Labor." *Crime, Media, Culture* 16, no. 2 (2020): 221–238. https://doi.org/10.1177/1741659019865309.

Fellner, Jamie. "Race and Drugs." In *The Oxford Handbook of Ethnicity, Crime, and Immigration*, edited by Sandra M. Bucerius and Michael Tonry), 194–223. New York: Oxford University Press, 2013.

Foucault, Michel. *Discipline and Punish: The Birth of the Prison*. New York: Pantheon Books, 1977.

Foucault, Michel. "Michel Foucault on the Role of Prisons." Interview by Roger-Pol Droit. Translated by Leonard Mayhew. *The New York Times* (August 1975). https://archive.nytimes.com/www.nytimes.com/books/00/12/17/specials/foucault-prisons.html.

Fredrikson, Annika. "Vocational Training in Prisons Can Fill Industry Gaps." *Christian Science Monitor* (September 2015). https://www.csmonitor.com/Business/2015/0908/Vocational-training-in-prisons-can-fill-industry-gaps.

Freeman, Richard. "Crime and the Employment of Disadvantaged Youth." In *Urban Labor Markets and Job Opportunity*, edited by George E. Peterson, 201–237. Washington, DC: Urban Institute Press, 1992.

Friedman, Brittany. "Toward a Critical Race Theory of Prison Order in the Wake of COVID-19 and Its Afterlives: When Disaster Collides with Institutional Death by Design." *Sociological Perspectives* 64, no. 5 (April 2021): 689–705. https://doi.org/10.1177/07311214211005485.

Garland, David. *Punishment and Modern Society: A Study in Social Theory*. Chicago: University of Chicago Press, 1990.

Garland, David. "Theoretical Advances and Problems in the Sociology of Punishment." *Punishment & Society* 20, no. 1 (January 2018): 8–33. https://doi.org/10.1177/1462474517737274.

Geller, Amanda, Irwin Garfinkel, and Bruce Western. "The Effects of Incarceration on Employment and Wages: An Analysis of the Fragile Families Survey." *Center for Research on Child Wellbeing, Working Paper* 1 (2006): 2006.

Gibson, Mary. "Global Perspectives on the Birth of the Prison." *The American Historical Review* 116, no. 4 (October 2011): 1040–1063. https://doi.org/10.1086/ahr.116.4.1040.

Gibson-Light, Michael. "Classification Struggles in Semi-Formal and Precarious Work: Lessons from Inmate Labor and Cultural Production." *Research in the Sociology of Work* 31 (2017): 61–89. https://doi.org/10.1108/S0277-283320170000031002.

Gibson-Light, Michael. "Ramen Politics: Informal Money and Logics of Resistance in the Contemporary American Prison." *Qualitative Sociology* 41, no. 2 (June 2018): 199–220. https://doi.org/10.1007/s11133-018-9376-0.

Gibson-Light, Michael. "Sandpiles of Dignity: Labor Status and Boundary-Making in the Contemporary American Prison." *RSF: The Russell Sage Foundation Journal of the Social Sciences* 6, no. 1 (March 2020): 198–216. https://doi.org/10.7758/RSF.2020.6.1.09.

Gibson-Light, Michael, and Josh Seim. "Punishing Fieldwork: Penal Domination and Prison Ethnography." *Journal of Contemporary Ethnography* 49, no. 5 (2020): 666–690. https://doi.org/10.1177/0891241620932982.

Gipson, Frances T., and Elizabeth A. Pierce. "Current Trends in State Inmate User Fee Programs for Health Services." *Journal of Correctional Health Care* 3, no. 2 (October 1996): 159–178. https://doi.org/10.1177/107834589600300205.

Goffman, Erving. *Asylums.* New York: Anchor Books, 1961.

Goldman, Emma. "Prisons: A Social Crime and Failure." In *Anarchism and Other Essays*, 115–132. New York: Mother Earth Publishing Association, 1911. http://dwardmac.pitzer.edu/Anarchist_Archives/goldman/aando/prisons.html.

Goodman, Philip. "'Another Second Chance': Rethinking Rehabilitation through the Lens of California's Prison Fire Camps." *Social Problems* 59, no. 4 (2012): 437–458.

Goodman, Philip. "Conclusion." In *Labor and Punishment: Work in and Out of Prison*, edited by Erin Hatton, 257–270. Oakland, CA: University of California Press, 2021.

Goodman, Philip. "Hero and Inmate: Work, Prisons, and Punishment in California's Fire Camps." *The Journal of Labor & Society* 15, no. 3 (2012): 353–376.

Goodman, Philip. "'It's Just Black, White, or Hispanic': An Observational Study of Racializing Moves in California's Segregated Prison Reception Centers." *Law & Society Review* 42, no. 4 (2008): 735–770. https://doi.org/10.1111/j.1540-5893.2008.00357.x.

Goodman, Philip. "Race in California's Prison Fire Camps for Men: Prison Politics, Space, and the Racialization of Everyday Life." *American Journal of Sociology* 120, no. 2 (September 2014): 352–394. https://doi.org/10.1086/678303.

Goodman, Philip, Joshua Page, and Michelle S. Phelps. *Breaking the Pendulum: The Long Struggle Over Criminal Justice.* New York: Oxford University Press, 2017.

Goodwin, Michele. "The Thirteenth Amendment: Modern Slavery, Capitalism, and Mass Incarceration." *Cornell Law Review* 104 (2018): 899–990.

Gottschalk, Marie. *Caught: The Prison State and the Lockdown of American Politics.* Princeton, NJ: Princeton University Press, 2016.

Gottschalk, Marie. "Cell Blocks & Red Ink: Mass Incarceration, the Great Recession & Penal Reform." *Daedalus* 139, no. 3 (July 2010): 62–73. https://doi.org/10.1162/DAED_a_00023.

Gottschalk, Marie. "Razing the Carceral State." *Social Justice* 42, no. 2 (140) (2015): 31–51.

Gottschalk, Marie. *The Prison and the Gallows: The Politics of Mass Incarceration in America.* Cambridge, UK: Cambridge University Press, 2006.

Gottschalk, Peter, and Robert Moffitt. "The Rising Instability of U.S. Earnings." *Journal of Economic Perspectives* 23, no. 4 (December 2009): 3–24. https://doi.org/10.1257/jep.23.4.3.

Gramsci, Antonio. *Selections from the Prison Notebooks*. Translated by Quintin Hoare and Geoffrey Nowell Smith. New York: International Publishers, 1971.

Grana, Sheryl J. *Women and Justice*. Lanham, MD: Rowman & Littlefield, 2010.

Granovetter, Mark. *Getting a Job: A Study of Contacts and Careers*. Chicago: University of Chicago Press, 1974.

Gray, Michael P. *The Business of Captivity: Elmira and Its Civil War Prison*. Kent, OH: Kent State University Press, 2001.

Green, Hardy. *The Company Town: The Industrial Edens and Satanic Mills That Shaped the American Economy*. New York: Basic Books, 2010.

Greenleaf, Thomas. *Laws of the State of New York: Comprising the Constitution, and the Acts of the Legislature, since the Revolution, from the First to the Twentieth Session, Inclusive*. New York: Thomas Greenleaf, 1797.

Guilbaud, Fabrice. "Working in Prison: Time as Experienced by Inmate-Workers." *Revue française de sociologie* 51, no. 5 (July 2010): 41–68.

Hagan, John. "The Social Embeddedness of Crime and Unemployment." *Criminology* 31, no. 4 (November 1993): 465–491. https://doi.org/10.1111/j.1745-9125.1993.tb01138.x.

Haley, Sarah. *No Mercy Here: Gender, Punishment, and the Making of Jim Crow Modernity*. Chapel Hill, NC: University of North Carolina Press, 2016.

Halpin, Brian. "Game Playing." In *Sociology of Work: An Encyclopedia*, edited by Vicki Smith, 311–312. Thousand Oaks, CA: SAGE Publications, 2013.

Haney, Lynne. *Offending Women: Power, Punishment, and the Regulation of Desire*. Berkeley: University of California Press, 2010.

Harcourt, Bernard E. "Neoliberal Penality: A Brief Genealogy." *Theoretical Criminology* 14, no. 1 (February 2010): 74–92. https://doi.org/10.1177/1362480609352785.

Harding, Richard. *Private Prisons and Public Accountability*. New York: Routledge, 2018. https://doi.org/10.4324/9781351308045.

Harmon, Mark G., and Breanna Boppre. "Women of Color and the War on Crime: An Explanation for the Rise in Black Female Imprisonment." *Journal of Ethnicity in Criminal Justice* 16, no. 4 (October 2018): 309–332. https://doi.org/10.1080/15377938.2015.1052173.

Harwell, Drew. "Honey Buns Sweeten Life for Florida Prisoners." *Tampa Bay Times* (2010). http://www.tampabay.com/features/humaninterest/honey-buns-sweeten-life-for-florida-prisoners/1142687.

Hatton, Erin. *Coerced: Work Under Threat of Punishment*. Berkeley: University of California Press, 2020.

Hatton, Erin. "'Either You Do It or You're Going to the Box': Coerced Labor in Contemporary America." *Critical Sociology* 45, no. 6 (September 2019): 907–920. https://doi.org/10.1177/0896920518763929.

Hatton, Erin. "When Work Is Punishment: Penal Subjectivities in Punitive Labor Regimes." *Punishment & Society* 20, no. 2 (April 2018): 174–191. https://doi.org/10.1177/1462474517690001.

Hatton, Erin. "Working Behind Bars: Prison Labor in America." In *Labor and Punishment: Work in and Out of Prison*, 17–50. Oakland, CA: University of California Press, 2021.

Heckman, James J., and Dimitriy V. Masterov. "The Productivity Argument for Investing in Young Children." *Applied Economic Perspectives and Policy* 29, no. 3 (October 2007): 446–493. https://doi.org/10.1111/j.1467-9353.2007.00359.x.

Hodson, Randy. *Dignity at Work*. Cambridge, UK: Cambridge University Press, 2001.

Holzer, Harry J. "Collateral Costs: Effects of Incarceration on Employment and Earnings Among Young Workers." In *Do Prisons Make Us Safer? The Benefits and Costs of the Prison Boom*, edited by Steven Raphael and Michael A. Stoll, 239–266. New York: Russell Sage Foundation, 2009.

Hsung, Ray May, Nan Lin, and Ronald L. Breiger. *Contexts of Social Capital: Social Networks in Markets, Communities and Families*. Oxfordshire, UK: Routledge Taylor & Francis Group, 2009. https://doi.org/10.4324/9780203890097.

Hymes, Dell. "Two Types of Linguistic Relativity." In *Sociolinguistics: Proceedings of the UCLA Sociolinguistics Conference, 1964*, edited by William Bright, 114–167. The Hague: Mouton & Co., 1966.

Ignatieff, Michael. *A Just Measure of Pain: The Penitentiary in the Industrial Revolution, 1750–1850*. New York: Pantheon Books, 1978.

Incarcerated Workers Organizing Committee. "IWOC's Statement of Purpose." *Incarcerated Workers Organizing Committee* (2014). https://incarceratedworkers.org/about.

Ingham, Geffrey. "Money Is a Social Relation." *Review of Social Economy* 54, no. 4 (December 1996): 507–529. https://doi.org/10.1080/00346769600000031.

International Labor Organization. Abolition of Forced Labour Convention (No. 105) (1957). https://www.ilo.org/dyn/normlex/en/f?p=NORMLEXPUB:12100:0::NO:12100:P12100_ILO_CODE:C105.

International Labor Organization. Convention Concerning Forced or Compulsory Labour (No. 29) (1930). https://www.ilo.org/dyn/normlex/en/f?p=NORMLEXPUB:12100:0::NO::P12100_ILO_CODE:C029.

International Labor Organization. "Use of Prison Labor." *Document. Q&As on Business and Forced Labour* (2016). http://www.ilo.org/empent/areas/business-helpdesk/faqs/WCMS_DOC_ENT_HLP_FL_FAQ_EN/lang--en/index.htm.

Irwin, John. *The Jail: Managing the Underclass in American Society*. Berkeley: University of California Press, 1985.

Irwin, John. *The Warehouse Prison: Disposal of the New Dangerous Class*. Oxford, UK: Oxford University Press, 2004.

Jackson, Steven J. "Mapping the Prison Telephone Industry." In *Prison Profiteers: Who Makes Money from Mass Incarceration*, edited by Tara Herivel and Paul Wright, 235–248. New York: The New Press, 2007.

Jacobs, James B. *Stateville: The Penitentiary in Mass Society*. Chicago: University of Chicago Press, 1977.

Jewkes, Yvonne. "Men Behind Bars: 'Doing' Masculinity as an Adaptation to Imprisonment." *Men and Masculinities* 8, no. 1 (July 2005): 44–63. https://doi.org/10.1177/1097184X03257452.

Joseph, Miranda. *Against the Romance of Community*. Minneapolis: University of Minnesota Press, 2002.

Kalleberg, Arne. *Good Jobs, Bad Jobs: The Rise of Polarized and Precarious Employment Systems in the United States, 1970s–2000s*. New York, NY: Russell Sage Foundation, 2011.

Karpova, Polina. "Predicting Inmate Economic Conflict in Female Housing Units: Individual Factors Versus Social Climate Factors." MS Thesis, Eastern Kentucky University, 2013.

Kim, Claire Jean. "The Racial Triangulation of Asian Americans." *Politics & Society* 27, no. 1 (1999): 105–138.

Kim, E. Tammy. "A National Strike Against 'Prison Slavery.'" *The New Yorker* (October 2016). https://www.newyorker.com/news/news-desk/a-national-strike-against-prison-slavery.

King, Roy, and Alison Liebling. "Doing Research in Prisons." In *Doing Research on Crime and Justice*, edited by Roy King and Emma Wincup, 431–454. New York: Oxford University Press, 2008.

Kirk, David S., and Sara Wakefield. "Collateral Consequences of Punishment: A Critical Review and Path Forward." *Annual Review of Criminology* 1, no. 1 (2018): 171–194. https://doi.org/10.1146/annurev-criminol-032317-092045.

Kruttschnitt, Candace, and Rosemary Gartner. "Women's Imprisonment." *Crime and Justice* 30 (January 2003): 1–81. https://doi.org/10.1086/652228.

Kruttschnitt, Candace, Anne-Marie Slotboom, Anja Dirkzwager, and Catrien Bijleveld. "Bringing Women's Carceral Experiences into the 'New Punitiveness' Fray." *Justice Quarterly* 30, no. 1 (February 2013): 18–43. https://doi.org/10.1080/07418825.2011.603698.

Kunda, Gideon. *Engineering Culture: Control and Commitment in a High-Tech Corporation*. Philadelphia: Temple University Press, 2006.

Kushner, Rachel. "Is Prison Necessary? Ruth Wilson Gilmore Might Change Your Mind." *The New York Times* (April 2019): sec. Magazine. https://www.nytimes.com/2019/04/17/magazine/prison-abolition-ruth-wilson-gilmore.html.

Kyckelhahn, Tracey. *State Corrections Expenditures, FY 1982–2010*. Washington, DC: Bureau of Justice Statistics, 2012.

LaBriola, Joe. "Post-Prison Employment Quality and Future Criminal Justice Contact." *RSF: The Russell Sage Foundation Journal of the Social Sciences* 6, no. 1 (March 2020): 154–172. https://doi.org/10.7758/RSF.2020.6.1.07.

Lacey, Nicola. "Punishment, (Neo)Liberalism and Social Democracy." In *The SAGE Handbook of Punishment and Society*, edited by Jonathan Simon and Richard Sparks, 260–280. London: SAGE, 2013.

Lageson, Sarah Esther, Mike Vuolo, and Christopher Uggen. "Legal Ambiguity in Managerial Assessments of Criminal Records." *Law & Social Inquiry* 40, no. 1 (2015): 175–204. https://doi.org/10.1111/lsi.12066.

Lageson, Sarah, and Christopher Uggen. "How Work Affects Crime—And Crime Affects Work—Over The Life Course." In *Handbook of Life-Course Criminology: Emerging Trends and Directions for Future Research*, edited by Chris L. Gibson and Marvin D. Krohn, 201–212. New York: Springer, 2013. https://doi.org/10.1007/978-1-4614-5113-6_12.

Lamont, Michèle. *The Dignity of Working Men: Morality and the Boundaries of Race, Class, and Immigration.* Cambridge, Massachusetts: Harvard University Press, 2002.

Lankenau, Stephen. "Smoke 'Em If You Got 'Em: Cigarette Black Markets in U.S. Prisons and Jails." *The Prison Journal* 81, no. 2 (June 2001): 142–161. https://doi.org/10.1177/0032885501081002002.

Leidner, Robin. "Work Identity without Steady Work: Lessons from Stage Actors." *Research in the Sociology of Work* 29 (January 2016): 3–35. https://doi.org/10.1108/S0277-283320160000029008.

Levenson, Laurie L., and Mary Gordon. "The Dirty Little Secrets about Pay-to-Stay." *Michigan Law Review First Impressions* 106 (2007): 67–70.

Levingston, Kirsten D. "Making the Bad Guy Pay: Growing Use of Cost Shifting as an Economic Sanction." In *Prison Profiteers: Who Makes Money from Mass Incarceration*, edited by Tara Herivel and Paul Wright, 52–79. New York: The New Press, 2007.

Lichtenstein, Alex. *Twice the Work of Free Labor: The Political Economy of Convict Labor in the New South.* London: Verso, 1996.

Liebling, Alison. "A New 'Ecology of Cruelty'? The Changing Shape of Maximum-Security Custody in England and Wales." In *Extreme Punishment*, edited by Keramet Reiter and Alexa Koenig, 91–114. New York: Palgrave Macmillan, 2015.

London, Jack. *The Road.* New York: Macmillan, 1907. https://www.gutenberg.org/cache/epub/14658/pg14658-images.html.

Lopez, Steven Henry. "Efficiency and the Fix Revisited: Informal Relations and Mock Routinization in a Nonprofit Nursing Home." *Qualitative Sociology* 30, no. 3 (2007): 225–247.

Losier, Toussaint. "The Movement Against 'Modern Day Slavery.'" *Jacobin* (September 2018). https://jacobinmag.com/2018/09/prison-strike-slavery-labor-jls-abolition.

Love, Margaret, Susan Kuzma, and Keith Waters. *Civil Disabilities of Convicted Felons: A State-by-State Survey.* Washington, DC: U.S. Department of Justice, Office of the Pardon Attorney, 1996.

Lundahl, Brad W., Chelsea Kunz, Cyndi Brownell, Norma Harris, and Russ Van Vleet. "Prison Privatization: A Meta-Analysis of Cost and Quality of Confinement Indicators." *Research on Social Work Practice* 19, no. 4 (July 2009): 383–394. https://doi.org/10.1177/1049731509331946.

Lynch, James, and William Sabol. "Prison Use and Social Control." *Policies, Processes, and Decisions of the Criminal Justice System* 3 (2000): 7–44.

Lynch, Mona. *Hard Bargains: The Coercive Power of Drug Laws in Federal Court.* New York: Russell Sage Foundation, 2016.

Lynch, Mona. *Sunbelt Justice: Arizona and the Transformation of American Punishment.* Stanford, CA: Stanford Law Books, 2009.

Lynch, Mona, and Marisa Omori. "Crack as Proxy: Aggressive Federal Drug Prosecutions and the Production of Black–White Racial Inequality." *Law & Society Review* 52, no. 3 (2018): 773–809. https://doi.org/10.1111/lasr.12348.

Maguire, Kathleen E., Timothy J. Flanagan, and Terence P. Thornberry. "Prison Labor and Recidivism." *Journal of Quantitative Criminology* 4, no. 1 (March 1988): 3–18. https://doi.org/10.1007/BF01066881.

Maldonado, Marta Maria. "'It Is Their Nature to Do Menial Labour': The Racialization of 'Latino/a Workers' by Agricultural Employers." *Ethnic and Racial Studies* 32, no. 6 (July 2009): 1017–1036. https://doi.org/10.1080/0141987090 2802254.

Maldonado, Marta María. "Racial Triangulation of Latino/a Workers by Agricultural Employers." *Human Organization* 65, no. 4 (Winter 2006): 353–361. http://dx.doi.org/10.17730/humo.65.4.a84b5xykr0dvp91l.

Marsden, David. *A Theory of Employment Systems: Micro-Foundations of Societal Diversity*. Oxford, UK: Oxford University Press, 1999.

Maruna, Shadd. *Making Good: How Ex-Convicts Reform and Rebuild Their Lives by Shadd Maruna*. Washington, DC: American Psychological Association, 2001.

Marx, Karl. *Capital: Volume One*. Edited by Friedrich Engels. Translated by Samuel Moore and Edward Aveling. Mineola, NY: Dover Publications, Inc., 2019.

Mathiesen, Thomas. *The Politics of Abolition*. London: Martin Robertson, 1974.

McCorkel, Jill. "Banking on Rehab: Private Prison Vendors and the Reconfiguration of Mass Incarceration." *Studies in Law, Politics, and Society* 77 (January 2018): 49–67. https://doi.org/10.1108/S1059-433720180000077003.

McCorkel, Jill. *Breaking Women: Gender, Race, and the New Politics of Imprisonment*. New York: NYU Press, 2013.

McCorkel, Jill. "Embodied Surveillance and the Gendering of Punishment." *Journal of Contemporary Ethnography* 32, no. 1 (February 2003): 41–76. https://doi.org/10.1177/0891241602238938.

McGrew, Annie, and Angela Hanks. "It's Time to Stop Using Our Mass Incarceration System for Free Labor." *Moyers* (October 2017). https://billmoyers.com/story/time-stop-using-mass-incarceration-system-free-labor/.

McLennan, Rebecca. *The Crisis of Imprisonment: Protest, Politics, and the Making of the American Penal State, 1776–1941*. Cambridge, UK: Cambridge University Press, 2008.

McLeod, Allegra M. "Prison Abolition and Grounded Justice." *UCLA Law Review* 62, no. 5 (2015): 1156–1239.

Melossi, Dario. "Gazette of Morality and Social Whip: Punishment, Hegemony and the Case of the USA, 1970–92." *Social & Legal Studies* 2, no. 3 (September 1993): 259–279. https://doi.org/10.1177/096466399300200301.

Melossi, Dario. "The Penal Question in 'Capital.'" *Crime and Social Justice* Spring-Summer, no. 5 (1976): 26–33.

Melossi, Dario, and Massimo Pavarini. *The Prison and the Factory: Origins of the Penitentiary System*. London: Macmillan, 1981.

Melossi, Dario, and Massimo Pavarini. *The Prison and the Factory: Origins of the Penitentiary System (40th Anniversary Edition)*. 2nd English Edition. Basingstoke, Hampshire: Palgrave Macmillan, 2018.

Meranze, Michael. *Laboratories of Virtue: Punishment, Revolution, and Authority in Philadelphia, 1760–1835*. 2nd edition. Chapel Hill, NC: University of North Carolina Press, 1996.

Miller, Reuben Jonathan. "Race, Hyper-Incarceration, and US Poverty Policy in Historic Perspective." *Sociology Compass* 7, no. 7 (2013): 573–589. https://doi.org/10.1111/soc4.12049.

Milman-Sivan, Faina. "Prisoners for Hire: Towards a Normative Justification of the ILO's Prohibition of Private Forced Prisoner Labor." *Fordham International Law Journal* 36 (2013): 1619–1682.

Mishel, Lawrence, Josh Bivens, Elise Gould, and Heidi Shierholz. *The State of Working America*. Ithaca, NY: Cornell University Press, 2012.

Morenoff, Jeffrey. "Racial and Ethnic Disparities in Crime and Delinquency in the United States." In *Ethnicity and Causal Mechanisms*, edited by Michael Rutter and Marta Tienda, 139–173. New York: Cambridge University Press, 2005.

Mulholland, Kate. "Workplace Resistance in an Irish Call Centre: Slammin', Scammin' Smokin' an' Leavin'." *Work, Employment and Society* 18, no. 4 (December 2004): 709–724. https://doi.org/10.1177/0950017004048691.

Murphy, Laura, and Jesselyn McCurdy. "ACLU Letter to the House Subcommittee on Financial Management, the Budget and International Security Expressing Concerns about S. 346, Which Prevents Offenders from Obtaining Job Skills and Benefitting from Opportunities for Rehabilitation." *American Civil Liberties Union* (2004). https://www.aclu.org/letter/aclu-letter-house-subcommittee-financial-management-budget-and-international-security.

National Advisory Commission on Criminal Justice Standards and Goals. *Task Force Report on Corrections*. Washington, DC: US Government Printing Office, 1973.

NPR Staff. "Behind Bars, Cheap Ramen Is As Good As Gold." *NPR* (November 2015). https://www.npr.org/sections/thesalt/2015/11/04/454671629/behind-bars-cheap-ramen-is-as-good-as-gold.

Oeur, Freeden. "Recognizing Dignity: Young Black Men Growing Up in an Era of Surveillance." *Socius* 2 (January 2016): 2378023116633712. https://doi.org/10.1177/2378023116633712.

O'Malley, Pat. "Rethinking Neoliberal Penality." SSRN Scholarly Paper (Rochester, NY: Social Science Research Network, August 2015): 1–25. https://doi.org/10.2139/ssrn.2644010.

Osborne, David. "Reinventing Government." *Public Productivity & Management Review* 16, no. 4 (1993): 349–356. https://doi.org/10.2307/3381012.

Osterman, Paul. "Choice of Employment Systems in Internal Labor Markets." *Industrial Relations: A Journal of Economy and Society* 26, no. 1 (1987): 46–67. https://doi.org/10.1111/j.1468-232X.1987.tb00693.x.

Page, Joshua. *The Toughest Beat: Politics, Punishment, and the Prison Officers Union in California*. Oxford, UK: Oxford University Press, 2011.

Page, Joshua, and Joe Soss. "The Predatory Dimensions of Criminal Justice." *Science* 374, no. 6565 (October 2021): 291–294. https://doi.org/10.1126/science.abj7782.

Pager, Devah. *Marked: Race, Crime, and Finding Work in an Era of Mass Incarceration*. Chicago: University of Chicago Press, 2007.

Pager, Devah, Bruce Western, and Bart Bonikowski. "Discrimination in a Low-Wage Labor Market: A Field Experiment." *American Sociological Review* 74, no. 5 (2009): 777–799.

Paynter, Ben. "Prison Economics: How Fish and Coffee Become Cash." *Wired* (January 2011). https://www.wired.com/2011/01/st_prisoncurrencies/.

Pedulla, David S., and Devah Pager. "Race and Networks in the Job Search Process." *American Sociological Review* 84, no. 6 (November 2019): 983–1012. https://doi.org/10.1177/0003122419883255.

Pettit, Becky, and Christopher J. Lyons. "Incarceration and the Legitimate Labor Market: Examining Age-Graded Effects on Employment and Wages." *Law & Society Review* 43, no. 4 (2009): 725–756. https://doi.org/10.1111/j.1540-5893.2009.00387.x.

Pettit, Becky, and Bruce Western. "Mass Imprisonment and the Life Course: Race and Class Inequality in U.S. Incarceration." *American Sociological Review* 69, no. 2 (April 2004): 151–169. https://doi.org/10.1177/000312240406900201.

Pfaff, John. *Locked In: The True Causes of Mass Incarceration-and How to Achieve Real Reform*. New York: Basic Books, 2017.

Pogorzelski, Wendy, Nancy Wolff, Ko-Yu Pan, and Cynthia L. Blitz. "Behavioral Health Problems, Ex-Offender Reentry Policies, and the 'Second Chance Act.'" *American Journal of Public Health* 95, no. 10 (October 2005): 1718–1724. https://doi.org/10.2105/AJPH.2005.065805.

Pryor, Frederic L. "Industries Behind Bars: An Economic Perspective on the Production of Goods and Services by U.S. Prison Industries." *Review of Industrial Organization* 27, no. 1 (August 2005): 1–16. https://doi.org/10.1007/s11151-005-4401-3.

Pugh, Allison J. *Longing and Belonging: Parents, Children, and Consumer Culture*. Berkeley: University of California Press, 2009.

Pyrooz, David C., Ryan M. Labrecque, Jennifer J. Tostlebe, and Bert Useem. "Views on COVID-19 from Inside Prison: Perspectives of High-Security Prisoners." *Justice Evaluation Journal* 3, no. 2 (July 2020): 294–306. https://doi.org/10.1080/24751979.2020.1777578.

Raher, Stephen. "The Company Store." *Prison Policy Initiative* (blog) (May 2018). https://www.prisonpolicy.org/reports/commissary.html.

Raher, Stephen. "Paging Anti-Trust Lawyers: Prison Commissary Giants Prepare to Merge." *Prison Policy Initiative* (blog) (July 2016). https://www.prisonpolicy.org/blog/2016/07/05/commissary-merger/.

Ray, Victor. "A Theory of Racialized Organizations." *American Sociological Review* 84, no. 1 (February 2019): 26–53. https://doi.org/10.1177/0003122418822335.

Reed, Adam. "'Smuk Is King': The Action of Cigarettes in a Papua New Guinea Prison." In *Thinking Through Things*, edited by Amiria Henare, Martin Holbraad, and Sari Wastell, 42–56. London: Routledge, 2007.

Reiter, Keramet. *23/7: Pelican Bay Prison and the Rise of Long-Term Solitary Confinement*. New Haven, CT: Yale University Press, 2016.

Reiter, Keramet. "Making Windows in Walls: Strategies for Prison Research." *Qualitative Inquiry* 20, no. 4 (April 2014): 417–428. https://doi.org/10.1177/1077800413515831.

Reskin, Barbara F. "The Proximate Causes of Employment Discrimination." *Contemporary Sociology* 29, no. 2 (2000): 319–328. https://doi.org/10.2307/2654387.

Reskin, Barbara F., and Patricia A. Roos. *Job Queues, Gender Queues: Explaining Women's Inroads into Male Occupations*. Philadelphia: Temple University Press, 1990.

Rhodes, Lorna. *Total Confinement: Madness and Reason in the Maximum-Security Prison*. Berkeley: University of California Press, 2004.

Richmond, Robyn, Tony Butler, Kay Wilhelm, Alexander Wodak, Margaret Cunningham, and Ian Anderson. "Tobacco in Prisons: A Focus Group Study." *Tobacco Control* 18, no. 3 (June 2009): 176–182. https://doi.org/10.1136/tc.2008.026393.

Rios, Victor M. *Punished: Policing the Lives of Black and Latino Boys*. New York: NYU Press, 2011.

Rocque, Michael, and Quincy Snellings. "The New Disciplinology: Research, Theory, and Remaining Puzzles on the School-to-Prison Pipeline." *Journal of Criminal Justice* 59 (November 2018): 3–11. https://doi.org/10.1016/j.jcrimjus.2017.05.002.

Rondinelli, Dennis A., and G. Shabbir Cheema, eds. *Reinventing Government for the Twenty-First Century: State Capacity in a Globalizing Society*. Bloomfield, CT: Kumarian Press, 2003).

Roodman, David. "The Impacts of Incarceration on Crime." SSRN Scholarly Paper (Rochester, NY: Social Science Research Network, September 2017): 5–143. https://doi.org/10.2139/ssrn.3635864.

Rothman, David J. *The Discovery of the Asylum*. New Brunswick, New Jersey: Transaction Publishers, 1971.

Roy, Donald F. "'Banana Time': Job Satisfaction and Informal Interaction." *Human Organization* 18, no. 4 (1959): 158–168.

Royster, Deirdre A. *Race and the Invisible Hand: How White Networks Exclude Black Men from Blue-Collar Jobs*. Berkeley: University of California Press, 2003.

Rubin, Ashley T. *The Deviant Prison: Philadelphia's Eastern State Penitentiary and the Origins of America's Modern Penal System, 1829–1913*. Cambridge, UK: Cambridge University Press, 2021.

Rubin, Ashley T. "Professionalizing Prison: Primitive Professionalization and the Administrative Defense of Eastern State Penitentiary, 1829–1879." *Law & Social Inquiry* 43, no. 1 (2018): 182–211. https://doi.org/10.1111/lsi.12263.

Rubin, Ashley T. "Resistance or Friction: Understanding the Significance of Prisoners' Secondary Adjustments." *Theoretical Criminology* 19, no. 1 (February 2015): 23–42. https://doi.org/10.1177/1362480614543320.

Rusche, Georg. "Labor Market and Penal Sanction: Thoughts on the Sociology of Criminal Justice." Translated by Gerda Dinwiddie. *Crime and Social Justice*, no. 10 (1978 1933): 2–8.

Rusche, Georg, and Otto Kirchheimer. *Punishment and Social Structure*. 5th edition. Piscataway, NJ: Transaction Publishers, 2009.

Ryder, Judith. "Auburn State Prison." In *Encyclopedia Britannica*. Springfield, MA: Merriam-Webster, 2013. https://www.britannica.com/topic/Auburn-State-Prison.

Sallaz, Jeffrey J. *Lives on the Line: How the Philippines Became the World's Call Center Capital*. New York: Oxford University Press, 2019.

Sallaz, Jeffrey J. "Permanent Pedagogy: How Post-Fordist Firms Generate Effort but Not Consent." *Work and Occupations* 42, no. 1 (February 2015): 3–34. https://doi.org/10.1177/0730888414551207.

Sallaz, Jeffrey J. "Service Labor and Symbolic Power: On Putting Bourdieu to Work." *Work and Occupations* 37, no. 3 (August 2010): 295–319. https://doi.org/10.1177/0730888410373076.

Sallaz, Jeffrey J., and Jane Zavisca. "Bourdieu in American Sociology, 1980–2004." *Annual Review of Sociology* 33, no. 1 (2007): 21–41. https://doi.org/10.1146/annurev.soc.33.040406.131627.

Santo, Alysia, and Andy Rossback. "What's in a Prison Meal?" *The Marshall Project* (July 2015). https://www.themarshallproject.org/2015/07/07/what-s-in-a-prison-meal.

Sawyer, Wendy. "How Much Do Incarcerated People Earn in Each State?" *Prison Policy Initiative* (2017). https://www.prisonpolicy.org/blog/2017/04/10/wages/.

Sawyer, Wendy. "Why Expensive Phone Calls Can Be Life-Altering for People in Jail—and Can Derail the Justice Process." *Prison Policy Initiative* (2019). https://www.prisonpolicy.org/blog/2019/02/05/jail-phone-calls/.

Sawyer, Wendy, and Peter Wagner. "Mass Incarceration: The Whole Pie 2020." *Prison Policy Initiative* (2020). https://www.prisonpolicy.org/reports/pie2020.html.

Scheck, Justin. "Mackerel Economics in Prison Leads to Appreciation for Oily Fillets." *Wall Street Journal* (October 2008): sec. Business. https://www.wsj.com/articles/SB122290720439096481.

Schlanger, Margo. "Civil Rights Injunctions over Time: A Case Study of Jail and Prison Court Orders." *New York University Law Review* 81 (2006): 630.

Schlosser, Jennifer A. "Bourdieu and Foucault: A Conceptual Integration Toward an Empirical Sociology of Prisons." *Critical Criminology* 21, no. 1 (March 2013): 31–46. https://doi.org/10.1007/s10612-012-9164-1.

Schwartzapfel, Beth. "A Primer on the Nationwide Prisoners' Strike." *The Marshall Project* (September 2016). https://www.themarshallproject.org/2016/09/27/a-primer-on-the-nationwide-prisoners-strike.

Schwartzapfel, Beth. "How Bad Is Prison Health Care? Depends on Who's Watching." *The Marshall Project* (February 2018). https://www.themarshallproject.org/2018/02/25/how-bad-is-prison-health-care-depends-on-who-s-watching.

Schwartzman, Kathleen C. *The Chicken Trail: Following Workers, Migrants, and Corporations across the Americas*. Ithaca, NY: Cornell University Press, 2013.

Seim, Josh. "Short-Timing: The Carceral Experience of Soon-to-Be-Released Prisoners." *Punishment & Society* 18, no. 4 (October 2016): 442–458. https://doi.org/10.1177/1462474516641377.

Seiter, Richard P., and Karen R. Kadela. "Prisoner Reentry: What Works, What Does Not, and What Is Promising." *Crime & Delinquency* 49, no. 3 (July 2003): 360–388. https://doi.org/10.1177/0011128703049003002.

Sexton, Lori. "Penal Subjectivities: Developing a Theoretical Framework for Penal Consciousness." *Punishment & Society* 17, no. 1 (January 2015): 114–136. https://doi.org/10.1177/1462474514548790.

Sharone, Ofer. *Flawed System/Flawed Self: Job Searching and Unemployment Experiences.* Chicago: University of Chicago Press, 2014.

Shemkus, Sarah. "Beyond Cheap Labor: Can Prison Work Programs Benefit Inmates?" *The Guardian* (December 2015): sec. Guardian Sustainable Business. https://www.theguardian.com/sustainable-business/2015/dec/09/prison-work-program-ohsa-whole-foods-inmate-labor-incarceration.

Shichor, David. *Punishment for Profit: Private Prisons/Public Concerns.* Thousand Oaks, CA: SAGE Publications, Inc, 1995.

Simmel, Georg. "The Stranger." In *The Sociology of Georg Simmel*, edited by Kurt Wolff, 402–408. New York: Simon and Schuster, 1950.

Simon, Jonathan. *Governing Through Crime: How the War on Crime Transformed American Democracy and Created a Culture of Fear.* Oxford, UK: Oxford University Press, 2007.

Simon, Jonathan. *Mass Incarceration on Trial: A Remarkable Court Decision and the Future of Prisons in America.* New York: The New Press, 2014.

Simon, Jonathan. *Poor Discipline.* Chicago: University of Chicago Press, 1993.

Simon, Jonathan. "The Second Coming of Dignity." In *The New Criminal Justice Thinking*, edited by Sharon Dolovich and Alexandra Natapoff, 275–307. New York: NYU Press, 2017.

Skarbek, David. *The Social Order of the Underworld: How Prison Gangs Govern the American Penal System.* Oxford, UK: Oxford University Press, 2014.

Smith, Chris. "The Short Overview of the Labour Process Perspective and History of the International Labour Process Conference." In *International Labour Process Conference, Leeds.* Leeds, UK, 2012.

Smith, Earl, and Angela J. Hattery. "Incarceration: A Tool for Racial Segregation and Labor Exploitation." *Race, Gender & Class* 15, no. 1 (2008): 79–97.

Smith, Julia Floyd. *Slavery and Plantation Growth in Antebellum Florida, 1821–1860.* Gainesville, FL: University Press of Florida, 1973.

Smith, Noah. "Paying Inmates Minimum Wages Helps the Working Class." *Bloomberg.com* (June 2017). https://www.bloomberg.com/opinion/articles/2017-06-02/paying-inmates-minimum-wages-helps-the-working-class.

Smith, Sandra Susan, and Jonathan Simon. "Exclusion and Extraction: Criminal Justice Contact and the Reallocation of Labor." *RSF: The Russell Sage Foundation Journal of the Social Sciences* 6, no. 1 (March 2020): 1–27. https://doi.org/10.7758/RSF.2020.6.1.01.

Smoyer, Amy B. "Making Fatty Girl Cakes: Food and Resistance in a Women's Prison." *The Prison Journal* 96, no. 2 (March 2016): 191–209. https://doi.org/10.1177/0032885515596520.

Smoyer, Amy B. "Mapping Prison Foodways." In *Experiencing Imprisonment: Research on the Experience of Living and Working in Carceral Institutions*, edited by Carla Reeves, 96–112. London: Routledge, 2016.

Smoyer, Amy B., and Giza Lopes. "Hungry on the Inside: Prison Food as Concrete and Symbolic Punishment in a Women's Prison." *Punishment & Society* 19, no. 2 (April 2017): 240–255. https://doi.org/10.1177/1462474516665605.

Snacken, Sonja. "Punishment, Legitimate Policies and Values: Penal Moderation, Dignity and Human Rights." *Punishment & Society* 17, no. 3 (July 2015): 397–423. https://doi.org/10.1177/1462474515590895.

Snow, David A., and Leon Anderson. *Down on Their Luck: A Study of Homeless Street People*. Berkeley, CA: University of California Press, 1993.

Social Security Administration. *What Prisoners Need To Know*. Washington, DC: US Government Printing Office, 2010.

Society for the Prevention of Pauperism in the City of New York. *Report on the Penitentiary System in the United States*. New York: Mahlon Day, 1822. https://archive.org/details/reportonpenitent00soci/page/n5/mode/2up.

Solinas-Saunders, Monica, Melissa J. Stacer, and Roger Guy. "Ex-Offender Barriers to Employment: Racial Disparities in Labor Markets with Asymmetric Information." *Journal of Crime and Justice* 38, no. 2 (April 2015): 249–269. https://doi.org/10.1080/0735648X.2013.870492.

Solomon, Akiba. "What Words We Use—and Avoid—When Covering People and Incarceration." *The Marshall Project* (April 2021). https://www.themarshallproject.org/2021/04/12/what-words-we-use-and-avoid-when-covering-people-and-incarceration.

Solomon, Amy, Kelly Johnson, Jeremy Travis, and Elizabeth McBride. "From Prison to Work: The Employment Dimensions of Prisoner Reentry." In *Research Report Reentry Roundtable*. Washington, DC: Urban Institute, 2004. https://www.voced.edu.au/content/ngv:17453.

Steffensmeier, Darrell, Jeffery Ulmer, and John Kramer. "The Interaction of Race, Gender, and Age in Criminal Sentencing: The Punishment Cost of Being Young, Black, and Male." *Criminology* 36, no. 4 (1998): 763–798. https://doi.org/10.1111/j.1745-9125.1998.tb01265.x.

Stephan, James. "Census of State and Federal Correctional Facilities, 1990." In *Census of State and Federal Correctional Facilities*. Washington, DC: Bureau of Justice Statistics, 1992: 1–32. https://www.bjs.gov/index.cfm?ty=pbdetail&iid=4067.

Stephan, James. "Census of State and Federal Correctional Facilities, 1995." In *Census of State and Federal Correctional Facilities*. Washington, DC: Bureau of Justice Statistics, 1997: 1–31. https://www.bjs.gov/index.cfm?ty=pbdetail&iid=535.

Stephan, James. "Census of State and Federal Correctional Facilities, 2005." In *Census of State and Federal Correctional Facilities*. Washington, DC: Bureau of Justice Statistics, 2008: 1–28. https://www.bjs.gov/content/pub/pdf/csfcf05.pdf.

Stephan, James, and Jennifer Karberg. "Census of State and Federal Correctional Facilities, 2000." In *Census of State and Federal Correctional Facilities*. Washington, DC: Bureau of Justice Statistics, 2003: 1–19. https://www.bjs.gov/index.cfm?ty=pbdetail&iid=533.

Stevens, Mitchell L., Elizabeth A. Armstrong, and Richard Arum. "Sieve, Incubator, Temple, Hub: Empirical and Theoretical Advances in the Sociology of Higher Education." *Annual Review of Sociology* 34, no. 1 (2008): 127–151. https://doi.org/10.1146/annurev.soc.34.040507.134737.

Sutton, John R. "Imprisonment and Labor Market Outcomes: Evidence from 15 Affluent Western Democracies. Presented at the American Sociological Association Quantitative Methods in the Social Sciences Lecture Series, Tucson, Arizona, October 2002.

Sykes, Gresham. *The Society of Captives: A Study of a Maximum Security Prison.* Princeton, New Jersey: Princeton University Press, 1958.

Thompson, Christie. "Where Crossword Puzzles Count as Counseling." *The Marshall Project* (June 2017). https://www.themarshallproject.org/2017/06/12/where-crossword-puzzles-count-as-counseling.

Thompson, Heather Ann. "The Prison Industrial Complex: A Growth Industry in a Shrinking Economy." *New Labor Forum* 21, no. 3 (October 2012): 39–47. https://doi.org/10.4179/NLF.213.0000006.

Thompson, Heather Ann. "Rethinking Working-Class Struggle through the Lens of the Carceral State: Toward a Labor History of Inmates and Guards." *Labor* 8, no. 3 (September 2011): 15–45. https://doi.org/10.1215/15476715-1275226.

Thompson, Paul, and Kirsty Newsome. "The Dynamics of Dignity at Work." *Research in the Sociology of Work* 28 (2016): 79–100.

Travis, Jeremy, and Christy Visher. "Prisoner Reentry and the Pathways to Adulthood: Policy Perspectives." In *On Your Own without a Net: The Transition to Adulthood for Vulnerable Populations,* edited by D. Wayne Osgood, E. Michael Foster, Constance Flanagan, and Gretchen Ruth, 145–177. Chicago: University of Chicago Press, 2005.

Travis, Jeremy, Bruce Western, and Steve Redburn. *The Growth of Incarceration in the United States: Exploring Causes and Consequences.* Washington, DC: National Academies Press, 2014. https://academicworks.cuny.edu/jj_pubs/27/.

Ugelvik, Thomas. "The Hidden Food: Mealtime Resistance and Identity Work in a Norwegian Prison." *Punishment & Society* 13, no. 1 (January 2011): 47–63. https://doi.org/10.1177/1462474510385630.

United States General Accounting Office. *Prisoner Labor: Perspectives on Paying the Federal Minimum Wage.* Washington, DC: General Accounting Office, 1993.

U.S. Department of Justice. Justice Systems Improvement Act, Pub. L. No. 96-157 (1979). https://www.congress.gov/bill/96th-congress/senate-bill/241.

U.S. Department of Justice. Prison Industry Enhancement Certification Program, Pub. L. No. 96-157, Sec. 827 (1979).

Van Cleve, Nicole. *Crook County: Racism and Injustice in America's Largest Criminal Court.* Stanford, CA: Stanford Law Books, 2016.

Vitale, Alex S. *The End of Policing.* New York: Verso, 2017.

Von Zielbauer, Paul. "Private Health Care in Jails Can Be a Death Sentence." In *Prison Profiteers: Who Makes Money from Mass Incarceration,* edited by Tara Herivel and Paul Wright, 204–227. New York: The New Press, 2009.

Vuolo, Mike, Sarah Lageson, and Christopher Uggen. "Criminal Record Questions in the Era of 'Ban the Box.'" *Criminology & Public Policy* 16, no. 1 (2017): 139–165. https://doi.org/10.1111/1745-9133.12250.

Wacquant, Loïc. "Bourdieu, Foucault, and the Penal State in the Neoliberal Era." In *Foucault and Neoliberalism*, edited by Daniel Zamora and Michael Behrent, 124–143. Cambridge, UK: Polity, 2016.

Wacquant, Loïc. "Class, Race & Hyperincarceration in Revanchist America." *Daedalus* 139, no. 3 (July 2010): 74–90. https://doi.org/10.1162/DAED_a_00024.

Wacquant, Loïc. "Crafting the Neoliberal State: Workfare, Prisonfare, and Social Insecurity." *Sociological Forum* 25, no. 2 (2010): 197–220. https://doi.org/10.1111/j.1573-7861.2010.01173.x.

Wacquant, Loïc. "The Curious Eclipse of Prison Ethnography in the Age of Mass Incarceration." *Ethnography* 3, no. 4 (December 2002): 371–397. https://doi.org/10.1177/1466138102003004012.

Wacquant, Loïc. "Deadly Symbiosis: When Ghetto and Prison Meet and Mesh." *Punishment & Society* 3, no. 1 (January 2001): 95–133. https://doi.org/10.1177/14624740122228276.

Wacquant, Loïc. "The New 'Peculiar Institution': On the Prison as Surrogate Ghetto." *Theoretical Criminology* 4, no. 3 (August 2000): 377–389. https://doi.org/10.1177/1362480600004003007.

Wacquant, Loïc. *Prisons of Poverty*. Minneapolis, MN: University of Minnesota Press, 2009.

Wacquant, Loïc. *Punishing the Poor: The Neoliberal Government of Social Insecurity*. Durham, NC: Duke University Press, 2009.

Wakefield, Sara, and Christopher Uggen. "Incarceration and Stratification." *Annual Review of Sociology* 36, no. 1 (2010): 387–406. https://doi.org/10.1146/annurev.soc.012809.102551.

Waldfogel, Joel. "The Effect of Criminal Conviction on Income and the Trust 'Reposed in the Workmen.'" *The Journal of Human Resources* 29, no. 1 (1994): 62–81. https://doi.org/10.2307/146056.

Waldron, Jeremy. "How Law Protects Dignity." *SSRN Scholarly Paper* (Rochester, NY: Social Science Research Network, December 2011). https://doi.org/10.2139/ssrn.1973341.

Walker, Michael L. "Race Making in a Penal Institution." *American Journal of Sociology* 121, no. 4 (January 2016): 1051–1078. https://doi.org/10.1086/684033.

Walmsley, Roy. *World Prison Population List*. 11th Edition. London, UK: Institute for Criminal Policy Research, 2010.

Warner, Cody, Joshua Kaiser, and Jason N. Houle. "Locked Out of the Labor Market? State-Level Hidden Sentences and the Labor Market Outcomes of Recently Incarcerated Young Adults." *RSF: The Russell Sage Foundation Journal of the Social Sciences* 6, no. 1 (March 2020): 132–151. https://doi.org/10.7758/RSF.2020.6.1.06.

Weiß, Anja. "Racist Symbolic Capital: A Bourdieuian Approach to the Analysis of Racism." In *Wages of Whiteness & Racist Symbolic Capital*, edited by Wulf

D. Hund, Jeremy Krikler, and David R. Roediger, 37–56. Berlin, Germany: Lit Verlag, 2010.

Weiss, Robert P. "'Repatriating' Low-Wage Work: The Political Economy of Prison Labor Reprivatization in the Postindustrial United States." *Criminology* 39, no. 2 (May 2001): 253–292. https://doi.org/10.1111/j.1745-9125.2001.tb00923.x.

Western, Bruce. *Homeward: Life in the Year After Prison: Life in the Year After Prison.* New York: Russell Sage Foundation, 2018.

Western, Bruce. *Punishment and Inequality in America.* New York: Russell Sage Foundation, 2006.

Western, Bruce, and Katherine Beckett. "How Unregulated Is the U.S. Labor Market? The Penal System as a Labor Market Institution." *American Journal of Sociology* 104, no. 4 (January 1999): 1030–1060. https://doi.org/10.1086/210135.

Western, Bruce, Jeffrey R. Kling, and David F. Weiman. "The Labor Market Consequences of Incarceration." *Crime & Delinquency* 47, no. 3 (July 2001): 410–427. https://doi.org/10.1177/0011128701047003007.

Western, Bruce, and Becky Pettit. "Incarceration & Social Inequality." *Daedalus* 139, no. 3 (July 2010): 8–19. https://doi.org/10.1162/DAED_a_00019.

Wheelock, Darren, and Christopher Uggen. "Punishment, Crime, and Poverty." In *The Colors of Poverty: Why Racial and Ethnic Disparities Persist*, edited by Ann Chih Lin and David Harris, 261–292. New York: Russell Sage Foundation, 2008. https://www.jstor.org/stable/10.7758/9781610447249.

Whitman, James Q. *Harsh Justice: Criminal Punishment and the Widening Divide Between America and Europe.* New York: Oxford University Press, 2003.

Willis, Paul. *Learning to Labor: How Working-Class Kids Get Working Class Jobs.* New York: Columbia University Press, 1977.

Wilson, David B., Catherine A. Gallagher, and Doris L. MacKenzie. "A Meta-Analysis of Corrections-Based Education, Vocation, and Work Programs for Adult Offenders." *Journal of Research in Crime and Delinquency* 37, no. 4 (2000): 347–368. https://doi.org/10.1177/0022427800037004001.

Wimmer, Andreas. "The Making and Unmaking of Ethnic Boundaries: A Multilevel Process Theory." *American Journal of Sociology* 113, no. 4 (January 2008): 970–1022. https://doi.org/10.1086/522803.

Wright, Erik Olin. "Social Class." In *Encyclopedia of Social Theory*, edited by George Ritzer, 717–724. Thousand Oaks, CA: SAGE Publications, 2004.

Yglesias, Matthew. "Prison Currency." *Think Progress* (blog) (October 2008). http://thinkprogress.org/yglesias/2008/10/02/189810/prison_currency.

Zatz, Noah D. "Prison Labor and the Paradox of Paid Nonmarket Work." In *Economic Sociology of Work*, edited by Nina Bandelj, 18: 369–398. Bingley, UK: Emerald Group Publishing Limited, 2009. https://doi.org/10.1108/S0277-2833(2009)0000018017.

Zatz, Noah D. "Working at the Boundaries of Markets: Prison Labor and the Economic Dimension of Employment Relationships." *Vanderbilt Law Review* 61 (2008): 857–958.

Zyl Smit, Dirk van, and Sonja Snacken. *Principles of European Prison Law and Policy: Penology and Human Rights.* New York: Oxford University Press, 2009.

Acknowledgments

I am foremost grateful to the imprisoned participants who allowed me into their lives and shared their experiences and outlooks. This could not have happened without their acceptance, cooperation, and input. I also thank the institutional agents that enabled this study.

Many mentors helped along the way, beginning with Jody Miller, Teresa Guess, Nancy Gleason, and Dennis Bohnenkamp at the University of Missouri—St. Louis (UMSL). My doctoral committee—Jeffrey Sallaz, Ronald Breiger, Kathleen Schwartzman, Jennifer Carlson, and Philip Goodman—offered guidance that helped bring these ideas to fruition. Others at the University of Arizona, UMSL, and the University of Denver provided encouragement and assistance at various stages. Analysis was supported in part by the National Science Foundation and University of Arizona's School of Sociology.

Special thanks to all who read full or partial drafts at different stages. Josh Seim, Gustavo "Goose" Alvarez, and Phil Goodman offered invaluable comments. Many folks helped inspire and encourage my efforts, including Josh Page, Erin Hatton, Liam Martin, Jonathan Simon, Sandra Susan Smith, Michael Campbell II, and certainly others. I am additionally grateful to "Goose" Alvarez for allowing me to include an excerpt from *The Pawn*. Chelsea Nicolas helped improve visuals. Letta Page helped strengthen the opening and closing chapters. James Cook, Meredith Keffer, and several anonymous reviewers helped guide the final manuscript with Oxford.

Projects like this rely on not only scholarly support, but social support as well. I'm forever beholden to the best cohort: Angela, Eliza, Hannah, Jess, Julia, Kate, Krista, Paul, and Ricardo. Cheers! Other folks offered countless morale boosts, including Andrew, Joseph, Kyle, Amy, Peter, Kathryn, James, Simone, Morgan, Eric, Alex,

Hannah, Colin, and too many others to list. Thank you. Jon Lampe always backs me up while still challenging me—anyways, thanks. I'm also driven by encouragement from the fam: Mom, Dad, Jordan, Alex, and Tiffany.

Finally, my wife, Karyn, read untold chapter proposals, outlines, and drafts through the years, always offering perceptive questions and suggestions. She championed my successes, elevated me during periods of stress, and helped keep my eye on the true reasons for this work. Thanks, darlin'.

MGL
Denver, CO

Index